EMBRACING
CONTRARIES

Without contraries is no progression.

William Blake

The chief characteristic of the mind is to be constantly describing itself.

Henry Focillon

It is in the nature of an hypothesis when once a man has conceived it, that it assimilates everything to itself as proper nourishment; and, from the first moment of your begetting it, it generally grows the stronger by everything you see, hear, read, or understand. That is of great use.

Walter Shandy in Laurence Sterne's
Tristram Shandy

EMBRACING CONTRARIES

Explorations in Learning and Teaching

❀❀❀

Peter Elbow

New York   Oxford
OXFORD UNIVERSITY PRESS
1986

Oxford University Press

Oxford   New York   Toronto
Delhi   Bombay   Calcutta   Madras   Karachi
Petaling Jaya   Singapore   Hong Kong   Tokyo
Nairobi   Dar es Salaam   Cape Town
Melbourne   Auckland

and associated companies in
Beirut   Berlin   Ibadan   Nicosia

Published by Oxford University Press, Inc.,
200 Madison Avenue, New York, New York 10016

Oxford is the registered trademark of Oxford University Press.

Library of Congress Cataloging-in-Publication Data

Elbow, Peter.
Embracing contraries.

Bibliography: p.
Includes index.
1. College teaching.   2. Learning.   3. College
teaching—Evaluation.   4. Knowledge, Theory of.
I. Title.
LB2331.E48   1986   378′.125   85–15413
ISBN 0–19–503692–1

Printing (last digit):   9 8 7 6 5 4 3 2 1

Printed in the United States of America

For Abby and Benjy,
the most huggable contraries in the world.

May they fall in love with perplexity.

Acknowledgments

I would like to thank New Directions Publishing Corporation for permission to reprint "Song for Ishtar" by Denise Levertov, from *Poems 1960–1967*. Copyright © 1962 by Denise Levertov Goodman. Reprinted by permission of New Directions Publishing Corporation.

I am also grateful for permission to reprint essays of mine which appeared in the following books or journals:

Penn State Press and *The Journal of General Education* ("Real Learning and Nondisciplinary Courses," 23.2, July 1971).

College English ("Exploring My Teaching," 32.4, April 1971 and "Embracing Contraries in the Teaching Process," 45.4, April 1983).

Soundings ("The Pedagogy of the Bamboozled," 56.2, Summer 1973).

Jossey-Bass ("Trying to Teach While Thinking About the End," Chapter 3, in *On Competence,* 1979; "One-to-one Faculty Development," in *Learning About Teaching, New Directions for Teaching and Learning,* Vol. 4, 1980).

Ohio State University Press and *The Journal of Higher Education* ("More Accurate Evaluation of Student Performance," 40, March 1969).

Wesleyan University Press ("The Value of Dialectic," Chapter 7, in *Oppositions in Chaucer,* 1975).

Heldref Publications and *Change Magazine* ("Teaching Thinking by Teaching Writing," September 1983).

Contents

Introduction

I've always been drawn to the question of what *really* happens when we learn or teach: What goes on inside the mind? Behind appearances? What's the process? There is mystery here. I've been gnawing on this bone for a long time as a student and teacher. I've chewed on it especially in my writing—picking it up and tugging on it first one way, then another.

I've gathered here a small selection of essays about learning and teaching that I've written over almost twenty years.* I risk the hubris of collecting them in a book not only because I think they could be of use if they were more readily available, but also because they fit together better than I ever realized when I was writing them. They turn out to be engaged in a single enterprise.

All along in my writing I've been trying to do justice to the rich messiness of learning and teaching—to avoid the limitations of neat theories and pat positions. Yet these essays grow from an opposite impulse as well: a hunger to figure things out, to reach conclusions, to arrive at stateable, portable, and even neat insights. I've always been irritated at the prejudice among so many people in higher education (particularly in institutions of higher repute) that pedagogy doesn't bear thinking about: that there's something useless and *infra-dig* about studying the *processes* of learning and teaching themselves (as opposed to the *contents* of

---

* In preparing them for this collection I have made only minor changes: frequent small omissions and occasional changes or additions in wording. I have largely omitted any work about writing or the teaching of writing—for which see the "Bibliography of Works on Writing by the Author" at the end of this book.

the disciplines); and that whether someone learns or teaches well is mostly a matter of inborn talent, temperament, and character.

Pulling these essays together, I see more clearly than ever how long I've been squirming on the hooks of the dilemma implied here. That is, on the one hand, of course it's true that attempts to systematize and to devise theories of pedagogy tend to invite simplification or even shallow thinking. Yet on the other hand, people who like to make this complaint and turn up their noses as they talk about the "horrors of educationese" are often dismal teachers and insufferably condescending—all the while refusing to think about what actually happens (and doesn't happen!) in their own classrooms and lecture halls. Many academics like to throw a cloak of alleged intellectuality over their refusal to *think*—in this case, about something that badly needs thought, namely, whether students actually learn.

A hunger for coherence; yet a hunger also to be true to the natural incoherence of experience. This dilemma has led me more often than I realized to work things out in terms of contraries: to gravitate toward oppositions and even to exaggerate differences—while also tending to notice how both sides of the opposition must somehow be right. My instinct has thus made me seek ways to avoid the limitations of the single point of view. And it has led me to a commonsense view that surely there cannot be only *one* right way to learn and teach: looking around us we see too many diverse forms of success. Yet, surely, the issue cannot also be hopelessly relative: there must be *principles* that we must satisfy to produce good learning and teaching—however diverse the ways in which people satisfy them.

With regard to practice, I think these essays can serve teachers, curriculum planners, and administrators not so much by providing specific "things to do" (though I do suggest a few), but by setting up ways of looking at the learning and teaching process that will trigger *in them* specific things to do which they wouldn't otherwise have thought of. I believe these essays can encourage teachers and planners to be more courageous and inventive in experimenting. (Especially at a time when there are calls for greater "results" and even for greater "rigor"—justifiable calls, I would say; but they get mixed up with unjustifiable calls merely *to return*.) I will also call it a "practical outcome" if I succeed

in validating that sense of frustration and confusion which anyone must experience who really tries to teach well and who tries
to attend closely to what is happening in students and in herself. When I manage to experience my frustration and confusion
not just as problems but rather as accurate and valid responses
to the complexities of the task at hand, I am often strengthened—
and sometimes led quite naturally to figure out the right next
step.

⚙

Needless to say these essays about the perplexities of learning
and teaching grow out of the perplexities of my own experience.
On the one hand, I was characteristically a "good" student: I
was earnest and diligent, it mattered enormously to me that I
be "successful." Teachers called me smart. (A good student, as
my former colleague Nancy Dworsky observed, is a student who
makes a teacher feel like a good teacher.) Yet, on the other hand,
I never felt really comfortable in school—always a bit of an out-
sider: as though I didn't quite belong, as though I didn't quite
fit the expectations of my teachers or my fellows.

Learning and teaching seemed natural to so many of my colleagues. They always seemed to know what they were doing and
why they were doing it that way. But it never felt natural to me
and I never felt I understood what was happening—whether I
tried to do it their way or not. Too much magic, mystery. I always felt nervous, even afraid. If I got the steps right for the
rain dance, rain came, but I never knew till I was wet whether I
was close. I never seemed to have any sense of what a good rain
dance looked like.

I felt this perplexity whether I was engaged in the supposedly
straightforward task of remembering/learning (trying to get
words and ideas to go into me), or engaged in the supposedly
harder task of figuring out new thoughts and ideas (trying to get
words and ideas to come out of me). That is, I could never mem-
orize material or find it when I was asked for it—though I was
always discovering later that the stuff had been in there all along.
Figuring out new ideas, or "my own ideas," was usually more
fun, but the vagaries of success were even greater: when it worked
I was genuinely good at it; when it didn't I couldn't seem to

produce *anything* at all—where other students could usually produce something.

Then came the time in graduate school, twenty-six years ago, when my fantasy fears finally materialized: *all* attempts at rain dance brought drought. I couldn't study, couldn't figure things out, couldn't write anything. I gave myself a few months to see if I could fight my way clear but couldn't. I quit early in the next semester. I concluded I had to abandon books and the academy. I had lost any sense of why the enterprise had any importance—indeed I experienced a repulsion for books.

I knocked around with temporary jobs for six months (helping door-to-door on my bicycle with the 1960 census) and then tried to find a "real" job. I tried for jobs as a kindergarten teacher. I hid my motivation as well as I could (I wanted to *play*), but I suspect I looked too crazed to those who interviewed me. Then— through the luck of a kindly former teacher and a departmental purge resulting in a need for bodies in July—I fell into a faculty position at M.I.T. I wasn't sure it was honest to take the job, given my frame of mind, but I soon got caught up in my teaching. I discovered that even though the inability to write barred me from being a *student*, I seemed to be able to *teach* just fine. Before long I even came to like books, to love teaching, to want to be an intellectual. And so, five years later I returned to graduate study, eventually getting my degree.

Thus, a pattern emerges in my life as a student and a teacher— what from a writerly point of view I could now call the "habit of revision." Whether on the smaller scale of writing an essay or the larger scale of getting a Ph.D., I seem incapable of doing things right the first time. It was decades, however—and I had to drift into the field of writing and work out some theories—before I could think of these botches as "drafts." They simply felt like failures. And why not, since I was trying as hard as I could to get them right and not succeeding? Yet I couldn't seem to leave it at failure either—leave bad enough alone. I couldn't just quit (except that once—for I didn't know I'd come back five years later). I always went home again and licked my wounds, regrouped my forces, and came back with another version which in the end succeeded in one way or another.

❀

From my own experience and my reflections upon it, then, one issue emerges as central. What is *natural* in studying, learning, and teaching? And what are our assumptions about how the mind ought to function in learning and teaching?

I had always assumed, as I think most people do, that as students we should be organized, coherent, and know what we're doing. And that as teachers, in addition to being organized and coherent, we should teach only what we know well; and that we should present to students the main principles of what we are teaching—and thus (as a natural consequence) we should stick to one discipline. (The structure of a discipline emphasizes main principles.) I had assumed that input always precedes output: that first we learn things, then we can have ideas; that we should not invite students to give their own ideas till they have proved that they can learn the ideas of others; that accuracy should precede transformation. Not having examined these assumptions, I didn't have enough sense to notice that my experience had tended to be the other way round: that I could get things to *go in* better if I had first been invited to have them come out; and that I could be more accurate if I had first been invited to transform. I simply felt my experience as perplexing.

I couldn't work my way free of these assumptions till I had done a lot of exploring of the writing process and worked out quite a few conclusions on my own. For a long time it had seemed as though my own experience with writing was peculiar— the nature of my difficulties and the nature of the solutions to them seemed aberrational. But when I wrote about my difficulties and my solutions, I discovered that they applied widely—not just to many students and unskilled writers but also to many adults and skilled writers. Gradually I have concluded that we must *adjust* our picture of what is natural in learning and teaching— of what goes on in the mind: our picture needs to be messier, more complicated, more paradoxical. I conclude that my experience of perplexity in learning, teaching, and writing—and the solutions I've devised—can be of use.

For I've discovered in recent years that there are many other students and teachers whose minds are like mine—disorganized, jumping around, bad at remembering things, always sucked down the unknown path while gazing wistfully toward the known one, vacillating and unable to decide. When we support and respect these seemingly recalcitrant and aberrational cognitive impulses (and thereby learn somewhat to *harness* them)— when we see them as *intelligent* instead of naughty—they lead to coherence not mess. Things are remembered not forgotten. Good new insights come. The process leads eventually to genuine decisions (where we feared we would stay becalmed forever in indecision)—decisions which are usually richer and better than the options we originally vacillated among.

There are many such students and teachers walking around who are smart but not *recognized* as smart. They don't "do things right," they don't fit well into the existing models of thinking and intelligence in schools and colleges. For example, they cannot remember well till they think, but are asked not to think till they can remember well. Many English teachers have come up to me and said, "You know, I've always written in the way you describe, but I've never dared admit it to students: I've always thought I had to force them to write 'right.' "

Even if all these students and teachers were as perversely blessed as I seem to have been with an unrelenting hunger to be accepted in the academy, that would not be enough. For none of us can function at our best unless we are *seen* as smart by ourselves and others. One of the main reasons why smart students function well is that they are *seen* as smart. We cannot take advantage of complicated patterns of intelligence unless we experience them working for us, not against us.

Thus, these essays have a kind of subtheme which often I was not fully conscious of as I wrote—a kind of table-turning or underdogism—namely, that people who experience themselves as dumb, and are seen that way, are really smart. (I have also been tempted by the vindictive corollary, but I think I now see that *everyone* is smart—even, grudgingly, those who think they are.) Thus I cannot escape an *ad hominem* critical reading of this book, for in the end I am really engaged in trying to work out a definition of good learning and teaching that doesn't exclude me.

❁

I want to thank many friends and colleagues for help with these essays over the years. The essays all went through many drafts, and I often gave early versions (sometimes even successive versions) to friends for responses—which I was fortunate to receive in abundance. Often I had a chance to read a version to some group or conference, and again my requests for responses were generously answered. In particular, I've been pestering people for more than ten years with versions of my doubting/believing essay in an effort to think my way through it, and more than a couple of dozen people have sent me long and thoughtful letters in response—for which I'm enormously grateful.

Because so many people helped me, I cannot name them here, but I would particularly mention how thankful I am to colleagues and students at M.I.T., Franconia College, The Evergreen State College, Wesleyan University, The Bard Institute for Writing and Thinking, The Bread Loaf School of English, and SUNY at Stony Brook. Special thanks to Joan Bossert and Curtis Church, my editors at Oxford. I am most grateful of all to my family, Cami, Abby, and Benjy, for giving me the most precious richness and support of all.

August 1985   P.E.
Stony Brook, New York

EMBRACING
CONTRARIES

PART I

✿✿✿

THE LEARNING PROCESS

You might say that the three essays in this section are more about thinking than about learning. But I am interested in learning *as thinking*—learning even *as expression*. I want to resist our tendency to picture learning as merely "taking things in"—separate from thinking as "stirring things around in there" and expression as "pouring things out."

The three essays in this section approach the learning process from very different angles, but each one emphasizes the role of contraries in the mind's task of restructuring itself. All three are arguments for seeing coherence and fruitfulness in processes we often see as messy or useless. (For example, making intuitive or playful metaphors, guessing and free associating, inviting our writing to be messy and contradictory, moving back and forth between different modes of writing within the same piece, and telling stories and describing scenes in order to "think carefully.") Learning is slower this way, but deeper and more long-lasting. Disorientation is not so disorienting when we feel it as useful.

The first essay was the earliest written. It explores the two basic cognitive processes involved in the very ability to learn— the two contrary ways in which the mind manages to categorize or make sense of the information it encounters. Its context is cognitive psychology.

The second essay was written about ten years later. It's context is writing (it was part of a book about writing), but its subject is "cooking": how we can coax the mind to transform itself or restructure its own contents through various kinds of interaction between contraries. Where the first essay is highly theoretical, this one emphasizes the practical question of how to increase productivity in thinking.

The third essay is a recent one arguing for a larger and more inclusive *model* of thinking that includes contrary processes: structured, logical thinking that involves control or steering; and intuitive, unstructured thinking that involves the ability to relinquish control or take one's hands off the steering wheel.

CHAPTER 1

❀❀❀

I wrote this essay after my first five years of teaching. It grew out of the powerful impact I felt from the fact that this teaching was almost all interdisciplinary. Interdisciplinary study seemed to make learning "real" for me and for my students in a way that learning had not often been before. (Later in my career I taught nine years at an institution devoted primarily to interdisciplinary teaching, The Evergreen State College.)

My introduction to teaching (1960 to 1963) was in M.I.T.'s core course for freshmen. Harald Reiche, a classicist who designed and directed the course, called it "nondisciplinary" rather than "interdisciplinary" because we focused on texts which predated—and even called into question—the very intellectual divisions represented by our disciplines: the texts were from Greece, Rome, the New Testament, and the Middle Ages. I had just quit graduate school in English literature and these three years of nondisciplinary teaching renewed my interest in books and learning, enabled me to study again, and made me think once more that I would cast my lot with books and teaching.

My next two years I joined in the founding of Franconia College where I chaired our interdisciplinary core course. (I had more college teaching experience than any of my colleagues!) The entire faculty of seven collaborated in designing a required *two*-year course. We chose twelve critical moments or incidents in the history of our culture—each to serve as the occasion for five weeks of reading from various disciplines. (Our "moments" ranged from Moses deciding how to respond to the burning bush to Marilyn Monroe committing suicide.)

Franconia College, new and unheard of in 1963, was not a college that many students would choose who could choose another. As I was engaged in teaching in that large, white, nineteenth-century hotel

5

on a hill, I had a recurring vision of an archetypal high school classroom: in the front of the room were those M.I.T. students I had taught
for three years—hands raised eagerly, on top of everything; at the
back of the same classroom were my present students—completely
apathetic and resentful. As the first year wore on, I was moved to
notice how these back-of-the-room students gradually woke up and
showed themselves to be lively and smart when we provided this interdisciplinary course and a community of supportive and excited teaching. It was then that I realized that learning can always be exciting and
personally involving—for any student. Students who look dumb are
not, but schools often help make them feel dumb.

In short, the nondisciplinary curriculum at Franconia—where we
constantly blurred the distinction between the disciplines, and between what is academic and what is personal or "practical" or "everyday"—didn't just give students a sense of themselves as invested students, it also gave me a sense of direction as a teacher. The experience
confirmed my commitment to higher education not just as a place
to work but as a culture I felt a part of—and needed to push against.
Where nothing else had induced me to return to graduate school, this
did the trick: a desire to kibitz. I realized that no one would listen to
me about higher education if they could say, "Well he's just sour because he couldn't hack it." Paradoxically, this pragmatic reason for re-
turning to graduate school ("Who cares about literature, I just need a
'credential' ") provided the psychological safety within which I could
gradually rediscover my love of literature and words for their own
sake.

After my first year back in school, as a reward to myself for survival
and good behavior, I gave myself that first summer to study cognitive
psychology: I wanted to learn how to describe more fully and clearly
the essential nature of the nondisciplinary learning I'd been involved
with for five years. It seemed to me that a deeper *kind* of learning had
occurred, but I didn't know how to describe that learning or to make
that case for interdisciplinary learning except in personal and affective
terms. Of course the personal and affective dimension was important
to me, but I knew that a powerful case could be made in purely cognitive terms. It also seemed to me, naively, that if I could "say it in
cognitive psychology" it would be truer. For these were the heady
years of new curriculum planning efforts in science, spearheaded by
Bruner and Zacharias.

The following essay resulted. I'm arguing that, whereas plain,
garden variety, in-school learning consists of the ability to apply academic concepts to academic contexts, "real learning" consists of two

further skills: the ability to apply known concepts more widely—to situations never found in school; and the ability to *invent* new concepts never presented in school. By fostering these two skills, nondisciplinary teaching can teach the ability to learn.

Nondisciplinary Courses and the Two Roots of Real Learning

Socrates and St. Augustine argue about whether or not we always act on the basis of what we know. Experience reveals both are right: we learn certain things in Socrates' fully integrated fashion such that we never unwittingly contradict them in word, thought, or deed. Yet there are other things we learn—and *seem* to learn very well—which we nonetheless contradict: we sometimes think, talk, or act as though we didn't know them. The distinction between the two sorts of learning is real enough—often a matter of observable behavior—but difficult to define or explain. At the risk of Henry James' taunt, "oh, you and your Boston 'really's!'" I call it the difference between *real learning* and *learning*. Probably we should not disparage plain learning. Our efforts produce it so often, it must serve an important goal of the organism. Nevertheless, this paper is an attempt to understand real learning and how to get more of it.

It can often seem that noncurricular and nonacademic activity tend to produce more "real learning" than textbooks, lectures, and classes: personal, social, and political situations, jobs, getting into trouble, quitting or getting kicked out of school—all these seem to teach better, if (perhaps) less, than our classes. When students really learn in class, it often seems because their class at that moment was an instance of a social and affective situation—fighting or joining others about felt ideas.

This is a bleak point of view. But there is eminent company. One turns, for example, to well-thumbed passages in Whitehead, Einstein, and Riesman. Perhaps Dewey pours the most limpid distillation of cognitive skepticism: "No thought, no idea, can possibly be conveyed as an idea from one person to another (Dewey 188).

But this very skepticism produces the seeds for hope. It makes you notice the rare occasion when a purely intellectual transaction strikes home and produces real learning. We see the phenomenon in its purest state if we ignore all transactions that are in themselves affective or social—all inspiring or powerful lectures, all class situations that are genuinely interactive, all emotive, fictional, or poetic reading—and concentrate on the fact that *some* people on *some* totally solitary occasions are affected to the core by simply taking in information or an idea. (Such events tend themselves to produce affect.) It would seem then that the profound fact about education is not that most of what students read means very little, but that occasionally, for some students, something read means a great deal.

I put aside in this essay, therefore, all questions concerning the affective, social, or putting-into-action ingredient in learning, and restrict myself to a purely cognitive view of curriculum.* My argument is that curricular changes alone could increase real learning significantly—could help more students learn more profoundly from reading a book. (I do not mean to imply that curricular changes are enough.)

The sort of nondisciplinary course I advocate—to supplement disciplinary courses, not replace them—is one in which a single concrete particular is seen from the point of view of the widest range of conflicting models, metaphors, hypotheses, conceptual schemes, sets, and disciplines. Relatively current and loaded events would make natural choices for the focus of such courses, e.g., the close vote in the Senate for initial deployment of the ABM or some event in Gandhi's life.

* I succeed only partially, therefore, in sidestepping the cognitive/affective trap. Thus I feel I should summarize my own premises: "affective" and "cognitive" can usefully be treated as different and separable, yet they are really opposite terminals of a single continuum. More precisely, they are different points of view for looking at what is optimally a single complex process. If this is a valid model, affective and cognitive would be functions of each other except as you approach pathology at either end of the continuum: that is, if you achieve really good affective learning you will capture good cognitive learning in your nets at the same time, or with good cognitive learning get affective learning.

But it is important not to spend all efforts merely on trying to unearth all the contemporary details. Long tangential forays are at the heart of this nondisciplinary process. The study of the ABM vote might well lead to sustained examination of the technology itself, Defense Department budgeting, lobbying processes in Congress, deterrence theory and game theory, the cultural terrain of an ABM site, and others. The focus on some event in Gandhi's life might involve forays into the theory of nonviolence, Indian culture, Eastern Religion, the physiology and psychology of vegetarianism and fasting, psychoanalytic biography à la Erikson, and others. A class might sometimes break into subgroups which would move in separate directions and report back to the whole, but this process should not go so far as to let students fall into merely specializing.

These concrete events, objects, or people need not, however, be necessarily current or even real, e.g., Adam and Eve deciding to eat the apple; Newton's alleged encounter with a later apple. I don't know the best criteria for choosing the concrete particular other than that it be genuinely important both to students and faculty and that it be fruitful for exploration through the widest range of modes of conceiving it.

Such nondisciplinary courses immediately extend beyond the professional competence of any faculty member. This is an advantage as much as a disadvantage. A teacher must relinquish the role of "expert" or "professional." At most he can profess to bring special skills and experience to the basic process of wondering about something and deciding to do something about it. He must take the role of collaborator. He can only do this honestly and well to the extent that he sets an example to the students of demanding that the course serve his own self-interested curiosity.

The crucial question about such courses, however, is not how to plan them. That will work out. The real question, given the current power of our disciplinary structure in universities and our disciplinary training, is whether enough members of the university want this sort of course.

Learning as the Acquisition of Categories

I follow cognitive psychologists' functional, process-oriented model of the mind and its furniture—somewhat like Gilbert Ryle's attempts as a philosopher to exorcise the ghost in the machine. Ideas aren't things or even truths that the mind sits in the middle and knows, but rather activities that follow certain rules; or the dispositions to perform such activities. And the mind isn't a thing or a place or a knower but is the shape of those activities or rules.

The paradigm learning activity is *categorizing* or *learning concepts,* and what that means is illustrated by statements like these:

> "To categorize is to render discriminably different things equivalent, to group the objects and events and people around us into classes, and to respond to them in terms of their class membership rather than their uniqueness." (Bruner, Goodnow, and Austin 1)

> A category is a scheme for processing data, for coding information, for transforming input. [The models and metaphors from information theory and computer affairs are persuasive.]

> A category or concept "expresses something that can be done with objects; the concept of an object is a prediction about what it will do or what we can do with it." (Bruner 1964)

> A concept is a method for making inferences or for going beyond the information given.

The implication for learning is that you don't teach anyone by feeding him information. It's processed and "filed," but whether it can ever be found again is a function of his filing and processing system which is precisely what you have left unchanged and probably very bad: brute (short-term) memory is high in the competition for man's feeblest capacity (Miller). You only teach someone if you affect the way he files his data, processes his information, or makes his inferences. Teaching or learning involves introducing categories. It seems to be a matter of making the learner construct them: "seeing, hearing and remembering are all acts of construction . . ." (Neisser, 1967, 10). The relation is not accidental between this emphasis on categories in cognitive psychology and the curricular reforms in which Zacharias and Bruner have played an important role. Those reforms, with their emphasis upon the underlying shape or structure of a discipline, have been built on the insight that a discipline can best be defined in terms of categories or concepts (Cronbach, Ch. 10). Thus if physics were just a lot of information not structured by superordinate, organizing categories, it would only be a "field" where inquiry takes place, not a discipline. Presumably, if all our concepts were laid out and arranged into the most efficient taxonomies, we would have the profile of our disciplines—or of what our disciplines ought to be. By emphasizing the structure of a discipline, one emphasizes high-order categories which process a maximum of data. This is the source of transfer in learning. (Historically, this whole point of view has served as a rebuttal to a previous generation of psychologists who thought transfer in learning didn't happen.)

I quarrel, however, with the exclusive curricular emphasis on disciplinary structure or high-order generalization. The quarrel is limited because I accept the importance of disciplinary courses and even majoring; but I argue that they should be supplemented by the opposite approach. Good disciplinary courses concentrate on crucial, superordinate concepts and apply them to the broadest range of data: we could say loosely that they use fewer and fewer concepts on more and more data. This is the source of their power and precision. The opposite of disciplinary courses would use more and more concepts on fewer and fewer data. This would mean focusing on a concrete person, event, place, or thing—that is, the lowest level concept—and trying to see it from as many points of view as possible.*

---

* I venture upon thin ice by implying physics as a paradigm of all disciplines. The fact that Zacharias and Bruner made it across does not mean that the next man will not fall through. For example, one can develop a strong argument that courses in literature, music, or art are precisely what I call nondisciplinary: a prolonged, catholic contemplation of the concrete or unique. And the same for history. I admit in theory the force of this objection, and indeed hope to pursue it for clues about literature. Yet what I am calling for would only be served if an individual work of art—or *single* historical event—were exclusively studied in a course which directly involved as many disciplines as possible. This may suggest fruitful ideas for the teaching of, say, literature and the training of teachers of literature: the main point would seem to be

To see why a disciplinary curriculum is not enough and should be supplemented with nondisciplinary courses, it is necessary to explore more fully what is meant by real learning.

Learning is getting categories. Even changing them would mean getting new ones. But of course the most trivial learning consists of getting categories: Pavlov taught a category to his dog. And all too similarly, when teachers teach students to write comprehensible essays feeding back undigested ideas from lectures and reading, this too constitutes imparting concepts. True enough, it requires important and sophisticated skills to take in concepts well enough to reformulate them on an essay or exam; and it's hard enough, God knows, for a teacher to make even that happen.

But real learning, in contrast, is the phenomenon of so abundantly "understanding" the concept in the book or lecture that it becomes part of us and determines the way we see, feel, and act—the way we process the widest range of data. If all we can do is answer academic essay questions about it, that means it will only process data roughly similar to the data in which it came:

---

that some disciplines have an *a priori* vested interest in the concrete or unique—in and of itself—which disciplines in science do not share since they define unique things only as instances.

But even though literature has a different relation to the concrete, it should nevertheless continually seek to uncover ever more superordinate categories which render order among the "data" in the discipline—even if those categories do not exhaust the significance of each datum in its uniqueness. That is, categories like Northrop Frye's may only specify what Shakespeare's plays share with trivial works and hence seem entirely to ignore what makes them great. Yet categories like Frye's add enormously to our understanding of Shakespeare's plays. Not *everything* about those plays is unique, and though it would seem a necessary truth that the excellence in Shakespeare's plays lies in what they alone possess, a more roundabout way of putting it may not be wholly sophistical—namely, that the excellence in a great work may lie in qualities or effects which it shares with inferior ones, but that a great writer manages better to liberate these qualities, bring them to life, clarify them, or embody them. (This would explain why those interested in the *craft* of literature will often tend to emphasize the *uniqueness* in a great work.)

Only by working out better high-order categories or abstractions can the study of literature find its *own* identity as a discipline, and so cease to mimic the outward mannerisms of science—usually the nineteenth century brands. In short, disciplines like literature seem to invite theoretical development in the direction of both the concrete and the abstract.

a fairly narrow range of words and types of sentences. It won't process many of the words and types of sentences we come across outside of class, and even fewer of the nonverbal stimuli we bump into.

We can say now that there are two ingredients in real learning. The first is *the ability to apply already-learned concepts to the widest range of data;* or *to recognize the widest range of potential instances of the concept.* The concepts taught in most college courses are extremely potent, so there is scarcely a datum the student meets in his day that is not an instance or potential instance of one of the concepts he has "attained" in his academic work. But he tends to process only a fraction of these data with these concepts. If it were otherwise, good teachers would be relieved from the paradoxical function so many realize has come to be theirs—that is, to "educate" the student to the point where he is finally conscious that he doesn't really believe that the earth goes around the sun, that a moving body keeps moving at the same speed forever unless something stops it, that there ever was such a thing as the Middle Ages—much less the nineteenth century—or that the words in a poem symbolize sex or death or whatever. The good teacher realizes that he often has the choice of either getting to one hundred, but having it all mean nothing really, or spending most of his time just getting to zero—but meaningfully. All this is a matter of the first ingredient in real learning: how widely the student applies known concepts.

But when a person comes upon data that can't be processed with the concepts he has (or not processed to solve the given problem), then the ability to apply concepts widely does no good, and he needs instead the second source of real learning, *the ability to construct new concepts.*

Of course there is a continuum between applying known concepts widely and inventing new ones. The new ones must in some sense be transformations of present stock: the more they derive from high-order or abstract concepts, the more they will feel like transformations; the more they derive from low-order specific concepts, the more they will feel new. Translation is easier and more obvious as you move up the ladder of abstraction and schematization. But even though these two ingredients of real learning lie on a continuum we can usefully treat them separately.

In each of the next two sections I will isolate a root cognitive capacity behind each source of real learning.

The Ability to Apply Known Concepts or to Get Experience from Symbols

The ability to apply known concepts widely, I must admit, is in one sense definitely increased by studying a discipline and emphasizing its structure or superordinate categories. Bruner gives the example of showing students how a worm changes his path up an inclined plane, when the angle of the plane is changed, in order to maintain his ascent of fifteen degrees. This is for the sake of leading the student to the concept that an organism, as its external stimulation is varied, changes its locomotor action in order to maintain a constant. The student is then shown how this concept can be applied to a huge range of organism behaviors, e.g., the density of a swarm of locusts varies with the temperature (Bruner, 1960, 6).

This emphasis on a superordinate concept is not merely handy for getting and remembering lots of subordinate ones that fall under its sway. One feels in it a real power of application and understanding. "Grasping the structure of a subject is understanding it in a way that permits many other things to be related to it meaningfully (Bruner, 1960, 7).

But we must look twice. Is it the disciplinary emphasis upon the high-level concepts that *in itself* gives the power of applying concepts widely? The full fair answer is both Yes and No. Yes, it does, in the sense that emphasis on structure gives the power to apply the concept over a wide range of data. If the student were presented helter-skelter with only low-level concepts, he would be far less able to apply them to new data. But strictly speaking, this is only a *potential* power of application. To the extent that the student *has* the gift of applying concepts, he applies them better to an exponential degree. Yet the emphasis on structure or superordinate categories has done nothing to help directly the ability, in itself, to apply concepts. (As things work out, this is a slight exaggeration: helping a student get more mileage out of a skill will almost invariably improve that skill in the end.)

If, as I've heard, curricular reforms of this sort have often helped successful students strikingly more than others (some say they don't help poor students at all), one could explain the fact by my hypothesis that improved disciplinary structure helps students to the extent they already have the capacity to apply concepts, but does not directly improve this capacity.

It may be objected at this point that my attack is hasty; that of course disciplinary structure is not enough in itself; that everyone recognizes the need to supplement it with the inductive method; that Bruner himself devotes a compelling essay to the value of induction ("The Act of Discovery"). We can explore this objection and get to the heart of the matter by exploring induction. We will see that induction is valuable and important, but does not solve our main problem of enhancing the ability, in itself, to apply concepts widely.

What is induction? First the student is given a lot of data, but he doesn't know what it amounts to or is supposed to amount to. Then he gets the "click"—the "aha!": something has emerged for him in the data. It is definitely a third and separate step—often requiring still more data—for the student to arrive where he can *understand* or *say* what concept emerged with the click.

It is clear for many reasons that the click stage is the important one. For one thing, there is almost always a definitely physical response that accompanies the click: a smile, or tension, or release of tension, or sudden movement, or some such thing. What's more, a person can operate accurately on the basis of the "clicked" concept at this stage—process data by it—even if he never reaches the third stage of knowing what the concept is. There is nothing uncommon about this phenomenon. (I was going to say "nothing mysterious," but it seems mysterious: we can call it the principle of one's grasp always exceeding one's reach.) The linguists have shown us a ubiquitous example: everyone's use of his native language consists of behavior very accurately in accord with rules which few understand. (It's only the rules we know that we violate.)

Studies seem to show that induction is the most successful or foolproof way of learning concepts; next comes a compromise method—explaining the concept verbally, but then giving examples; fewest students can take their concepts neat (Hendrix). Now we can understand why. For induction produces the experience—the "feel"—of a concept *before* there are any words for it. It is this *nonverbal experience* of a concept which enables one to recognize a huge range of instances of the concept: one doesn't need verbal cues as mediation.

We can refine our understanding of the process at the heart of induction by pausing over an interesting fact: when examples of a concept are presented after the concept has been verbally explained, sometimes these examples *don't* produce the crucial, nonverbal experience that would have occurred if the examples had come first; yet sometimes these post-explanation examples *do* produce the click. Therefore, we must avoid any oversimple answer, such as that words (the explanation) prevent the nonverbal experience. The truth of the matter would seem to be that the full nonverbal experience of a concept requires that instances be experienced doubly: not merely as instances of the concept but also as instances of conflicting concepts or *gestalten;* there must be the shift effect as in an ambiguous optical illusion. This is the source of the click. In short, examples of X given after it has been verbally explained, sometimes refuse to feel like anything but instances of X, and so we have gained not at all in our ability to see something as an instance of X that we didn't already see that way.

Analyzing the virtue of induction shows precisely the condition behind the ability to apply concepts widely: the possession of a strong and definite nonverbal experience of the concept and a strong tie between this experience and the words—each should readily call up the other. But if this is what we need for the ability to apply concepts widely, then induction is not the way to get it. For one thing, life is too short to learn by induction everything we would "really know"; and for college teachers, especially, there is always "too much to cover." But more important than this, induction *puts* the experience there by means of setting up the "real" experience; whereas what we need is the ability to put the experience there "artificially" and vicariously with words alone—without, that is, having *had* the experience. Induction *gives* the student the experience instead of getting him to construct the experience for himself out of his repertoire of word meanings. In short, behind the capacity to apply concepts widely is *the capacity to construct new experience from symbols.*

A "neo-behaviorist" explanation of verbal behavior provides a possible model for seeing this ability in more detail (Staats and Staats). It would amount to the process of constructing out of word meanings—or more precisely, out of the "implicit responses to verbal stimuli"—a response to a stimulus never experienced. It might also be called "mediated tacting": the child who has learned by direct experience to associate "book" and "purple" with their referents, but who has never seen a purple book, succeeds in fetching one from the next room when asked because he has been able to construct the experience to match a concept he has learned only verbally. In short, it is the root ability in the use of language as a "second signalling system" to overcome limitations of experience.

L. S. Vygotsky gives us a useful way of understanding the more complex forms of this ability to get experience from symbols—as it might be involved in college learning. He describes the development of the thought of the child as the continual interpenetration of "scientific concepts" and "spontaneous concepts." Scientific concepts have nothing necessarily to do with science: they are simply the concepts that the child learns formally and verbally—usually in school. "These concepts are schematic and lack the rich content derived from personal experience" (Vygotsky 108). He writes of the Russian child who knows "slavery" and "exploitation" in this fashion (especially schematic in a Marxist context) but who has not experienced them. Spontaneous concepts on the other hand are everyday ones that the child learns operationally by immediate confrontation with experience; they are thus "saturated with experience," but often cannot be formulated or explained. Piaget talks of the child who can use "brother" or "because" correctly, but cannot explain or, seemingly, understand them. The child has them as spontaneous concepts.

Vygotsky asserts then that two contrasting motions are necessary for the interpenetration of these two types of concepts. Spontaneous or experientially-learned concepts are helped "upward," as it were, to self-conscious understanding by the path of the scientific or formally-learned concepts "downward." But scientific concepts are only helped downward or fully experienced—and thus fully able to be applied to unfamiliar instances—to the extent that spontaneous concepts have worked their way up to actualize them.

This is a useful model for understanding the performance of students in college. To illustrate, I would make three crude categories:

1. The "turned on" student who is very interested, productive, and full of insights. He gets inside the subject and lives it; sees instances of the concepts everywhere. His output is sometimes not efficient or extensive because he is so enmeshed: he has to fight hard for perspective, and sometimes does not achieve it. In this student the interpenetration of spontaneous and scientific concepts is rich.

2. The student who does competent, decent work but is not particularly interested or involved. He has no trouble turning out an acceptable curricular product but seldom comes up with original insights. He gets only enough experience from the symbols to operate in the context of their classroom uses.

3. The student who isn't quite getting it. He feels he can understand the individual words, sentences, even books in the course, but can't seem to put them together to make any overall sense. He often can do decently on objective tests of short focal length. In such a student the interpenetration is clearly insufficient; he can work with the school concepts only in the very form they are presented. He can't put the words or sentences together to generate more than the narrowest experiences—that is, he is poor at constructing experience from symbols.

This model would help explain why there seemed to be an increasing number of students of the second sort (decent competence with no sense of involvement) even as early as the early sixties before political issues turned many away from their courses. For there had been considerable sophistication and structuring at a higher conceptual level of the concepts taught in college: college curricula became more high-powered. Yet there had not been a corresponding increase for many high-school and college students of the kind of activity that brings corresponding development of spontaneous concepts: leisure for just living, having unstructured experience, thinking and talking in simple response to the environment bumped into. Indeed the importance of academic success in high school and college had probably reduced free time and loose experience for most college-bound students.

The interpenetration of spontaneous and scientific concepts—the ability to get experience from symbols—would help give a sense of personal involvement or a sense of self in relation to what is being studied. And a deficiency in this capacity would help produce the common feeling that the thing being studied, though perfectly well understood, is not quite "real." This is Lionel Trilling on students in a seminar on Victorian England:

> Despite the vivacity of their minds, they found it almost impossible to imagine the actuality of personal and social situations in the fairly recent past. The distant past might perhaps have given them less trouble, as being nearly in the realm of fantasy and comprehensible as such. Many of them, as it happened, had concerned themselves with the study of religion, and they were surely most gifted in their understanding of the more arcane aspects of theology; but if we raised questions about the Thirty-Nine Articles, or the disabilities of Dissenters, or the functions of a bishop, they were not merely impatient of such Philistine considerations; we had the distinct impression that, whatever religion *was* for them, it clearly had nothing to do with an (actual) religious community, a church, or prayer. (Quoted in Bell 167)

Students, too, remark of this phenomenon. The glib use of high-order conceptualizations seems a hallmark of our time—even the one that refers to the phenomenon itself: "dissociation of sensibility." Hegel puts it in philosophical terms:

> Nowadays, the task before us consists not so much in getting the individual clear of the state of sensuous immediacy, and making him a substance that thinks and is grasped in terms of thought, but, rather the very opposite: it consists in actualizing the universal, and giving it spiritual vitality by the process of breaking down and superseding fixed and determinate thoughts. (Quoted in Bell 167)

The diagnosis has got out of hand to imply so many of the ills of our time that it would be unlikely to find any single, neat disease. But if there is any strength in my previous argument, one important ingredient of this general problem would consist of a weakness in one root of "real learning"—that is, in the ability to apply concepts widely (or recognize all instances); and behind it an insufficient interpenetration of scientific and spontaneous concepts: a weakness in the ability to get experience from symbols.

If the diagnosis is valid, what is the remedy? Obviously, "nature's way" is "just living," particularly "really living." This would explain why there are often such beneficial effects—even from the narrow point of view of success in studies—from dropping out of school for a year, from going out for a sport or an activity, and from "getting involved" in some action group. But because continual upward sophistication of disciplinary curricula widens the gap between formally-learned and experientially-learned concepts, and because time for "just living" is harder and harder for students to get, there would be great value in nondisciplinary courses.

The main process in such courses would be the sustained examination and contemplation of the concrete. There are a number of ways of talking about the beneficial effects of this activity. (1) The concrete in this sort of course serves as the intersection for the widest possible range of scientific and spontaneous concepts. Thus there is an interaction and fertilization among concepts producing in the student a richer repertoire of, if you will, "implicit responses to verbal stimuli." (2) The student will learn to see and feel the concrete as an instance of a huge range of different and conflicting concepts, and this experience will increase his ability to get the cognitive click which is the root of the ability to produce a *nonverbal* experience of a concept. (3) Increased structure in disciplines yields a huge *potential* gain in the ability to apply concepts widely. These interdisciplinary courses would bring such potential power to fruition.

It often happens these days that when a new, vociferously "relevant" course is given, students discover that the "relevance" of the new course somehow mysteriously evaporates just as it is getting under way. Now we can see one reason why. Frequently the cognitive strategy of the new course is no different from that of the preceding ones. "Let them study the inner city, but, by

God, they better do so in a way that maintains first-rate academic standards." "First-rate academic standards," unfortunately, has too often come to mean using a cognitive strategy and course model derived from our high-powered disciplines. "Academic study" and "disciplinary study" can seem almost synonymous. Anything else is likely to feel "sloppy" to most academics—trained as they are in disciplines. And so the new course on the inner-city or the counter-culture may be fruitlessly abstract and only emphasize powerful, high-order concepts. It then turns out to be no help (labeled "irrelevance") to the problem of the lack of inter-penetration of formally-learned and experientially-learned con-cepts—nothing at all, that is, to help the student to improve at getting experience from symbols.

The Ability to Invent New Concepts or to Think with Metaphors

We turn from the first to the second source of real learning—from the ability to apply concepts widely to the ability to invent new concepts. Again the strategy will be to explore its relation to induction.

There is no doubt that induction is perfect for getting the student started in the process of inventing concepts. That's what induction is: the student doesn't know the concept; he is fed data; he invents it. It gives him practice and also the experience of success, both of which are crucial in learning anything. But induction as it is used in an academic, pedagogical setting—that is, planned induction in a discipline—is a severely restricted busi-ness. Indeed most of what is called the inductive method in school and college is really only pretending: the most striking example is laboratory science—exercise, often, in making it come out the way the book says it should. But even when the answer is not known ahead of time, the data are chosen because they imply the answer, and sufficient data are almost always given to make the new concept pop up without much difficulty. Also the range of data and of concepts is restricted and comparatively predict-able because it is a course in a discipline.

But our interest in real learning—the relation of what the student studies to the rest of what he thinks, sees, feels, and does—forces us to be interested in the contrasting state of affairs: where there are not enough data—or do not seem to be enough—to imply the concept that is needed. In other words, the student doesn't know what his data really are, and he has no hints about what sort of concept the "answer" will be. This is the situation of someone working at the frontiers of research; and it is the situation of the student faced with a problem or the need for a decision in his life outside his academic work. If he doesn't know what to do, doesn't know how to solve his problem or make his decision, it means either that he hasn't been able to bring to bear the necessary concepts he knows, or that he doesn't have the necessary concept for processing the situation and thus needs to invent it.

It is illuminating to consider the latter situation hypothetically and very abstractly: inventing a new concept. (It is also illuminating to translate this proposal into timely language—"What is the strategy for a machine to solve problems that are too hard for it?") A person has a problem, which is, in effect, data he cannot process. This problem or data we'll call X. We know that none of the concepts he has will work. Therefore he needs to invent a new one he's never heard of or conceived of—a real act of creation like Galileo turning around his way of thinking and conceiving a frictionless body moving in abstract space. We will call his answer Z—this concept he has never conceived of and which thus probably goes against the grain of his thinking. And as in these cases, though he is aware of his problem data, X, he's not aware of what would constitute the other data he needs to help him to his answer.

We can now construct his ideal strategy and thereby see what we can learn about inventing categories or learning how to learn. We'll call the concepts he knows A . . . Q. Of the concepts in this whole range, A, B, and C are the ones he really knows well, and P and Q are ones he can operate with but doesn't understand and is not conscious of.

In trying to find something he doesn't know, he will no doubt start by considering the possibility that he does know: he'll try A, B, and C. But they won't work. Now he feels stuck. If he just wanders around looking for Z—something he's never conceived and which isn't a transformation of his known concepts (relatively speaking)—he will spend his whole life in a futile search. Yet he isn't really stuck. If he were, we would still be living in the trees. *Though he cannot look for Z, he can look for things that are in some way functions of, or vary with, X on the basis of Z.*

First, he will probably "discover" P and Q—the concepts he possesses only operationally. Since they are among the concepts that give the shape to his thinking, his eye will first be caught by things that are functions of X and P and Q—things that vary with X and P and Q.

All is going well. For all this while he has been developing his sensitivity to X, and now he will begin to be able to notice things that vary ever more faintly and unexpectedly with it. He will be able to notice things that vary with X otherwise than according to the concepts he already possesses, otherwise than according to A . . . Q. This is now the stage of wrong but original answers—perhaps S, U, and Y. But finally, his eye will now be faintly caught by things that vary with X on the basis of Z; and as he gets the smell or the feel of these things and finds more of them, he will get the smell of Z. If he just wants to solve X, he may stop with finding and using Z. If he is a self-conscious collector of concepts, he will keep at the adumbrating—metaphor collecting—process till he can consciously conceptualize Z. Thus we see that from a group of analogues or metaphors that suggest Z obliquely by triangulation, he will finally be able to formulate Z directly.

The speed and directness with which he performs this creative or inventive task depends on his sensitivity to the process. To the extent that he insists on proceeding logically, it will take him perhaps forever. To the extent that he knows and trusts his ability to proceed analogically—by feel of functionality—he will get there more quickly.

This analogical process can be related to the fact that people who are good inventors of concepts—who make breakthroughs that require the forging of original concepts or new ways of thinking—seem mysteriously but characteristically to have what is called a good nose for data. When one looks back over their activity, it seems they have been collecting relevant data for years, even when they weren't conscious that it was relevant data.

It is perhaps clear now that this ideal strategy for inventing concepts is really the metaphoric process. Investigators of invention and creativity have been on the track of metaphor for years. The approach to metaphor outlined above brings into relief a fact that is often overlooked, however: *metaphor is not a case of two-termed resemblance, but rather of three-termed functionality.* The idea of "resemblance" obscures the important, three-part structure that is metaphor's source of power. The hidden or implicit third term by which the two noticed members are functional is the power by which one's grasp can exceed one's reach. When, for example, the child learns to use "because" correctly in sentences but doesn't understand the meaning of the concept, he is perceiving a functionality between certain kinds of phrases and operating on the basis of the hidden third term. In fact, any time we inductively grasp a concept, we are exercising our natural sensitivity to functionality in order to use that implicit third member which we do not explicitly understand. The analogy or sense of relationship *constructs* or *invents* the third member (which is always on a higher level of abstraction). By making other similar analogies, we can come to understand the third member. What this means is that the organism is capable of responding to a functionality between two concepts on the basis of a third, *before it has any acquaintance with that third member,* i.e., responding to *potential* functionality. What occurs, presumably, is an act of construction whereby the organism builds or invents the new concept—builds or invents a relationship between the two given concepts—but does so operationally or intuitively. We can construct and use new concepts in this way far in advance of our ability to be conscious of what we have made and are using. This is precisely the aspect of metaphor by which it is the source of originality in thought.*

Let me explain this metaphorical or analogical process less abstractly and schematically. It is mostly poets and children who are given to saying that things remind them of seemingly unrelated things and they don't know why. But in fact we all engage

---

* I was not aware when I wrote this passage that corroboration of a sort was to be had in Michael Polanyi's *Personal Knowledge* and *The Tacit Dimension*. But he does not work out the process so fully in relation to metaphor and analogy.

in this crucial process of sensing functionality—constructing meta-phors on the basis of implicit third terms we are not aware of. Every element in a dream is such a metaphor or analogy. Dreams are tricky, however, because often one of the first two terms is hidden as well as the third term: often I can only say "I dreamed last night I was chased by a zebra" and so I am faced by a three-termed equation with two unknowns; but if I can say "I dreamed about you last night but you were a zebra chasing me," then only the middle term is unknown—the category which links "you" and "zebra."

But in waking life, many people don't often experience this three-termed, constructive character of metaphor. They've been taught too often that it's cuckoo to think two apparently unre-lated things are the same and not know how or why—so they've stopped doing it. We're not supposed to talk beyond our means. Therefore, when most people think of metaphor, they think of traditional metaphors in which either there's not much of a three-termed structure or else the third term doesn't tell us any-thing we didn't know. If, for example, we say we "plowed" through the morning's work, there isn't usually much genuine plowing in it, and thus not much interaction between two sepa-rate elements to produce a third concept. Or if we compare our girl to a flower, we are usually (not necessarily, of course) ritually calling upon an already hallowed conglomerate third term hav-ing to do with beauty, desirability, smell, delicacy, and natural-ness. But the capacity is in us all. Every time someone has a feel-ing about something, he can be sure that there is an implicit analogy or metaphor buried there—and the more unexpected and difficult-to-explain the feeling, the greater the payload.

The generative power of metaphor's three-termed structure is only clear in the case of an unfamiliar metaphor. Consider "the moon is a sow." (For this kind of discussion, the simplest, Aris-totelian definition of metaphor is best: any use of a "wrong" word on purpose or any implied comparison.) "The moon is a sow" may seem simply opaque at first. But if the words are en-couraged to reverberate and if one forces oneself to try to link them, the interaction will bring to mind potential aspects of each that might not otherwise have been thought of: e.g., the moon as heavy, dirty, mottled, female; a sow as permanent, archetypal, shining, the focus of everyone's eyes. Someone else might read in different highlights. (My view already has a "set," as will become clear.) For the thing to notice about a remote comparison like this one is that if there are no focusing clues, if one didn't make the comparison by oneself, and if it doesn't immediately touch off some already-responsive chord, it seems as though there are both too many and too few points of comparison and nothing clicks into place.

But if one does force oneself to read in links, new highlights, qualities, or perceptions are brought to mind. So if one wanted to have as many ideas as possible about the moon, it would be productive to go around comparing it to everything one can think of to see what potential aspects are invented and forced to light. (The same for "sow.") This process makes it clear why the third, more abstract, middle concept of a metaphor is usually not noticed: it usually remains merely implicit, serving only to bring to light some more concrete potential aspect of one of the overt terms.

But it is precisely this implicit third term that the present analysis tells us to investigate. If I hear "the moon is a sow" for the first time and it seems merely opaque, I am liable to end up with any number of different third terms—or perhaps none. But suppose that click of recognition occurs when I hear it; or suppose I had spoken the metaphor myself out of some feeling (even though I didn't understand why I said it). Then it would be true to say that the third term is already there waiting to be brought to birth. Sometimes pondering will do it. But often it won't. Then it is a good idea to keep the metaphor in the back of my mind—and the feeling of it—and try to keep my eyes out for other situations and other metaphors which remind me of it or have the same flavor. Strictly speaking, these would be other metaphors with the same third member. But if the implicit concept is at all new and obscure, if it goes at all against the grain of my present stock of concepts, such direct hits will be rare. I would probably have to edge up to it by making other metaphors involving moon and sow (as well as other concepts that get sucked in). It is by such operations that I would be able to put my finger on and perhaps articulate the point of intersection—the implicit third term—that gave the comparison resonance for me. It is the process that leads to new concepts.

We get a picture of just such a process in the poem by Denise Levertov whose first line we've been considering:

Song for Ishtar*

The moon is a sow
and grunts in my throat
Her great shining shines through me
so the mud of my hollow gleams
and breaks in silver bubbles

She is a sow
and I a pig and a poet
When she opens her white
lips to devour me I bite back
and laughter rocks the moon

In the black of desire
we rock and grunt, grunt and
shine

Of course I do not claim to give a picture of the actual process of writing this poem. Merely that it illustrates in an idealized form what might happen if you started with a felt metaphor and brought to birth its implicit third term. In this case, the third term is a complex concept built of the intersection of concepts like poetry making, divinity, female, sexual desire, darkness, laughing, biting, etc. Of course there is no single word or phrase for it. In fact a possible definition of success in a poem of this sort is that it constitutes the most economical formulation of its concept.

For the sake of a neatly simple example, I truncated what is actually the operative opening metaphor: "The moon is a sow / and grunts in my throat." It is really a metaphor within a metaphor or a complex, four-termed metaphor (moon, sow, *me making sounds,* and the implicit new concept). Such complex metaphors are common. The extra term or metaphor in the second

* From *O Taste and See,* New Directions, 1962. Quoted by permission of the publisher.

line gives more direction and suggestiveness to moon and sow by bringing to mind potential aspects of each and suggesting a triangulation on where they might intersect: the second line would keep most readers from responding to the first line as opaque. But with regard to the focus of this essay on real learning, I would also stress another, perhaps more important lesson from the complication of the second line: the self is often a crucial item in the metaphorical process. It is well to remember that even if one has a question (X), that is impersonal, and even if the answer (Z) is likely to be impersonal, nevertheless, personal items and feelings should be included in the search for metaphors (i.e., the search for metaphors for X which might have Z as their implicit third term). Perceptions, feelings, and associations connected with the self are apt to be the most cognitively rich and powerful at our disposal. (See the chapter Appendix for an exercise that applies the generative property of metaphor to self-conscious heuristic search.)

Thus, behind the capacity for inventing new concepts is the more fundamental capacity that we call metaphoric or analogical ability: sensitivity to functionality. Metaphor—a necessarily *verbal* phenomenon—is really only a subset of analogy which may be purely conceptual or even visual or aural. But it is useful here to use the term "metaphor" now and again because it happens to connote better than "analogy" does the wild, idiosyncratic, and nonlogical quality which this cognitive process can have. "Functionality" is the most precise term: two things may be functional to an organism in many different ways, some of which involve more remoteness than we usually mean by "analogous." Night and day are functional simply by succeeding each other; the bell and the meat are functional for Pavlov's dog. But we must contribute what we know about analogy and metaphor to this category of functionality.

Thus the activity itself is very basic, even if on the one hand "metaphor" suggests poetic, verbal subtlety; and on the other hand "analogue" and "functionality" suggest scientific, technical, or logical expertise. When we remember that every image in a dream and every feeling that a person has about something is produced by his sensitivity to functionality, we cannot help concluding that we share this root cognitive ability with most animals, even if not with our machines. There is a lesson here. We abuse our machines in the same fashion that we do our children: by trying to make them in our image of ourselves as fully rational cogitators.*

But to get the benefit of this basic capacity, a person must practice it, learn to develop trust in it, and be encouraged to sense enough analogies and metaphors to bring the implicit third term to birth. He must try to learn to give the process itself its head—sometimes to let the words and concepts themselves seem to give birth to other words and concepts, while he feels as though he's merely a bystander. The qualities of *play* and *fooling around* must be helped to flourish. We see now why children and poets are good at it. Academic work, on the other hand, tends often to squash all these necessary and prior activities— play, practice, trust, and proliferation—to stress exclusively the last and admittedly important step in the chain: testing your answer. Many of the answers or concepts produced in this sort of process will be wrong. Metaphorical thinking is the source of good guessing and is in fact hard to distinguish from guessing— an activity felt as taboo in most institutions of learning. The need to test for correctness has led schooling too often to inhibit

* Machines are not able (yet?), as animals are, to respond to functionalities on the basis of third concepts never introduced or programmed—even, that is, on the basis of concepts that have never been thought of. In short, we are dealing with induction. It is this root capacity that gives animals the tendency to reflect within themselves redundancies in their environment (or more precisely, to reflect redundancies in the history of their experience, most of which will have been in relation to their environment). An astounding range of phenomena can be seen as instances of this process of redundancy-mapping. The physical evolution of species is a reflection at the grossest level of redundancies in experience. At a level that is presumably neural, instincts are permanently "wired-in" reflections of redundancy. Conditioning is an impermanent kind of instinct built on redundancy. And the sort of functionality-sensing discussed above, such as verbal metaphor-making, is merely the most delicate form of redundancy-mapping.

Needless to say, I have ventured here a bit beyond the enclaves shared by psychologists, information theorists, and linguists. My speculations, however, are not so far from the spirit of what can be found in: O. H. Mowrer, *Learning Theory and the Symbolic Processes,* C. E. Osgood, *Nebraska Symposium on Motivation, The Measurement of Meaning,* and *Approaches to the Study of Aphasia;* G. A. Miller, E. Galanter, K. H. Pribram, *Plans and the Structure of Behavior.*

all wrong answers, thereby conditioning students to produce only those answers they know are right and understand the derivation of.* How common it is for a student to think and even feel that his mind is blank when he "doesn't know the answer to a question"—instead of bursting with "wrong" answers some of which may be right or potentially right. We can see how foolish it is to insist on the primacy of testing your answer if we simply reflect on the fact that logic and order are not vehicles for yielding a new product—they can never produce anything but what is already implicit in the premises. Rather they are the tools of testing and are useless unless you have fecundity to impose on them.

The same kind of nondisciplinary course that focuses on a concrete particularity would serve here too as training in the capacity for inventing new concepts: metaphoric ability or sensitivity to functionality. In the first place, if a student needs a genuinely new concept and not just a transformation of the ones he already has, he must seek analogues in a *different* hierarchy of concepts from the one his problem is in. This means either investigating concretes—as concretes—or investigating concepts in an entirely different conceptual hierarchy or discipline. In the second place, the most fruitful source of the widest range of metaphors is in concretes or low-level concepts. They contain the richest source of idiosyncracies and peculiarities in which to find a diverse range of relationships. Thus, it may be fruitful to compare the two concepts "astronomical body" and "common animal"—but not as fruitful as "the moon is a sow."

I am tempted to insist here on a fine but real distinction between "nondisciplinary" and "interdisciplinary." Nondisciplinary (or perhaps predisciplinary)—what I am pressing for—means starting always with something concrete or unique, and *then*

---

* We meet here in its simplest form the reason for the change in foreign-language teaching from learning grammar to massive listening and talking. People can learn to use the rules of a language much more quickly than they can learn to know what those rules are: we cripple a person if we restrict his performance to that tiny fraction of the things he knows which he *understands, knows that he knows, or knows why he knows*. The reader should not mistake this for an anti-intellectualist argument: I am not arguing against trying to know what you know but rather arguing for more grist for the mill.

bringing to bear (among other things) the guns of the fully developed disciplines; whereas interdisciplinary means starting with disciplines—superordinate concepts—and simply bringing them together to see what relationships can be found. The distinction reveals the paradox that interdisciplinary activity is liable to be the ultimate flowering of the *essential disciplinary process*—the process of abstraction: seeking to work out a new larger hierarchy that contains existing disciplinary hierarchies. This emergent metadiscipline will have to do with language, logic, epistemology, cognition, and heuristic. Such an interdisciplinary process is *like* the disciplinary process in its usefulness and importance: it gives power and precision—the power of getting above categories and seeing their limits, seeing them in perspective. But it has the limitations of disciplinary study: even though it may promote an intellectual sophistication in which there is a great integration among *"scientific"* categories, it is liable to *fail* to promote the interpenetration of "scientific" and "spontaneous" categories (Vygotsky's distinction). The interdisciplinary enterprise, in this sense, is in danger of beginning to rise from the earth and float impotently because of not being grounded in the concrete and unique. It seeks connections by moving as it were upward, while the nondisciplinary enterprise seeks them by moving downward.

Daniel Bell, in his diagnosis of educational problems in colleges, does trenchant if brief justice to this ailment of *overabstraction* inherent in the disciplinary process. But the remedies he proposes, though helpful as far as they go, don't do enough about this problem of overabstraction. He doesn't see the sense in which the interdisciplinary curriculum he proposes is an intensifying of the abstractive process rather than an antidote to it. His impulse is wholly upward, and there is a danger in his curriculum of losing touch with the concrete. I don't think he has fully integrated his curricular proposal with his insights about disciplines and their relation to thinking and culture.

But I don't press this distinction between interdisciplinary and nondisciplinary for the same reason that I am hesitant to quibble with Bell. For both kinds of interaction between disciplines are desperately needed. In the light of the present politics of disciplines, we will do well to get any of either variety.

Nondisciplinary Courses to Increase Traffic Between Verbal and Nonverbal Experience

Behind the first source of real learning—applying known concepts widely—we found a more basic process: getting experience from symbols by means of the effective interpenetration of spontaneous and scientific concepts. Behind the second source of real learning—inventing new concepts—we found again a more basic process: the metaphoric process or the ability to sense functionality.

These two root cognitive processes are complementary and the basis of real learning from the most primitive to the most sophisticated. The reason they are so crucial is that they represent the two directions of traffic across the border between verbal and nonverbal experience. Where the first consists of constructing new experience from words, the second—sensing functionality—consists in effect of constructing new words from experience: searching for felt relationships among experiences in order to bring to birth new implied concepts. Of course a brand new word is seldom invented especially for the new concept. Usually the new concept is embodied in a new arrangement of words or in a new metaphorical sense of an old word.

These two abilities correspond to the two qualities that most teachers naturally notice in a good student or good learner of any sort: on the one hand, with a seeming passivity, he gets rich experience from the words he reads or hears; and on the other hand, with a seeming active quality, he characteristically manipulates, pushes and pulls into different perspectives, and transforms any data he comes up against.

These two processes—applying concepts widely and inventing new ones—also correspond to Piaget's two basic processes of assimilation and accommodation: as it were, eating the environment and being eaten by the environment.

Two caveats before closing. First, this is no argument against induction in teaching. Much more is needed, not less. But induction is not enough.

Second, this is no argument against disciplinary courses or further increases in the high-powered structuring of disciplines. Only the most sophisticated study in disciplines can exploit the potential power and organization of concepts. Without training in a discipline, it is hard to attain the power or precision with an important concept that comes from using it critically and exhaustively on a huge range of data. And every student should have the experience of attaining this sort of mastery over at least one hierarchy of concepts. This will help to give him a sense of what he doesn't have when he is using concepts less exhaustively exploited.

Thus, by the way, we see that it defeats the purpose of majoring to major in a single geographical area or historical period instead of in a discipline (which is a hierarchy of concepts applied to as *many* geographical and historical areas as possible). A person who majors, say, in the Renaissance in Italy, though he may amass a great concentration of data and is certainly apt to develop a great tact for the area, will nevertheless tend not to gain real mastery of *any single* hierarchy of concepts involved in his study, e.g., history, art, literature, economics, science, philosophy. The validity of what he does with any of these data is in danger unless he escapes parochialism in at least some concepts. And a set of concepts is likely to remain untrustworthy and not fully developed until it is applied to as diverse a range of data as possible. (It is easier to say this in theory than to decide in practice to deflect a student with a passion for an area-study.)

To sum up. The problem has been how to increase real knowing. Disciplinary curricula—the study of concepts organized into hierarchies—yields power over more potent concepts: they are potentially capable of being applied more widely, fruitfully, and creatively. But *the ability in itself to learn*—that is, to grasp, apply, and invent concepts—should also be pursued even in college by the nondisciplinary focusing on concrete particulars. If we seek consciously to develop these root learning abilities, more of our classroom and library learning will produce Socrates' sort of knowing.

The argument can be schematically represented by two contradictory geometric models for knowledge (suggested by Dante's treatment of the Spheres and the Intelligences of the Spheres). On the one hand each discipline, or hierarchy of concepts, serves as a center which ultimately unifies and organizes around it all others: i.e., an ideally complete physics or literature will eventually lead to everything. But on the other hand it is also true that each unique, concrete event or thing is a still center around which all the hierarchies of concepts merely revolve in humble service. The present "professional," disciplinary, emphasis in curricula does justice to the former picture, but not to the latter. The problem is one which Whitehead long ago recognized: ". . . in the modern world, the celibacy of the medieval learned class has been replaced by a celibacy of the intellect which is divorced from the concrete contemplation of complete facts" (quoted in Bell 155).

Appendix

What follows is an exercise from a book in preparation in collaboration with Dwight Paine* designed to help someone "be smarter": to have more ideas about things and to be better at coming up with answers he never thought of. In this one the reader is asked to make a wide range of conflicting metaphors and conceptualizations about a person—perhaps an historical figure he is trying to understand better. Making the metaphorical responses would produce many implicit third terms relating to the historical figure—some obvious and some unhelpful. But he would be learning to be on the lookout for metaphors or responses that seem, however obscure, somehow to resonate or to ring some sort of bell. In these cases the implicit third term might be the "answer"—that is, a link between the historical figure (the problem data) and some sensed uncertainty or question about him. (For of course the inquirer ought to assume he doesn't yet know what will turn out to be his real question about the problem data.) The inquirer should then fasten on these loaded or pregnant responses and try to worry the third terms to birth by pondering and making other metaphors by association. Most people need practice at this whole process before they are good at making fruitful metaphors and sensing which ones bear pursuit.

* Never completed, but see "Metaphors for Priming the Pump," in my *Writing With Power*.

Think of a person

1. Think of an event in _____'s life. Close your eyes and spend a moment imagining you are _____ while this event is occurring. Experience as many details as you can—even seemingly unimportant background details: What is the time of day? Feel the weather, temperature, sounds, light, shadows, smells, and so forth.

2. Which object or person in the previous scene would you be if you wanted to be the ideal observer? Be it and speak for a moment in its voice about what it sees.

3. Imagine _____ as an animal. What animal? In this form, _____ falls in love with a different animal. What animal? What do they have for children?

4. Imagine _____ as a food. What food? In this form, _____ falls in love with a different food. What food? What do they have for children?

5. Imagine _____ as a place. What place? In this form, _____ falls in love with a different place. What place? What do they have for children?

6. Think of three things that would never happen to _____.

7. Imagine one of those things happening to _____ and describe it.

8. Imagine _____ had a totally different name. What is it? How would _____ be different with this name?

9. Imagine _____ was of the opposite sex. Describe how the new _____ would dress, wear his or her hair, move, and talk.

10. Be one of _____'s parents. Describe _____.

11. Be a child of _____ and describe _____.

12. Be the psychiatrist of _____ and describe _____.

13. Be the pet of _____ (specify what pet) and describe _____.

14. Imagine you are someone who understands _____ as having had problems which are now mostly solved or worked out: i.e., you see _____'s character as a solution to problems. Be this person and describe _____.

15. Imagine you are someone who understands _____ as someone who is *coming* to serious problems: you see _____'s

present character as bearing the seeds of future problems he cannot see. Be this person and describe _____.

16a. Think of _____ as part of an ecological system: tell as many things as you can that go into _____. What is his input? What, in every sense of the word, does _____ eat.

16b. Tell as many things as possible that *come out of* _____. What is his output?

16c. Name as many things as possible that _____ *comes out of*. What is the output for? What, in every sense of the word, emits ———?

16d. Name as many things as possible *that* _____ *goes into*. What is he input for. What, in every sense of the word, eats _____?

17. Tell a sad story about _____.

18. Tell a funny story about _____ that has the same events as the preceding sad one. Imagine, in short, that you are someone who sees the preceding story as funny and tell it from your new point of view.

19. Close your eyes and see _____'s face as clearly and vividly as you can.

CHAPTER 2

⚜⚜⚜

When I returned to graduate study for the second time after five years of teaching, I was nervous that maybe I'd *still* find myself unable to write the papers my teachers would assign me. It's true that I'd written in the meantime—ambitious memos and curricular proposals and even a tiny pamphlet for students on writing—but no academic papers. Therefore during the next three years of graduate study, I watched myself closely as I worked at each of the many papers I had to write. Because of my nervousness, I had a heightened sensitivity to whether things were starting to go in any sense badly—or well. I got my papers all written (mostly even on time)—in the end a dissertation—but for a couple of years I used to set fictional deadlines for myself. I'd make a deal with myself that the paper was really due one week before the official due date—making it more or less a life-and-death matter that I have *something* completed for my deadline, no matter how terrible. Then I had a week to fix things up. I fell into keeping a kind of a journal (though often only extended entries on stray pieces of paper) in which I tried to say what was happening when I noticed something going on in my writing. Most of my entries were explorations of one or another kind of stuckpoint or breakthrough.

These pieces of writing became the basis for *Writing Without Teachers*—from which the present chapter is taken. Thus, though the book tries to present a theory of how the mind gets things written—and gives plenty of normative advice—it grew out of an impulse that was essentially autobiographical and empirical: an attempt to write as honestly and accurately as I could about *what's going on* in my mind and feelings as I write—particularly at moments of frustration. This activity which I've come to call "process writing" has remained the most fruitful and trustworthy source of learning for me—in the personal realm or in matters of learning and teaching. I think of process writing as the main source for all the essays here.*

What follows is a portion of Chapter III of *Writing Without Teachers*. The chapter which precedes it ("Growing") asks the reader to think of a piece of writing as alive—as something which *wants* to grow and develop through stages. In the excerpt that follows, I describe the "cooking" process that makes growth possible.

* Three examples:

1. *October 10.* I badgered them and pushed and pulled to get them to give feedback. (First just to read things they had written.) I hated doing it. Feels so awful to have to push people, badger, wait, demand. BUT THEY DID IT. IT WORKED. They read some important stuff they had just written. It was there. I had been feeling perhaps it isn't there, but it is always there. Remember that.

2. *March 5.* Conference with ———. Realized that I had been feeling she was "out of it." Mad at her for not trying, holding back. Feeling she is fighting me, fighting the course; that I am failing with her; that she is going to get me; I've got to wrestle with her and get her to stop doing this thing.

Tried pulling back and getting her to talk. Asking her what does she need from me. It worked. The crucial breakthrough was when it finally came clear that she needed to say, "I need to do it *myself.*" (And, by implication, I have to stop pushing her.) It really worked, even though she was having a hard time. It started out with me in the familiar rut: bothered, angry, but pretending to be rational with her. Her, locked into a held-back silence. I broke out of that.

How can I remember this and reproduce it?

3. *November 3.* Stalled by being bugged cause people didn't have their writing on Anne Frank. Just takes the wind out my sails. I just want to give up. Refuse to try. I have lots of stuff to give, I'm well prepared, I was all ready—but now I just don't want to try.

I'm sulking.

I'd rather sulk than chew them out. It seems like it would be better maybe to cuss them out. But I'm giving up.

Cooking: The Interaction of Conflicting Elements

Growing is the overall larger process, the evolution of whole organisms. Cooking is the smaller process: bubbling, percolating, fermenting, chemical interaction, atomic fission. Cooking drives the engine that makes growing happen. It's because of cooking that a piece of writing can start out X and end up Y, that a writer can start out after supper seeing, feeling, and knowing one set of things and end up at midnight seeing, feeling, and knowing things he hadn't thought of before. Cooking is the smallest unit of generative action, the smallest piece of anti-entropy whereby a person spends his energy to buy new perceptions and insights from himself.

At first I thought that writing freely was the secret of cooking. If someone who has always written in a controlled way takes off the editorial lid, he tends to produce a burst of cooking. Yet often this is not enough in itself to produce cooking. Sometimes it just makes a barren swamp.

Then I thought the heart of cooking was energy. It's true that it takes energy to cook. And sometimes a big burst of energy seems to be what makes cooking happen. But as everyone knows who has tried to write, sometimes no amount of energy suffices to get something written.

I think I've finally figured it out. Cooking is the interaction of contrasting or conflicting material. I try in what follows to specify various *kinds* of interaction that are important in writing. But in any of them cooking consists of the process of one piece of material (or one process) being transformed by interacting with another: one piece of material being seen through the lens of another, being dragged through the guts of another, being reoriented or reorganized in terms of the other, being mapped onto the other.

Cooking as Interaction Between People

The original, commonest, easiest-to-produce kind of interaction is that between people. If you are stuck writing or trying to figure something out, there is nothing better than finding one person, or more, to talk to. If they don't agree or have trouble understanding, so much the better—so long as their minds are not closed. This explains what happens to me and many others countless times: I write a paper; it's not very good; I discuss it with someone; after fifteen minutes of back-and-forth I say something in response to a question or argument of his and he says, "But why didn't you *say* that? That's good. That's clear." I want to shout, "But I *did* say that. The whole paper is saying that." But in truth the whole paper is merely implying or leading up to or circumnavigating that. Until I could see my words and thoughts refracted through his consciousness, I *couldn't* say it directly that way.

Two heads are better than one because two heads can make conflicting material interact better than one head usually can. It's why brainstorming works. I say something. You give a response and it constitutes some restructuring or reorienting of what I said. Then *I* see something new on the basis of your restructuring and so I, in turn, can restructure what I first said. The process provides a continual leverage or mechanical advantage: we each successively climb upon the shoulders of the other's restructuring, so that at each climbing up, we can see a little farther. This is the process by which a discussion or argument "gets somewhere"—and it shows clearly why some discussions get nowhere. When people are stubborn and narrow-minded, they refuse to allow the material in their head to be restructured by what the other person says: they simply hang on to the orientations thay have and are too afraid to relinquish any of them.

Cooking as Interaction Between Ideas

Just as two people, if they let their ideas interact, can produce ideas or points of view that neither could singly have produced, a lone person, if he learns to maximize the interaction among his own ideas or points of view, can produce new ones that didn't seem available to him.

The way to do this is to encourage conflicts or contradictions in your thinking. We are usually taught to avoid them; and we cooperate in this teaching because it is confusing or frustrating to hold two conflicting ideas at the same time. It feels like a dead end or a trap but really it is the most fruitful situation to be in. Unless you can get yourself into a contradiction, you may be stuck with no power to have any thoughts other than the ones you are already thinking.

It turns out that in your normal round of thinking and perceiving—especially if you are trying to write—you drift into conflicts and contradictions all the time. If you don't seem to, it merely means you have trained yourself not to see them. Follow streams of thought, metaphors, and associations better—drift better—and look for disagreements rather than agreements.

Cooking as Interaction Between Words and Ideas, Between Immersion and Perspective

I've spent a lot of time in a debate with myself about whether it's better to work things out in the medium of words or in the medium of ideas and meanings.

When I first discovered the virtues of writing a lot I thought I had discovered that it was always a bad thing to work at the idea level, to make outlines, or to work in terms of "points" or meanings. And that it was always better just to keep on writing at the word level. I clung to this idea for a long time. Even in the face of huge word-swamps I got into and could scarcely get out of. "I haven't written things out in words *enough,*" I said to myself. But finally I had to admit to myself that working in thoughts could be a good thing. Here is a diary entry from a time when this lesson was being driven home to me:

I'm stuck with a bad article. I'm trying to rewrite it and can't. It doesn't work; and I can't get anyone to publish it; I finally have to admit that I can feel something weak and wrong or fishy about it. But I can't seem to improve it. Finally a breakthrough from translating my *words* into *thoughts*—forcing myself to restate in *simple brief* form the thoughts that exist in the thing—usually by paragraph: find plus-or-minus one thought in each paragraph. But only genuine thoughts. Be tough about admitting there's no thought in some paragraphs.

It's remarkably liberating. I realize I'd been hypnotized by the words, phrases, and sentences I'd worked out with such pain—and I really like them and value them.

And so I came to decide that both levels are good, but for different purposes: perspective and immersion. Working in ideas gives you perspective, structure, and clarity; working in words gives you fecundity, novelty, richness. Two passages from one entry:

I was hung up in words, enmeshed in them and not seeing around them or with perspective. I cured it by getting *out from under* words and saying "but what *idea* is this really asserting? . . .

What is bad about this process of being mired up in the mess of words is what is good about it: when you are writing along, riding on the rhythms of speech and the energies of syntax, you often wander off the track. Even if you are writing from an outline, you still wander off the track. But this is precisely the process by which I come up with new ideas I could never have known to put in an outline.

But even that view of the two processes didn't always hold true. One day I was forced to notice that sometimes word-writing leads you to just the summing-up you were looking for and couldn't get by trying to "sum-up." And sometimes idea-thinking produces fecundity by giving you a new angle where writing-out was keeping you stuck in one potato patch. It's not that one is better than the other; not even that each has a different function. It's the interaction between the two that yields both clarity and richness—cooking. Start with whichever you prefer. But make sure you use both and move back and forth between them. For when you sum up a long set of words into a single thought (even if you do it badly), you always find new things in the words: new implications, relationships, and places where they don't make sense. And when you take a single thought and turn it into a full set of words—put it into someone's mouth—you also find things in that thought you hadn't seen before. Each time you switch modes, you get a new view and more leverage.

Cooking as Interaction Between Metaphors

Interaction between metaphors is interaction of the most fine-grained, generative sort. When you make a metaphor, you call something by a wrong name. If you make a comparison, an analogy, or an example, you are thinking of something in terms of something else. There is always a contradiction. You are not just calling a house a house, but rather a playground, a jungle, a curse, a wound, a paradise. Each throws into relief aspects of the house you might otherwise miss. You are seeing one thought or perception through the lens of another. Here again is the essence of cooking. As in all cooking, new ideas and perceptions result. Connections are loosened so that something may develop or grow in whatever its potential directions are.

If you find it hard to use metaphors, it merely means you are out of the habit of listening to them. Make the ones you can, and keep trying to hold your mind open to register the others that are there.

Perhaps you've listened too much to warnings against mixed metaphors. A mixed metaphor is never bad because it's mixed, only because it's badly mixed. (This is only a consideration for final drafts: for earlier drafts, the more "bad" mixing, the better.) Anyone who is against mixed metaphors because they are mixed is like someone who is against kissing twice: he probably doesn't really like kissing once. He's entitled to his taste but he mustn't be taken as a judge of kisses.

Cooking as Interaction Between Modes

Try to encourage the same thing with different modes or textures of writing. Allow your writing to fall into poetry and then back

into prose; from informal to formal; from personal to impersonal; first-person to third-person; fiction, nonfiction; empirical,
a priori. When it starts to change modes on you, don't shrink
back and stop it. Let it go and develop itself in that mode. Even
if it seems crazy. It will show you things about your material and
help it to cook, develop, and grow. First you are writing about
a dog you had; then you are writing about sadness; then you are
writing about personalities of dogs; then about the effect of the
past; then a poem about names; then an autobiographical self-
analysis; then a story about your family. Each way of writing will
bring out different aspects of the material.

Cooking as Interaction Between
You and Symbols on Paper

Language is the principal medium that allows you to interact
with yourself. (Painters do it with shapes and colors, composers
with musical sounds.) Without a symbol system such as language,
it is difficult if not impossible to think about more than one thing
at a time, and thus to allow two thoughts to interact and cook.
Putting a thought into symbols means setting it down and letting the mind take a rest from it. With language you can put an
idea or feeling or perception into words—put it in your cud
or put it in the freezer—and then go on to have a different one
and not lose the first. In this way, you can entertain two thoughts
or feelings at the same time or think about the relationship between two thoughts or feelings. A principle value of language,
therefore, is that it permits you to *distance* yourself from your
own perceptions, feelings, and thoughts.

Try, then, to write words on paper so as to permit an interaction between you and not-you. You are building someone to
talk to. This means two stages: first put out words on paper as
freely as possible, trying to be so fully involved that you don't
even think about it and don't experience any gap between you
and the words: just talk onto the paper. But then, in the second
stage, stand back and make as large a gap as you can between
you and the words: set them aside and then pick them up and
try to read them as though they came out of someone else. Learn

to interact with them, react to them. Learn to let them produce a new reaction or response in you.

One of the functions of a diary is to create interaction between you and symbols on paper. If you have strong feelings and then write them down freely, it gives you on the one hand some distance and control, but on the other hand it often makes you feel those feelings *more*. For you can often allow yourself to feel something more if you are not so helpless and lost in the middle of it. So the writing helps you feel the feeling and then go on to feel the next feelings. Not be stuck.

Noncooking

You can help cooking happen by making it more overt. For this it helps to understand why cooking sometimes doesn't happen.

There are two kinds of noncooking. The first is when there aren't any contrasting or conflicting elements to interact. This is the situation when you know what you have to say, you say it, and it is perfectly straightforward. If you already have brilliant fully-cooked material lying around in your head, you are fine. But usually what you have isn't very interesting, satisfactory, or sufficient. You need better material, you need some good ideas, you need some good things to say. This can usually be cured by writing a lot, lifting the editorial lid, babbling or doing ten-minute exercises.

The first kind of noncooking is illustrated by a group of people who all agree with each other. No one can do anything but nod his head or else say, "And here's another reason I agree with you." Sometimes you get the same effect when everyone is excessively "nice" and there is nothing but agreement in the room: no energy, no ideas, no different perceptions.

But there is a different kind of noncooking where there is plenty of conflicting material but it won't interact. This kind of noncooking can also be vividly illustrated by a group of people. This time the group is full of disagreement, but whenever someone starts to say something, he is immediately interrupted by someone else starting to say why he disagrees with what (he thinks) the person was starting to say. There is no fruitful interaction, there is none of the productive phenomenon of one idea or perception refracted or seen through the lens of another. There is only deadlock and stalemate. Two strong men arm-wrestling: great energy expended, muscles bulging, sweat popping out on the foreheads, but no movement.

I warm to this second sort of noncooking: being caught in irons between a lot of contrasting material but being unable to cook it. Instead of interacting, the material just locks horns. You start to follow one idea or train of thought or way of writing but then you see it's no good; then another, but you see it, too, doesn't work; then another and the same thing. You try the first one again, but don't get any farther. Frustration.

The problem of the argumentative group illustrates how to get cooking going. They need to stop all the interrupting: make sure each speaker finishes what he is saying before someone else speaks. In this way they can maximize the chance of one person's view actually getting inside the head of the other people and being transmuted or reoriented there.

So, too, if you are stuck because your ideas won't interact. Take each idea singly. Pretend to espouse each one wholeheartedly. See everything in terms of it. Pretend you are a person who is convinced of it. This amounts to giving each idea a full hearing and ensures that the interaction happens—that the other material is seen through its lens.

You get a similar kind of noncooking when there is no interaction between writing-out and summing-up—working in words and working in meanings. You start writing but before you get very far you stop writing because you sense something wrong. This happens again and again. I can only break out of this sort of noncooking—which is perhaps *my* major stuckpoint—if I quite consciously force myself to make the interaction overt in two painfully separated steps. This means that if I am writing I must consciously prevent myself from switching to the sitting-back-wondering-whether-it-makes-sense mode. If I see it doesn't make sense I must keep writing—perhaps about *why* it doesn't make sense or if possible start saying things that do make sense. But not stop. Only after a full cycle of writing—ten or twenty minutes at least—can I let myself stand back and think in perspective. And when I start this contrasting mode, I must also force myself to keep at it till it too completes its cycle.

If you want to ensure cooking you have to make more than one interaction: if you start with words, it's not good enough just to translate into assertions; it's the movement from immersion to perspective and *then back to immersion*—or vice versa—that really strengthens and refines what you are producing. And the more transitions, the more strengthening, the more refining.

A stuckpoint:

All these ideas rolling around in my head about motives for teaching and reasons why my plan is good. I can find words for them separately but I am going crazy spending tons of time, because I can't write them down—can't figure out where to begin. It's like a tangled ball of string and I can't find the end. I can only find loops. If I were in a conversation or argument, I would express all these points—I could bring them out when they were needed in response to the words of the other person. But here I've got no other person. I feel like I'm in a terrible vacuum, in a sensory-deprivation room, trying to fight my way out of a wet paper bag when there are endless folds of wet paper and though I fight through each fold, there's still more soggy, dank, sodden, smelly paper hanging all over me.

Here was a situation where I let myself remain stuck at the same intermediate distance from my words: I allowed myself to remain halfway between dealing with my words as me and as not-me, instead of forcing an interaction between the two modes. I needed to get closer—write faster and make the words merely me; and then move back and treat them as not-me. By building someone to argue with, I would have managed to get all my ideas into words. Admittedly, they would have been a great mess—as in an argument—but eventually I would have seen some workable shape for what I was trying to say and finally would have found somewhere to start. (Or—if you want to see this as a problem in starting—I couldn't find a place to *start* until I started anywhere and wrote a great deal first.)

Out of this strategy for dealing with noncooking we can see a more universal piece of advice for all cooking and growing. Almost always it is good to use extremes and let moderation arrive eventually. Being in the middle is being stuck, barren, held between opposites. When there are cycles to be gone through, do each one to the extreme—keep yourself from being caught in the middle. You can't be a good, ruthless editor unless you are a messy, rich producer. But you can't be really fecund as a producer unless you know you'll be able to go at it with a ruthless knife.

External Cooking or Desperation Writing

I know I am not alone in my recurring twinges of panic that I won't be able to write something when I need to, I won't be able to produce coherent speech or thought. And that lingering doubt is a great hindrance to writing. It's a constant fog or static that clouds the mind. I never got out of its clutches till I discovered that it was possible to write something—not something great or pleasing but at least something usable, workable—when my mind is out of commission. The trick at such times is to do all your cooking out on the table: your mind is incapable of doing any inside. It means using symbols and pieces of paper not as a crutch but as a wheelchair.

The first thing is to admit your condition: because of some mood or event or whatever, your mind is incapable of anything that could be called thought. It can put out a babbling kind of speech utterance, it can put a simple feeling, perception, or sort-of-thought into understandable (though terrible) words. But it is incapable of considering anything in relation to anything else. The moment you try to hold that thought or feeling up against some other to see the relationship, you simply lose the picture—you get nothing but buzzing lines or waving colors.

So admit this. Avoid anything more than one feeling, perception, or thought. Simply write as much as possible. Try simply to steer your mind in the direction or general vicinity of the thing you are trying to write about and start writing and keep writing.

Just write and keep writing. (Probably best to write on only one side of the paper in case you should want to cut parts out with scissors—but you probably won't.) Just write and keep writing. It will probably come in waves. After a flurry, stop and take a brief rest. But don't stop too long. Don't think about what you are writing or what you have written or else you will overload the circuit again. Keep writing as though you are drugged or drunk. Keep doing this till you feel you have a lot of material that might be useful; or, if necessary, till you can't stand it any more—even if you doubt that there's anything useful there.

Then take a pad of little pieces of paper—or perhaps 3 × 5 cards—and simply start at the beginning of what you were writing, and as you read over what you wrote, every time you come to any thought, feeling, perception, or image that could be gathered up into one sentence or one assertion, do so and write it by itself on a little sheet of paper. In short, you are trying to turn, say, ten or twenty pages of wandering mush into twenty or thirty hard little crab apples. Sometimes there won't be many on a page. But if it seems to you that there are none on a page, you are making a serious error—the same serious error that put you in this comatose state to start with. You are mistaking lousy, stupid, second-rate, wrong, childish, foolish, worthless ideas for no ideas at all. Your job is not to pick out *good* ideas but to pick out ideas. You were conscious and therefore your words will be full of things that could be called feelings, utterances, ideas— things that can be squeezed into one simple sentence. This is your job. Don't ask for too much.

After you have done this, take those little slips or cards, read through them a number of times—not struggling with them, simply wandering and mulling through them; perhaps shifting them around and looking through them in various sequences. In a sense these are cards you are playing solitaire with, and the rules of this particular game permit shuffling the unused pile.

The goal of this procedure with the cards is to get them to distribute themselves into two or three or ten or fifteen different piles on your desk. You can get them to do this almost by themselves if you simply keep reading through them in different orders; certain cards will begin to feel like they go with other cards. I emphasize this passive, thoughtless mode because I want to talk about desperation writing in its pure state. In practice, almost invariably at some point in the procedure, your sanity begins to return. It is often at this point. You actually are moved to have thoughts or—and the difference between active and passive is crucial here—to *exert* thought: to hold two cards together and *build* or *assert* a relationship. It is a matter of bringing energy to bear.

So you may start to be able to do something active with these cards, and begin actually to think. But if not, just allow the cards to find their own piles with each other by feel, by drift, by intuition, by mindlessness.

You have now engaged in the two main activities that will permit you to get something cooked out on the table rather than in your brain: writing out into messy words, summing up into single assertions, and even sensing relationships between assertions. You can simply continue to deploy these two activities.

Desperation writing seemed magic when I discovered how to do it. As though I had found secret powers and was getting something for nothing: new ideas where formerly I was barren; structure where formerly I remained stuck in chaos. Gradually I began to fear there must be some catch—I would be punished for violating nature, my own powers would be cut off:

It's scary. I think I'm developing a dependency on this prosthesis for the mind. My mind is turning to slush. I can no longer seem to hold three ideas in my mouth at the same time like I used to. I'm always resorting to prosthesis. And I can't seem to make myself write well any more. I just write flabby, mushy, soupy. No backbone in my head. I'll go blind and insane if I indulge myself in this easiness—if I continue to use this crutch, my organs will dry up and atrophy.

Is it really true? I think I'm able to do more complicated things now—work at a higher level—but is this wishful thinking to disguise the fact that I'm writing badly and slowly and something seems screwed up about my attempts to write this book?

As far as I can tell I still have all my powers. But I was right to sense something was fishy. It is possible to abuse this approach and I was tending to do so. The mistake hinged on failing to distinguish between *cooking* and *external cooking*. Since external cooking got me out my bind, I mistook it for the goal. Finally I began to distinguish the two.

I may be falling in love with the process, the externalizing of the organic process outside the organism. But it's only the means to an end: cooking. If you're not cooking, externalize it to make it happen; but once you get yourself cooking, don't make the mistake of

thinking that it's better to have it external; the truth is that it's better to have it *internal:* things cook at a hotter temperature and you
get a more permanent, magical, fine-grained, extensive transmuta-
tion of elements than you could ever get externally.

The extreme of external cooking is "desperation writing." The
extreme of internal cooking is what I call "magic writing":
cooking which is wholly internal, hidden, and sometimes in-
stantaneous. Think of Mozart writing out a completed sym-
phony as fast as he could write; or A. E. Housman ending up
with a perfectly polished poem after a lunch of beer and a sleepy
walk in the sun.

External cooking is like mixing up dry ingredients in a bowl,
whereas internal cooking is like dissolving them in water so they
integrate at the molecular level. Internal cooking produces more
force and voice in the words: this integrated texture is more clear
and powerful; every cell of the final product contains a plan or
microcosm (gene) of the whole. This is why freewriting can produce writing that is better than most slow careful writing.

Also, internal cooking is in fact quicker and takes less energy.
External cooking is like low gear on a bicycle. When you first
discover low gear, it seems as though you are getting something
for nothing: you now easily conquer a hill you couldn't get up
before. But in actual fact, if you had been able to *stay* in high
gear, you would have gotten up the hill with far less energy. It
was wasteful to take all those strokes in that lower gear. But you
would have had to be *much* stronger to save this energy. (Only
the rich can afford to economize.) Similarly, internal cooking
means getting the whole pot boiling at once and having it go
through changes as a whole. Whereas external cooking means
taking it into separate little pots and cooking each one with less
fuel—but the total fuel bill is greater. You save energy if you
cook the whole thing at once—and spill less, too—but you need
a bigger burst of energy or strength. And you need to endure a
hotter temperature.

Moral: use external cooking when you need it. Be good at using it. Use it especially to get cooking going. But don't think you
can use it to beat the system and avoid cooking. If you want to
write, you must cook. There is always a *crunch* in writing. The

crunch feels to me like lifting the Empire State Building; like folding up a ten-acre parachute on a windy field. You can't avoid the crunch. It takes heat, electricity, acid to cook. If you can't stand the heat, get out of the kitchen. If you don't like the excitement or energy that is building up in your guts, your head, your forearms, it is possible to abuse external cooking and use it to dissipate this heat, acid, electricity.

For most people, external cooking usually increases cooking. It gets you cooking at last. It sets higher but reachable standards for you: you insist on cooking whatever you write. If you get to the point where you are abusing it—where you are cooking too many things in thimbles with matches when you could actually throw it all into a pressure cooker and put the heat on high—you will know it and move in that direction.

CHAPTER 3

⚘⚘⚘

This essay (one of the most recent) emphasizes a different pair of opposites at the heart of learning. I am trying to broaden our conception of thinking or purposive rationality. Instead of characterizing it as a single effort in more or less one direction, I portray it as the interaction between two efforts in two conflicting directions. That is, instead of seeing rationality as primarily the attempt to make inferences that are careful and conscious, I portray it as the interaction between that attempt and a contrary one—sometimes thought of as non-rational—toward association, digression, and the relinquishing of control. In short, the contrary I'm interested in here is that between *careful* and *careless* thinking—the process of learning how to move back and forth between imposing control and relinquishing it.

The theme of the present book is overt here. Thinking in contraries usually holds us back because it so often leads us to stalemate or warfare; yet, if well managed, it is the very source of progress.

Talk about the nature of thinking or rationality is usually too abstract and disembodied, but we can make it concrete and practical by looking at the actual behavior of people as they write, and at the actual texts they produce. Thus writing can serve thinking not only by giving students more and better opportunities to practice it. Writing can also help thinking in a more theoretically oriented way by giving us a more detailed and accurate movie of the mind at work—if only we exploit the full range of *kinds* of writing available to us.

❀❀❀

Teaching Two Kinds of Thinking by Teaching Writing

When I celebrate freewriting and fast exploratory writing on first drafts—the postponing of vigilance and control during the early stages of writing—it seems to many listeners as though I'm celebrating *holidays* from thinking. Some say, "Yes, good, we all need holidays from thinking." Others say, "Horrors! Their vigilance muscles will get flabby and they'll lose their ability to think critically." But I insist that I'm teaching thinking.

Of course it's not the only way I teach thinking through writing. I also teach it by teaching careful, conscious, critical revising. Thus I teach two kinds of thinking. I'll call them first-order thinking and second-order thinking.*

First-order thinking is intuitive and creative and doesn't strive for conscious direction or control. We use it when we get hunches or see gestalts. We use it when we sense analogies or ride on metaphors or arrange the pieces in a collage. We use it when we write fast without censoring and let the words lead us to associations and intuitions we hadn't foreseen. Second-order thinking is conscious, directed, controlled thinking. We steer; we scrutinize each link in the chain. Second-order thinking is committed to accuracy and strives for logic and control: we examine our premises and assess the validity of each inference. Second-order thinking is what most people have in mind when they talk about "critical thinking."

Each kind of thinking has its own characteristic strengths and weaknesses. I like to emphasize how second-order thinking often

* This account of first- and second-order thinking owes something to my reading of Peter Medawar's *Induction and Intuition in Scientific Thought*. Medawar is building on the approach of Karl Popper.

brings out people's worst thinking. If you want to get people to seem dumber than they are, try asking them a hard question and then saying, "Now think carefully." Thinking carefully means trying to examine your thinking while using it too—trying to think about thinking while also thinking about something else—which often leads people to foolishness. This is one of the main reasons why shrewd and sensible students often write essays asserting things they don't really believe and defending them with wooden reasoning they wouldn't dream of using if they were just talking thoughtfully with a friend.

First-order thinking, on the other hand, often heightens intelligence. If you want to get people to be remarkably insightful, try asking them the hard question and then saying, "Don't do any careful thinking yet, just write three or four stories or incidents that come to mind in connection with that question; and then do some fast exploratory freewriting." It turns out that such unplanned narrative and descriptive exploratory writing (or speaking) will almost invariably lead the person spontaneously to formulate *conceptual* insights that are remarkably shrewd. These are fresh insights which are rooted in experience and thus they usually get around the person's prejudices, stock responses, or desires for mere consistency; they are usually shrewder than the person's long-held convictions. (See "The Loop Writing Process" in my *Writing With Power*.) In addition (to bring up a writerly concern), these insights are usually expressed in lively, human, and experienced language. In short, to use Polanyi's terms, we know more tacitly than we do focally. Finally (to raise another writerly concern), when someone really gets going in a sustained piece of generative writing and manages, as it were, to stand out of the way and relinquish planning and control—when someone manages to let the words and images and ideas choose more words, images, and ideas—a more elegant shape or organization often emerges, one more integral to the material than careful outlining or conscious planning can produce. It's not that the rough draft writing will itself be well organized in its totality—though that occasionally happens. What's more common is that the exploratory zigzagging leads finally to a click where the writer suddenly sees, "Yes, that's the right handle for this whole issue, now I've got the right point of view, and now

I see the right organization or progression of parts. I couldn't find it when I just tried to think, plan, and outline."

Yet despite my fascination with the conceptual power of creative intuitive thinking—of what might seem to some like "careless thinking"—I have learned not to forget to tell the other side of the story. That is, we are also likely to be *fooled* by first-order thinking. In first-order thinking we don't reflect on what we are doing and hence we are more likely to be steered by our unaware assumptions, our unconscious prejudices, our unexamined point of view. And often enough, no shape or organization emerges at all—just randomly ordered thoughts. We cannot *count on* first-order thinking to give us something valuable.

Thus the two kinds of thinking have the opposite virtues and vices. Second-order thinking is a way to check our thinking, to be more aware, to steer instead of being steered. In particular, we must not trust the fruits of intuitive and experiential first-order thinking unless we have carefully assessed them with second-order critical thinking. Yet we probably won't *have* enough interesting ideas or hypotheses to assess if we use only our assessing muscles: we need first-order thinking to generate a rich array of insights. And first-order thinking doesn't just give us more; it is faster too. Our early steps in second-order thinking (or our early steps at a higher level of second-order thinking than we are practiced at) are often slow backward steps into wrongheadedness (Bruner, 1966.) Yet this is no argument against the need for second-order thinking. Indeed I suspect that the way we enlarge the penumbra of our tacit knowledge is by searching harder and further with the beam of our focal knowledge.

We are in the habit—in the academic culture anyway—of assuming that thinking is not thinking unless it is wholly logical or critically aware of itself at every step. But I cannot resist calling first-order thinking a bona fide kind of thinking because it is a process of making sense and figuring out: though not consciously steered or controlled, it is nevertheless purposive and skillful.

❁

There is an obvious link between the writing process and these two kinds of thinking. I link first-order intuitive or creative thinking with freewriting and first-draft exploratory writing in which one defers planning, control, organizing, and censoring. I link second-order thinking with slow, thoughtful rewriting or revising where one constantly subjects everything to critical scrutiny.

But I'm not content merely to assert a link. The two writing processes enhance the two thinking processes.

It is obvious how careful revising enhances second-order thinking. If having any language at all (any "second signaling system") gives us more power over our thinking, it is obvious that a *written* language vastly increases that power. By writing down our thoughts we can put them aside and come back to them with renewed critical energy and a fresh point of view. We can criticize better because writing helps us achieve the perennially difficult task of standing outside our own thinking. Thus outlines are more helpful while revising than at the start of the writing process because finally there's something rich and interesting to outline. Revising is when I use the "X-ray" or "skeleton" exercise—asking both the writer and her readers to isolate the central core of inference in a paper: What is the assertion and what premises and reasons does it rest on? This is the best practice for critical thinking, because instead of being a canned exercise with artificial ingredients unconnected to the student, it is an exercise in assessing and strengthening the thinking which is embodied in one's own or someone else's live discourse. Since we are trying for the tricky goal of thinking about our subject but at the same time thinking about our thinking about it, putting our thoughts on paper gives us a fighting chance. But notice that what most heightens this critical awareness is not so much the writing down of words in the first place, though of course that helps, but the *coming back* to a text and re-seeing it from the outside (in space) instead of just hearing it from the inside (in time).

But does freewriting or uncensored, generative writing really enhance creative first-order thinking? You might say that speaking is a better way to enhance creative thinking—either through brainstorming or through the back and forth of discussion or debate. But that only works if we *have* other people available, people we trust, and people skilled at enhancing our creative thinking. Free exploratory writing, on the other hand, though we must learn to use it, is always available. And since the goal in creative thinking is to harness intuition—to get the imagination to take the reins in its own hands—solitary writing for no audience is often more productive than speaking. Speaking is almost invariably to an audience, and an audience puts pressure on us to make sense and avoid inferences we cannot explain.

You might also argue that intuitive thinking is better enhanced by silent musing; or going for a walk or sleeping on it or any of a host of other ways to push a question away from focal attention back to the preconscious. But such attempts at nonlinguistic processing often merely postpone thinking instead of actually enriching it. Freewriting and exploratory writing, on the other hand, are almost invariably productive because they exploit the autonomous generative powers of language and syntax themselves. Once you manage to get yourself writing in an exploratory but uncensored fashion, the ongoing string of language and syntax itself becomes a lively and surprising force for generation. Words call up words, ideas call up more ideas. A momentum of language and thinking develops and one learns to nurture it by keeping the pen moving. With a bit of practice, you can usually bring yourself to the place where you can stop and say, "Look at that! I've been led by this unrolling string of words to an insight or connection or structure that I had no premonition of. I could never have proposed it if I were just musing or making an outline. I wasn't steering, I was being taken for a ride." Heuristic prewriting techniques that involve only list-making or diagram-making tend to lack the generative force that comes from the use of actual syntax—speech on paper.*

I'm not trying to disparage spoken discourse or nonverbal back-burner work. They can be wonderful. But they are not as reliable as writing for enhancing first-order thinking.†

---

* There is an interesting piece of research in which a heuristic consisting of freewriting was more effective on almost all counts than a problem-solving heuristic that didn't harness actual syntax. (See Hilgers.)

†There are interesting ways for subject-matter teachers to help students unleash first-order thinking about whatever subject they are teaching—ways that do not necessarily demand careful grading or correcting of papers. See my "Teaching Writing by Not Paying Attention to Writing."

"Taken for a ride." The metaphor evokes what's good but also what's fearful about first-order thinking and uncensored writing. It is dangerous to be taken for a ride, literally by a horse or metaphorically by a shark. "Eternal vigilance." But the goal of first-order thinking or writing is to *relax* vigilance and be taken on as many rides as possible: *as long as* we remember that this is only half the process. We must assess the results with second-order thinking or revising. In short, by using the writing process in this two-sided way, I can foster contraries: our ability to let go and be taken on surprising rides; yet also our ability critically to assess the resulting views.

Practical Consequences

I am not concluding from all this that there is only one right way to think or write. We all know too many good thinkers or writers who contradict each other and even themselves in their methods. But this notion of opposite extremes gives a constructive and specific picture of what we're looking for in good thinking and writing. That is, even though there are many good ways to think and write, it seems clear that excellence must involve finding *some* way to be both abundantly inventive yet toughmindedly critical. Indeed this model of conflicting goals suggests why good writers and thinkers are so various in their technique: if they are managing to harness opposites—in particular, opposites that tend to interfere with each other—they are doing something mysterious. Success is liable to take many forms, some of them surprising.

As a teacher, it helps me to have these two clear goals in mind when I come across a student about whom I must say, "She clearly *is* a smart person, but why is she so often wrong?" Or "She clearly thinks hard and carefully, but why is she so characteristically uninteresting or unproductive in her work?" I can ask of any person or performance, "Is there enough rich material to build from?" and "Is there a careful and critical enough assessment of the material?"

If I am careful to acknowledge to my students that things are complex and that there is no single best way to think or write—and that excellence in these realms is a mystery that can be mastered in surprising ways—then I may justifiably turn around and stress simplicity by harping on two practical rules of thumb.

First, since creative and critical thinking are opposite and involve mentalities that tend to conflict with each other, it helps most people to learn to work on them separately or one at a time by moving back and forth between them. If we are trying to think creatively or write generatively, it usually hinders us if we try at the same time to think critically or to revise: it makes us reject what we are engaged in thinking before we've really worked it out at all—or to cross out what we've written before we've finished the sentence or paragraph and allowed something to develop. But if we hold off criticism or revising for a while, we can build a safe place for generative thinking or writing. Similarly, if we devote certain times to wholehearted critical thinking or revising, we can be more acute and powerful in our critical assessment.

For one of the main things that holds us back from being as creative as we could be is fear of looking silly or being wrong. But that worry dissipates when we know we will soon turn to wholehearted criticism and revising and weed out what is foolish. Similarly, one of the main things that holds us back from being as critical as we could be is fear that we'll have to reject everything and be left with nothing at all. But that worry also dissipates when we know we've already generated an extremely rich set of materials to work on (or if we haven't, we know we can do so quickly whenever we turn to wholehearted generating). In short, even though creative and critical thinking can magically coalesce in the hands of masters and at certain special moments when the rest of us are at our best, it usually helps us to work on them separately so they can flourish yet reinforce each other.

Second rule of thumb. It usually helps to *start with* creative thinking and exploratory writing and then engage in critical assessment and revision afterward—after we have gotten ourselves going and there is already lots to assess. It's not that we should necessarily try to force our writing into two self-contained steps (though I aim for this when all goes smoothly). Often I cannot finish all generating or all first-order thinking before I need to do some revising or criticizing—which will sometimes force a new burst of generating. We are never finished with generating—and having generated, we always need to criticize and revise. I used to think that I should try to finish getting my students good at creative generating before I went on to work on revising and being critical. But I've discovered that some students won't let go and allow themselves to be creative till after we do some hard work on critical thinking and revising. They don't feel safe relaxing their vigilance till I demonstrate that I'm also teaching heightened vigilance. Sometimes, early in the semester, I ask students to rethink and revise a paper in order to prove to them that they are not stuck with what they put down in early drafts, and that careful critical thinking can make a big difference.

But the fact remains that most people get more and better thinking—and less time-wasting—if they start off generating. My main agenda for the beginning of a semester is always to enforce generating and brainstorming and the deferral of criticism in order to build students' confidence and show them that they can quickly learn to come up with a great quantity of words and ideas. Then gradually we progress to a back-and-forth movement between generating and criticizing. I find I help my own writing and thinking and that of my students by consciously training ourselves to start with first-order thinking and generating and to take it on longer and longer rides—to hold off longer and longer the transition to criticizing and logic. Back and forth, yes, but in longer spells so that each mentality has more time to flourish before we move on to its opposite.

Mutual Reinforcement

Because the history of our culture is often experienced as a battle between reason and feeling, between rationality and irrationality, between logic and impulse—and because intuitive first-order thinking is indissolubly mixed up with feeling, irrationality, and impulse—we end up with disciplined critical thinking and uncensored creative thinking dug into opposed trenches with their guns trained on each other. Logic and reason have won the battle to be our standard for thinking, but not the battle for hearts and minds, and therefore champions of logic and reason understandably criticize all relaxations of critical vigilance. Similarly, champions of creative first-order thinking sometimes feel they must criticize critical thinking if only to win some legitimacy for themselves. But this is an unfortunate historical and developmental accident. If we would see clearly how it really is with thinking and writing, we would see that the situation isn't either/or, it's both/and: the more first-order thinking, the more second-order thinking; the more generative uncensored writing, the more critical revising; and vice versa. It's a matter of learning to work on opposites one at a time in a generous spirit of mutual reinforcement rather than in a spirit of restrictive combat.

PART II

❁❁❁

THE TEACHING PROCESS

The four essays in this part (presented in the order in which they were written) represent a twelve-year wrestle with what is probably the deepest and most human issue for teachers: the issue of *authority* in teaching. In a sense the previous part is a story about *what* I have taught; this one is a story about *how* I taught.

Wrestling seems inevitable to me because of the inherent paradox of authority in learning and teaching: students seldom learn well unless they *give in* or submit to teachers. Yet they seldom learn well unless they *resist* or even reject their teachers.

In these essays I tend to speak of myself as a teacher, but it seems clear to me now that whatever *sense* I manage to make about this tricky matter of authority probably comes from the fact that I am also speaking about myself as learner—my past self as student (and how I reacted to *my* teachers) as well as my present self as someone who learns or doesn't learn in my own classroom. (Again, the insight was crystallized for me in the realm of writing: it scarcely helps at all for teachers to work on "techniques for the teaching of writing" unless they also work on their *own* writing and their own feelings about it.)

The vicissitudes and perplexities in my own life as a student and teacher may stem from the extremity with which I inhabited both sides of the authority paradox: I didn't just "go along" with my teachers, I hungered to please them, I fell in love with them, I wanted to *be* them. Similarly, I didn't just engage in "independent thinking" (thereby earning approving pats on the head from them); eventually I seemed driven to reject, spit out, and indeed hate those teachers and all they stood for. And then subsequently back and forth. Without the extremities of these responses, I probably would not have made teaching and learning so deep a part of me.

CHAPTER 4

❀❀❀

In my first bout of teaching (that interdisciplinary teaching at M.I.T. and Franconia College from 1960 to 1965), I simply tried to imitate the good teachers I'd had—to be Socrates and a good guy at the same time. My first essay about teaching (not collected here) grew out of this teaching and my realization that few faculties took teaching as seriously as my teachers had done at Williams College. In that essay I argued that it's not good enough for teachers just to "show up with the goods," they must "produce learning" in students. If the student doesn't learn, it is the teacher's fault.

The hubris of that position grew out of the excitement and naive confidence I felt in my first five years of teaching. It had been such a pleasure to *stop* being a student and start teaching—to stop having to seek help and start giving it, to stop paying and start being paid!—that I'd rocketed off with a kind of pent up animal/intellectual energy. I loved pacing in front of the class trying to "get my points across" and trying to orchestrate a "well run discussion." I think the teaching process helped heighten my excitement with what I was reading and teaching—I suppose by providing me with a constant audience. I remember often trying to hide a choke in my voice and a mist in my eyes—emotional reactions which crept up on me as I read aloud favorite passages from the text.

But that stage of teaching was behind me when I wrote the essay which follows. This essay grew out of my *second* bout of teaching and is about a different kind of excitement with teaching and sharing-with-students. When I returned to teaching in 1968 with my new Ph.D., it happened that I returned to the very same classrooms at M.I.T. that I'd taught in from 1960–63. I found myself with some perplexing and unexpected responses to my authority as a teacher. No doubt, there is some naiveté here—and it was after all 1968 and Vietnam and M.I.T. and Cambridge, Massachusetts. But it's sad to see how difficult it is for the educational world (and at times even for me) to acknowledge the validity of the ideas and feelings expressed here.

❁❁❁

Exploring My Teaching

I possess in good measure the impulse to nail down the truth about teaching once and for all, and on that basis to tell everyone else how to teach. Much in this essay hovers on the brink of being plain, pushy, normative advice. Nevertheless, the main thing I've come to believe through the exploration described here—and the main thing I wish to stress—is that better teaching behavior comes primarily from exploring one's *own* teaching from an experiential and phenomenological point of view: "What did I actually do? What was I actually experiencing when I did it? Can I say what feelings, ideas, or experiences led me to do it?" This approach leads to very different teaching behaviors for different people and even different teaching behaviors for the same person at different times. All these behaviors will indeed be "right," I would guess, so long as they rest upon a symmetrical premise: an equal affirmation of the *student's* experience, his right to ground his behaviors in his experience, and thus his right, like the teacher's, to embark on his own voyage of change, development, and growth as to what is right for him.

After five years of regular college teaching—trying to be Socrates and a good guy at the same time—and after three years of nonteaching while I was finishing my Ph.D. but thinking a lot about teaching (see *College English,* Vol. 30, Nos. 2 and 3), I reentered the classroom to discover an unexpected set of reactions. I found I couldn't stand to tell students things they hadn't asked me to tell them. I knew I knew things that were both true and important, but that only made me feel all the more gagged and mute. I even found I couldn't stand to ask questions—except the question, "What is your question?" Nothing seemed worth saying in a classroom till a student had a question he took seriously. I was no longer willing to listen to the thud of my question lying dead on the classroom floor. I refused to coax interest. I also felt it as a refusal to pedal alone. If they won't pedal, neither will I. No source of energy seemed bearable except their motivation. And not only motivation but experience. If they are not talking from the experience of the text read—even the felt experience of getting no experience from it—then count me out.

These were troublesome feelings. Giving in to them seemed to mean abdicating my role as a teacher. But they wouldn't go away and I was feeling ornery. So with respect to most of the leadership activities of teachers, I'd become by Christmas a kind of drop-out, a conscientious objector, a giver-in to repugnance.

I'm prepared to consider the hypothesis that these feelings are some kind of pathology. Some kind of petulant backlash at having finally submitted to graduate school. Or some kind of atrophy of the deep sexual hunger to tell people things. But on the other hand, perhaps the real pathology is the hunger to tell people things they didn't ask you to tell them. If this turns out to be true, if *unsolicited telling* turns out to hinder rather than help our goal of producing knowledge and understanding in students, then we will have to be honest enough to set up other arenas where teachers can work off this appetite.

Perhaps my metaphor is too unsavory. But not too sexual. The one thing sure is that teaching is sexual. What is uncertain is which practices are natural and which unnatural, which fruitful and which barren, which legal and which illegal. When the sexuality of teaching is more generally felt and admitted, we may finally draw the obvious moral: it is a practice that should only be performed upon the persons of consenting adults.

But since I am not sure which is pathology—unsolicited telling or holding back—and since I don't yet know the grounds for deciding the question, I am merely asserting that it is possible to have these feelings, act on them, and live to tell the tale. Not go blind and insane. It is not a trivial point since so many teachers share these feelings but scarcely entertain them because they feel them unspeakable.

My present introductory literature course is the latest product of these feelings. It is a sophomore course, but comparable to freshman English since it is more or less required and is the first English course taken. Most courses are structured around a class hour, a set of books, and a teacher's perception of the content. If a student's goals, perceptions, and motivation can fit into that structure, fine; if not, too bad. I have tried to stand that model on its head. The core of my course is each student's goals, perceptions, and willingness to do something about it. The other ingredients—the class hour and the teacher's perception of the content—are invited to fit into that structure if and where they can; and if not, too bad.

The course has three rules: (1) The student must state on paper, for everyone to read, at the beginning, what he wants to get out of the course; at mid-term and end of term, what he thinks he is getting and not getting. Each student may pursue his own goals; read anything and go in any direction. The only constraints are those imposed by reality. For example, I make it clear I am not going to spend any more time on the course than if I taught it in a conventional way. (2) Each student must read something each week: either literature or about literature. I offer my services in helping people find things suitable to their goals. (3) Each student must put words on paper (even if only to say he does not wish to write) once a week and put it in a box in the reserve reading room where everyone can read everyone else's and make comments. (There are about 20 in the class.) The writing need not be on what was read that week, though I ask the student to jot his reading down somewhere on the paper. Attendance is not required. Anyone who follows these rules is guaranteed an A. If not, he is not taking the course and I ask him to drop it or flunk it. (I try not to be coercively non-directive: if a student's goals are to read what the teacher thinks most suitable for an introductory course and to get out of it what the teacher thinks he ought to get out of it, I try to help him with these goals.)

☘

I wish to describe my experience in this course in terms of five beliefs I end up with.

1. Much teaching behavior really stems from an unwarranted

fear of things falling apart. When I started to act on my new feelings and to refrain from unsolicited telling and asking, I discovered that that fear lay behind much of my previous teaching. I began to realize I'd always been "running" or "structuring" a class with the underlying feeling that if I ever stopped, some unspecifiable chaos or confusion would ensue. In all my teaching, there had been a not-fully-experienced sense of only precariously holding dissolution at bay.

But the unnamed disaster somehow doesn't happen. There is some confusion, desultoriness, and recurring silence, but the new class texture has an organic structure and stability. The class finds a new and stabler center of gravity. And I discover a mental or emotional muscle I've always been clenching to keep the ship from sinking or the plane from crashing. I discover it by feeling all of a sudden how tired it is.

But fears die hard. There are still days when it returns—my security may be low and my refusal flagging. I come in and ask, "Well, what is the question? How can we use our time?" The silence wells up. I reach for my pipe and throw myself into carefully prying out the old tobacco—which it is important to leave there for these situations—cleaning it, filling it, tamping, and managing never quite to get it well lit so I can have something to keep busy with. All the while trying not to gulp. Not even cool enough to ask myself, "So what is this impending thing that is so scary? What's the disaster if nothing productive gets accomplished? You know perfectly well that they don't carry away anything much useful from your 'well run' classes."

Some students share this anxiety and some do not. Interestingly, it is usually the ostensibly "good" class—the productive and conscientious one—which persists longest in keeping up some kind of nervous chatter and prevents the class from finding its real center of gravity—usually silence at first and then some question about why in hell they are in this class doing what they are doing: with respect first to the class hour, then to the course, and only then to genuinely assented-to questions about the subject matter. It's so slow. And yet since I won't settle for any but genuinely assented-to questions, it represents a huge improvement and I'm not tempted to go back to the-show-must-go-on.

Surely many others must be trapped as I was by *unfelt* fears in their running of a class.

2. An actual audience is crucial for writing. English teachers know it helps for the student to *imagine* an audience. But this is nothing compared to the benefit of actually having one. The best thing about my course is the fact that each student writes something weekly he knows the rest of the class will read and, for the most part, comment on.

An audience acts as suction. Only a few lucky or diligent souls find an audience *because* they write well. As often as not, people write well because they find an audience. They may not find a large and discriminating audience until after they get pretty good. But they had to start by being lucky, pushy, or driven enough to find a genuine audience—even if small and informal. Writers like to say that a compulsion to write is the only necessary condition for being a good writer. The formula is elliptical and can be expanded in two directions: (1) the compulsion to write makes you find an audience and then you get better; or (2) the presence of an audience produces the compulsion to write.

I sense everywhere a huge *potential* desire to be heard which the presence of an audience can awaken. A genuine audience can be tiny—even one person. But only exceptional teachers can succeed in being a genuine audience for more than a couple of their students. And a larger audience is better.

I have had the experience more than once of having thought I had finished writing something; sending it around and finally finding someone who would print it; and only then discovering a willingness to revise it again. Lack of character, perhaps, but a common disease which no college course can hope to cure.

The necessity of an audience is supported by the evidence about how children learn to speak: the audience is layed on for free and is eager for all productions; the child doesn't have to *deserve* it. Whether the infant's audience gives correction doesn't matter much. What matters is ongoing interaction: answering and talking, i.e., nonevaluative feedback. And no audience, no speech. Imagine the sorry results of an infant trying to learn to speak by a process equivalent to our freshmen English or writing courses.

The writing of the students in my course improves noticeably. They do not necessarily work on the kind of writing that someone else thinks they ought to. Few work consistently on critical, analytic essays. The majority write explorations of their own experience. More poetry than I expected. But it is clear they are learning the basic elements or atoms for any sort of writing: how to work out thoughts and feelings into words; how to get words on paper such that the meanings get into the reader's head; and how to make the effects of those words on a reader more nearly what the writer intended.

The most solid evidence for the quality of their writing is that I actually enjoy reading the papers in the box each week. And they get more enjoyable each week. The voice and self of each writer continually emerge more forcefully.

3. Students learn more about literature through writing than through reading. Many students don't really believe in the reality of words that come in books studied in school. I remember discovering, the first moment I was in France, that I hadn't really believed there were real people who spoke that funny language I studied in school and college. That unexpected, faint surprise revealed that part of me suspected all along that French was an elaborate hoax by schools and teachers to give me something difficult to learn. Paranoia, if you will, but again, a common disease.

And so in the case of literature, I feel students in this class doing with each other's writing the one thing—and a rare thing—that is a precondition for the appreciation and study of literature: taking the words seriously; giving full inner assent to their reality. I phrase the writing assignment as a requirement to "put words on paper such that it's not a waste of time for the reader or the writer." At last students wrestle with the main question—especially in an introductory course: What real value is there in putting words down on paper or in reading them? If a teacher feels the value is self-evident, he should look to some of our cultural and literary critics who have serious doubts. Students share these doubts and it's no good saying they're not allowed to take them seriously till they know as much or write as well as, say, George Steiner. I suspect many English teachers insist so loudly on the importance of reading and writing because of an inner doubt that is too frightening to face. I'm stuck by the quiet relief with which many English and writing programs swing into film. Students came to *enjoy* literature more than they ever have done in a course of mine because this question of whether it's worth putting words on paper at last became the center of the course—and operationally, not intellectually or theoretically.

4. For learning, empirical feedback is a good thing and normative evaluation is a bad thing. Empirical feedback, in the case of writing, means learning what the words did to the reader. Normative evaluation means having the words judgmentally ranked according to some abstract standard. I have found that empirical feedback seems to encourage activity; to release energy. Presumably when one gets accurate, honest, human feedback—with all the inevitable contradictions between responders—one learns not to be scared to put forth words. Normative evaluation seems to inhibit words.

The value of having everyone in the class reading everyone else's writing is that it inevitably brings out empirical feedback and diminishes normative evaluation. Students often start out giving normative judgments: they've learned in school that "commenting" on a paper means saying whether it is good or bad. But these judgments are so diverse and conflicting that the writer can see how normative evaluations are usually skewed forms of personal, empirical feedback. When there are many comments on a paper, it is perfectly clear that a statement like, "This is disorganized and uninteresting and doesn't really amount to anything," really means, "You bored me and I didn't perceive any organization or meaning here." For other comments show that other readers reacted entirely differently. The effect of this situation—and my urging—is that students get better at giving honest empirical feedback. (They did not, however, usually give *enough* commentary or feedback to satisfy me and some of them.)

I grade as I do because of this distinction between feedback and judgment. When the grade is as meaningless as possible, the student can better believe, assimilate, and benefit from the feedback he gets from me and his classmates. I am frankly trying to channel my responses into personal, honest reactions, and keep them from being channeled into institutional normative judgments. Students write more than they have to, I think, because of a setting with maximum feedback and minimum judgment.

5. It is good to separate constraints from freedoms with absolute clarity. I am tempted to think that the amount of freedom in a course makes less difference than how clearly it is distinguished from constraint. Almost any course contains more freedom than is first apparent, but if there is any ambiguity, the freedom ends up inhibiting rather than liberating energy.

I cannot resist speculating on the obscure dynamics here. I find myself and many students reading in constraints that are not there. "If I do such and such I'll get on the bad side of Smith," when in fact Smith couldn't care less. "If I teach in such and such a way, I will lose my job," when the teacher knows deep down that his latitude is immense if he is not needlessly inflammatory. "I wouldn't be reading this crap except that he might put it on the exam," when the student knows deep down he would do better on the exam if he spent a fraction of the time seriously reading a "trot" and discussing it with a couple of friends. "I've got to take this course because they require it in graduate school" when he doesn't take the trouble to find out whether it is really so—and it usually isn't.

There must be good reasons for fooling ourselves in this way. For one thing, it may be a form of reacting to past occasions when we were stung: we were offered free choice but there were covert constraints. Students have had this experience many times. There is hardly a high school course that doesn't begin with the announcement, "Now you people can make what you want to out of this course."

Desires may also make one read in constraints that do not exist: it is hard—especially these days—to accept and experience the universal desire simply to be told what to do—to be held by arms too strong to break out of.

I can think of a third reason for feeling constraints that aren't there: if I feel some task as constrained rather than free, then I don't have to feel how much I care about it and fear failing. In short, I am spared the risk of investment and caring. Whatever the reason for this failure to experience the full degree of freedom or choice that exists, it causes a subtle, pervasive insulation against real learning—a covert non-assent or holding back from genuine participation in the knowledge that is seemingly attained.

As I see it, then, when choice is available, there is usually an initial resistance and tendency to do nothing at all. It is a threatening investment for many students simply to do something school-like when they don't have to. If this can be gotten past, if the choice or freedom can be finally assented to and the investment made, there turns out to be a liberation of energy. But if there is any haziness or ambiguity about the choice, many students get stuck at the stage of feeling subtly constrained. They resent and resist the freedom. The freedom is not assented to, the hump is not gotten over, and there is no liberation of energy.

Such ambiguity can come from a teacher's unspoken doubts and hedges: "You can read whatever you want." ("So long as you don't read trash.") Or, "I am giving you this choice to exercise as you see fit." ("Only I wish I didn't have to give it to those of you who are lazy and don't give a damn about this subject because you won't use the freedom well and don't deserve it.") These unspoken thoughts get through to students—presumably through tone of voice, phrasing, and even physical gestures.

It follows from the idea that freedom and constraints should be clearly distinguished that rules are often a good thing. I used to feel rules were childish. We're in college now. Let's not go around making rules. But there are in fact many constraints at play upon us and our students—from the society, the institution, the teacher's idea of what is proper, or simply from the teacher's character or prejudices. It is liberating to get them into clear rules.

Students only learn to choose and to motivate themselves in spaces cleared by freedom. These spaces can be very small and still work, so long as they are not clouded by ambiguity. A teacher can give meaningful freedom even if he works within a very tightly constrained system. Suppose, for example, that every aspect of a course involves a constraint stemming either from the institution's rules or the teacher's sense of what is non-negotiably necessary. If, in such a situation, the teacher decides nevertheless that the last fifteen minutes of each class period are genuinely free to be used as the class decides—or one full class a week—a new degree of freedom and learning will result.

I use class time for my example because it is usually the area of greatest ambiguity about freedom. So often we are trying for two goals at the same time: to create a free, unconstrained feeling ("free discussion"), and to *cover* points chosen in advance. (Sometimes, in fact, even to *conclude* things concluded in advance.) It is crucial in running a so-called free discussion to make up our minds—and make it clear to the class—what the rules really are. Almost any rules are workable so long as they are clear: "We can talk about anything so long as it has something to do with the assignment"; or, "I reserve the right to decide what the questions will be, but we can do anything in treating these questions"; or, "It can go where the class wants it to go, but I reserve the right to decide we are wasting time; but I admit I don't know exactly what my criteria are for the decision; in fact I admit my criteria will vary with my mood."

The only unworkable rule is a common unspoken one: "You must freely make my points." When I finally sensed the presence of this rule and how unworkable it was, I was forced to see that, if I feel certain points *must* be made in class, then I should make them as openly as I can—even through lectures—and not try to coax others to be my mouthpiece.

The problem of class time illustrates the fact that even though it is helpful and liberating to try to get things into a binary system of being either totally free or totally constrained, most of us want some aspects of our course to be somewhere in between. For such grey areas of reality, we have a favorite phrase: *"It would be a good idea* if you did such and such." I find it hard to break the habit, but I can now see it as one of the most self-defeating ways to ask students to do something. Even though the matter is not fully free or constrained, that is no excuse, it now seems to me, for not making up my mind whether I am saying, "You will get a lower mark if you don't"; or, "You will learn less if you don't"; or, "You will develop less character if you don't"; or, "You will personally disappoint me or make my life harder if you don't." Each of these messages is perfectly valid and causes students little difficulty. But to fudge the issue of which is the true one has the effect of producing needless resistance.

In my efforts to distinguish clearly between areas of freedom and constraint and to make unambiguous, accurate messages about those things that lie somewhere between, I discovered why I hadn't naturally stumbled into these practices before. They are hard. In particular, they put me more personally on the line and make me feel risk. For instance, in the case of sending messages, one of my favorites is, "I think it would be better for you to do X, but it is your choice and it doesn't matter to me." It's unambiguous, all right. But unfortunately it is seldom accurate in my case. I seldom *am* indifferent about whether they do X. As I began to notice this, I began to realize that in many cases the only thing I was sure of was that *I* would feel better if they did X; and *not* that X was necessarily the best possible thing for all of them. But it is threatening to send the new, more accurate message. It makes me feel more vulnerable. And it permits students who probably ought to do X to say the hell with it—sometimes purely out of a spirit of contrariness. But I feel it helps in the long run. It begins to make my word more trustworthy.

Similarly in the case of trying to make unambiguous rules, I found I was more likely than before to be thought of as a dirty rat by the student. I want the area of freedom to be very large, but nevertheless authority is more naked when one is unambiguous. Therefore more students are apt to be very angry about something or other—even about the freedom itself. As this made me very uncomfortable, I began to sense how much of my characteristic teaching behavior is an attempt to avoid being the object of the student's anger.

I suppose this whole exploration of the importance of being unambiguous about freedom and constraint—this renewed attack upon the old problem of freedom and necessity—is merely an extended way of saying that I find an inescapable power relationship in any institutionalized teaching. I feel this power relationship hinders the sort of learning situation I seek—one in which the student comes to act on his own motivation and comes to evaluate ideas and perceptions on their own merits and not in terms of who holds them. I feel I can best minimize this power relationship by getting the weapons out on the table. Trying to pretend that the power and weapons are not there—however swinging I am and however groovy the students are—only gets the power more permanently and insidiously into the air.

It may be, of course, that it is misguided and perverse of me to want to get rid of the power relationship: my own hang-up about authority. Certainly the power relationship can be viewed as a potent audio-visual aid for a mature teacher to welcome and use honestly and constructively. Either verdict, however, points to the importance of recognizing the power relationship.

❁

Because I'm confident the course is working at an important level, I want to share my frustrations. First, inevitably, not enough gets *covered* in class. It's all very well to make fun of the teacher's itch to "cover" a lot, but the itch is so real. Allowing everyone to choose his own reading makes it harder for the class to come together in a focused discussion. In the future I may ask that we somehow come up with a mechanism for focusing one class a week upon a common text or planned topic of discussion.

There were times when I could honestly have said, "Damn it, this desultory, wandering small talk and local gossip is downright boring to me. Can't we do something more interesting and substantive? Otherwise I'll simply go on sitting here wishing my alarm hadn't gone off." I didn't dare say it, but now I suspect I should have. Reticence about these feelings probably made more oppressive vibrations than expressing them would have done. It's as though I feared I had some super, demolishing power and they were nothing but weak and defenseless. Whereas if I had just said it, maybe it would have helped us all sooner to get past a loaded and awkward way of behaving with each other—strengthened their autonomy and reduced my self-consciousness. To carry this off, however, I'd have to succeed in saying it and meaning it as one person who feels dissatisfied—not as someone who harbors the insistence that the class follow my feelings.

I found, by the way, that longer classes of this sort are more productive than shorter ones. It's worth trying to change three 50-minute classes a week into two longer ones. It's too easy for everyone to wait it out for 50 minutes and avoid the effort and investment of overcoming inertia—holding the breath till the end of the period.

But I'm sure the problem of low productivity in class won't disappear. Students display strong reactions to past teaching.

They do a lot of testing because they have historical reason for suspecting there is a catch. They will inevitably spend considerable time pushing the limits to see whether they are in the presence of that hidden rule underlying so many current educational experiments: "You may do whatever you want—*so long as it's not something I feel is a waste of time.*"

I was also frustrated by what I perceive as a rampant individualism. At the operational level, this took the form of an aversion to working together in subgroups with common reading. Even though many of them had similar goals, this never happened. It discouraged me. The individualism took an epistemological form as well: a tendency to operate on the unspoken premise that "I know what I perceive, feel, and think; if I try to get any of these into words or into someone else's head, there is only distortion and loss, and it's not worth the effort." They were scarcely willing even to entertain the opposite premise, namely, "I don't know what I perceive, feel, or think *until* I can get it into language and perhaps even into someone else's head."

So students didn't seem to doubt their own individual perceptions of a text. They seemed uninterested in testing one individual's perceptions against another's. But I persist in thinking I shouldn't force this activity. I feel less worried about their emerging from my course with skewed perceptions of texts than about their persistence in not wanting to do anything about it. I see their wrongheaded, or at least parochial, point of view itself as a kind of proof that required corrective discussions haven't worked in the past. Why should they work better now?

During the term I saw no cure except patience for this student stance of I-don't-need-anybody's-help-to-see-accurately. I had already sensed a quiet refusal in it: they understood perfectly well, as anyone does, that their perceptions were liable to be skewed. The refusal annoyed me. But as I think about it now, I see I can do more. First, I am led to try to guess what experience might produce this epistemological arrogance. And then try to see if I can experience it vicariously myself. This is what I come up with: "Look! For years and years, you English teachers have been saying things and forcing us to do things which all tended to make us feel we have defective sensing mechanisms: our very perceptions are wrong—our own responses invalid. Almost invariably, the poem or character I preferred was shown less worthy of preference than one which left me cold. I was always noticing things that you seemed to show unimportant, and failing to notice things you seemed to show most important. You may be able to convince me I have defective perception in literature; but you can't make me want to rub my nose in it. So now you tell me I can do what I want with a literature class and you want me to go in for more of that? Not on your life!"

So where I once felt indifference and even arrogance about individual perception, I now feel a pervasive defensiveness and doubt. Where I once saw teachers as too unconvincing, I now see they were too convincing. I wish I'd felt this earlier because it dispels my annoyance and that annoyance probably made things worse. For I now see as healthy and positive their refusal to joust publicly with their own responses until they are a bit confident, or at least comfortable and self-accepting, about them. For myself, certainly, I can't really expose my own responses for refinement or correction (as here) until I feel pretty good about them. Only then, paradoxically, can I truly open myself to the possibility that they are seriously skewed, and allow myself ungrudgingly to move on to different, more accurate perceptions.

Another frustration is that I feel much less useful in such a teaching situation. My head is bursting with fascinating things that the dirty rats didn't ask me. (Half way through the term, however, I saw I should join in the activity of putting words on paper once a week for the box. So that gave me a forum that seemed appropriate.) As teachers we tend to assume we are useful to students, and that the more we are used—the more they get from us—the better we are doing. I think we should take a ride on the opposite premise and see where it leads—the premise that we can be of very little use and that we may not be doing badly if they get very little from us. Einstein put it bluntly in a letter:

> Incidentally, I am only coming to Princeton to research, not to teach. There is too much education altogether, especially in American schools. The only rational way of educating is to be an example—of what to avoid, if one can't be the other sort. (21–22)

Another frustration is that one must put up with great naiveté. But I am convinced, now, that when you allow real choice and self-motivated learning, the student reverts to the point at which real learning last took place. This often means going way back. They revert to what they really feel and think—not to what they normally produce in classes, papers, and tests. John Holt talks shrewdly of how primary school arithmetic teachers often find themselves keeping the class discussion within channels implied by the textbook because the children can thereby produce correct answers; whereas if things wander into novel or unexpected byways, the teacher is forced to confront the overwhelmingly discouraging fact that the children don't really understand the most elementary concept of arithmetic which they have already "mastered." I feel I often see students demonstrate that they don't really understand many things they have a competent academic mastery of. That is, they haven't "really learned" them—they haven't been willing or able to digest, assent to, or participate in the knowledge of these things. For this reason I feel we should view as progress this reversion to naive stations where real learning stopped.

❁

In the end, I am led back to a new perception of those original pesky feelings: something has been motivating me all along which only now comes to awareness. I sense differently now those refusals to tell things unsolicited, to ask questions, and to pedal alone. I feel them now as more positive. Behind the reticence and sense of being gagged lies a need to be genuinely listened to, to carry some weight, to make a dent. I want a chance for my words to penetrate to a level of serious consciousness. And that need is great enough that I'll pay a large price. I'll settle for very few words indeed. Behind my ostensible openness lies an intense demandingness. If I didn't really want to be demanding, I could teach the old "well-run" course that students let roll off their backs so easily. It's my desire to be heard that makes me insist that the students figure out what they want to know.

I am like the teacher of the noisy class who says, ever so sweetly, "Now boys and girls, I'm not going to say another thing until you are quiet enough for me to be heard." (Stifled cheers!) But my intuition had enough sense to take things into its own hands and insist that I didn't have a chance of being heard until they made *more* noise. I think this is true even at the literal level: in my few good classes, I have to fight to be heard, but my words carry more real weight—the weight of a person and not just a teacher. If I want to be heard at all, I've got to set up a situation in which the options of whether to hear me or tune me out—whether to take me seriously or dismiss me—are more genuine than in a normal classroom field of force. I'm refusing, therefore, to be short-circuited by a role which students react to with the stereotyped responses to authority: either automatic, ungenuine acceptance or else automatic, ungenuine refusal.

I don't know whether this underlying need to be truly heard is a good thing or a bad thing: whether the ineffectual parts of my teaching come from not fully inhabiting this basic feeling, or from not having gotten over it. I imagine two different answers from students. I imagine them saying,

> Well, it's about time you had the guts to feel and admit your mere humanity—your desire to get through and your need to make a difference. There's no hope for you as a teacher as long as you come on with this self-delusion about being disinterested, nondirective, and seeking only the student's own goals and motivation. In that stance, you can never succeed in being anything for us but cold, indifferent, and a waste of our time—ultimately enraging.

But I also hear them saying,

> Get off our back! We've got enough to think about without your personal need to make a dent on us. What do you think we are? Objects laid on to gratify your need to feel your life makes a difference?

My teaching has benefited in the past from experiencing more fully the feelings which generate what I try to do. So I trust this new clarification of feeling must be progress even if I don't yet know what to think of it.

CHAPTER 5

❀❀❀

I am in effect replying here to that excited teacher who wrote "Exploring My Teaching" a few years earlier. And I am speaking, in a sense, for my *third* bout of teaching. For I wrote the essay which follows while I was in the process of changing academic universes: moving from M.I.T. to The Evergreen State College. (Evergreen is an experimental state college in Washington. It was then in its second year; it had no departments, no academic ranks, no tenure, no grades, and instead of courses, full-time academic programs. I wanted to move from an institution where I had the luxury of being a gadfly to one where I had the responsibility of being in the mainstream.)

As I reflected on the small part my humanities courses played in the overall education of my M.I.T. students, and the large part my full-time, full-year interdisciplinary programs played in the education of my Evergreen students, I was struck with my *responsibilities* as a teacher to take on authority. Oddly enough, teachers at Evergreen had to take on more authority *because* it was an experimental culture: there were no traditions that permitted most of the "rules" to be left unstated. (These thoughts about authority also crystallized for me because I was writing at a time when I was making some larger sense out of my own life—marrying for a second time and learning somewhat better than before to acknowledge my own dependencies on others.)

But I wrote the first draft of this essay before I left M.I.T. For even there I began to be struck with how confused students could be about authority. I remember one particular course toward the end of my time at M.I.T. where (following my advice in the previous essay) I decided to spell out the authority situation completely and explicitly. I thought this would make my students feel freer and more autonomous: not only because these things are usually left so vague, but also because I was in fact giving them so much authority which teachers usually retain. Nevertheless, I wanted to be absolutely clear about which decisions *still* rested with me and with the institution. The effect of my little speech and hand-out, oddly enough, was that my students experienced me as intimidating, almost dictatorial. They weren't used to so much talk about power—about power being, as it were, nakedly acknowledged. To "give away" power was somehow to flaunt the fact that I had it to give away.

⚙⚙⚙

The Pedagogy of the Bamboozled

This is not a book review. I am not trying to do justice to the fullness and complexity of Freire's *The Pedagogy of the Oppressed*.* In what follows I am only trying to ask how the major principles of his book relate to my situation: a teacher hired by an educational *institution* to teach mostly non-adult, middle-class students.

My argument can be summarized as follows. Freire gives principles which I think very few institutional teachers in this country follow. But I think many teachers, both in high school and college, *imply* in subtle ways that they do follow these principles. In this way they bamboozle students and themselves. Thus there are two possible reforms: start really doing what Freire describes; or stop implying that you do. Both courses of action would be excellent. But I find myself more excited at the prospect of the latter because it is so much more feasible. It is revolutionary in that it could actually happen this Monday morning.

The book strikes me most as a description of what an education would have to be like if it were *really* designed to liberate people. I abstract four major requirements:

First, the *teacher* must work as a collaborating ally of the student, not as a supervisor. Second, the *subject* of the study must

---

* I have occasional doubts which I don't know how to settle: Are his own practices, which he only faintly alludes to, fully in accord with the principles that form the substance of the book? And isn't there something suspicious about a book which emphasizes so much the importance of concrete reality, and yet in its language, style, and structure is so wholly abstract, deductive, and without *any* concrete people, places, or incidents?

be the lives of the students or, more precisely, the students' perceptions of their own lives—always reflected back to the student as a problem or a source of contradictions. Third, the *goal* of the study must be not just to change the student, though that will happen, but to work with the student to change the world: objective, external reality. Fourth, the *process* must be primarily rational and cognitive (rather than affective): critical thinking, problem-posing, looking for contradictions, and achieving greater awareness of one's own awareness and thinking.

1. The teacher must be an ally of the students. If we follow this principle we tend to get into what feels like chaos (more chaos than Freire implies). It takes so long to decide what to do and how to do it; and decisions are always having to be redecided. But if a teacher is willing to open himself to this mess—and clearly it can be a valuable and productive mess—then he can seem genuinely to collaborate with the student. But I insist on "seem." There is a crucial contradiction in the role of almost every institutional teacher that prevents our being genuine allies of the student: we are both credit-giver and teacher. As credit-giver we are the hurdle the student has to get over; as teacher we are the person who helps the student get over hurdles. It is very common for teachers to imply that they are more truly allies of the student than this contradiction permits. This is a source of bamboozlement for students, especially in their relations with experimental, liberal, open teachers who profess to be entirely "on the student's side." Freire's teaching in South America is outside an institution and no credit is involved.

2. The object of study is the actual lives of the students and their perceptions of their lives—always reflected back as problems to be solved and sources of contradiction. Freire proposes that the teacher and students spend half the time of the educational transaction investigating the students' lives as piercingly as possible: looking and looking, taking notes, trying to notice things that aren't usually noticed—almost as an anthropologist might do. And then look at this material and try to find the "generative themes" and the latent contradictions in their lives. Then build collaboratively a curriculum around those issues.*

---

* Here he is not strict with himself. He says the teacher can slip in some issues he thinks are important, even if they did not come up through the

Here, too, the difficulties are great. For one thing, the student may not *want* to study his own life or perception of it. When I come across students intent on self-liberation, they often have some external goal of study—e.g., learning some skill or trade, or even reading Hesse—which they think will lead them to liberation. As Freire says, the teacher must respect these goals and even help the student with them, but he can also continue to push his own conviction. That is, in addition to helping the student work toward the other goal, the teacher can constantly say, "But what do you see in your own life? What do you think about your perception?" But I think that any teacher-as-ally can push his conviction successfully here only if he is equally intent on exploring his *own* life and his *own* perception of it in collaboration with the student. Otherwise the student will tend to see him merely as a meddler, voyeur, and manipulator.

When we order books and set up themes which *we* decide (or publishers decide, or even past students decide) are relevant to the real lives of the students, we are often pretending to make our subject the lives and perception-of-lives of our students, but are actually falling short in a bamboozling way. And again it is those teachers who feel themselves most on the side of the student, most interested in open education, who are most likely to bamboozle in this fashion. The student has a hard time denying that these issues and books are relevant to his own life. He is often in the position of feeling them boring, somehow feeling they have nothing to do with him in a way he can't put his finger on, and feeling very baffled, blaming himself. The teacher *thinks* these books and issues really are about the student's lives (e.g., drugs; sex; suburbs!). The student, too, is convinced. Yet somehow it all seems unreal. He's bamboozled into thinking "What's the matter with me? Aren't I even interested in my own life? My own problems?" Yet, as Freire points out, these books and issues may not really represent the students' lives accurately. Certainly they may not represent their *perception* of their lives.

---

collaborative process of exploration. He even says that you can skip the collaborative planning and come in with a ready-made curriculum if you are short of money or time. This is the universal evasion of liberal curriculum planners, for one is always short of both time and money.

But again the student is liable to be bamboozled into thinking he doesn't even feel his own feelings right.

3. The goal is not changing the student but working with the student to change external, objective reality. Freire is insisting here on an epistemological claim that there are certain things you cannot see, feel, understand, or intend until you are engaged with allies in actually trying to change the world. He is going one further than the Dewey tradition of learning-by-doing: he is insisting that the action must be more than a "laboratory" or "practice" kind of action. It must be sincerely designed to make a difference in the real world. Otherwise the deeper changes in the head and heart of the individual do not take place.

I don't think there's much bamboozlement here. Not many teachers define as the goal of their course a particular set of partisan activities designed actually to change some social, personal, or political situation. And certainly most educational institutions are not comfortable accepting partisan action as the goal; especially not if the action starts to be effective.

4. The process is primarily rational and cognitive (rather than affective): critical thinking, problem-posing, looking for contradictions, and achieving greater awareness of one's own awareness and thinking. Freire's insistence on rationality here is connected with his insistence that education must be engaged in changing reality: you don't change reality effectively without making plans, models, goals; without instrumental behavior and deferred gratification; without words, abstractions, critical thinking, and heightened self-awareness. In Freire's words,

> To exist, humanly, is to *name* the world, to change it. Once named, the world in its turn reappears to the namers as a problem and requires of them a new *naming*. Men are not built in silence, but in a word, a work, in action-reflection. (76)

Freire's insistence on rationality is a healthy corrective to the reaction against it in much experimental ("affective," "experiential") education. For him "subjectivity," "irrationality," "partisanship," and "immersion" are bad words; "split," "separate," and "awareness of consciousness of self" are good words.

I am struck with the strength of the distrust of rationality among many students. In its extreme form, the student feels

there is no use arguing any question at all; there is no use talking; any answer is as good as any other no matter what the question; what is "true for you" is what is true, and that is the only
significant way to use the word "true." A mild form of this distrust seems epidemic.

There must be many complex cultural reasons for this condition. But I cannot help thinking there are two things which
teachers often do that help bamboozle students into this distrust
of rationality: teachers hide their authority and run away from
their authority, and in both cases allow rationality to serve as a
smoke screen to mask the process, fooling both themselves and
their students.

The first process I have in mind is the way many teachers settle arguments between students and themselves about some substantive issue. Often the teacher asserts his answer is better than
the student's and thereby ends an argument. Perhaps the teacher
is right. Perhaps the argument was getting tedious and starting
to go around in circles. Perhaps the teacher has to settle on a
judgment in order to grade a test or paper. Perhaps the teacher
likes to have his own way. In any case, the teacher sincerely is
convinced that his answer is better than the student's. The problem comes when he asserts that he has *demonstrated* that his
answer is better—on the grounds of rationality. Usually he has
not. It is extremely hard to do. It's not that he is necessarily
wrong, though often he is. It's that he professes to have demonstrated he is right when he has done nothing of the sort. In
short, he has exercised *authority* to end an argument or make a
decision, but he has pretended it was not an exercise of authority—who wants to be pushy and authoritarian?—but only an exercise of rationality. An honest exercise of authority, even if
hated, would not bamboozle.

Rationality is also tainted by the baby-sitting function of
school. Society is not willing to let adolescents run loose and
parents are not willing to tend them at home. Therefore they
must go to school. Almost all teachers, from kindergarten to
graduate school, are to a greater or lesser degree being paid to
keep students in a room or busy with homework who don't want
to be there. There are various solutions to this problem, from
naked force, to withering intimidation, to charismatic intensity.

But few teachers can really manage those three solutions well. The best way to keep students there and have the fewest fights and the least unpleasantness is to fall into being someone more or less sincerely interested in getting them involved and concerned in learning, talking, and thinking. It's my bet that this is the way most teachers who have livable or even pleasant classrooms have managed it. The schools that most middle-class students attend are not really cruel or oppressive; teachers sincerely ask for thinking, problem-posing, doubting, rationality, critical thinking, and genuine discussion among students. Nothing makes the teacher's life easier than truly to interest students in these activities. But all these activities, and rationality itself, are tainted because deep down so many teachers are also using them instrumentally in order to kill time and baby-sit. I think the real animus students feel against school and rationality stems from the fact that so many teachers *succeeded* in getting them involved and excited. At some level, they feel taken in. If their school life had been merely hateful or dull, they would only feel good old-fashioned dislike and scorn.

In truth this tainting of rationality by the baby-sitting function has more to do with elementary and secondary education than college. Yet we too are not exempt from trying to keep an answer from coming up too soon: what would we do with the rest of the hour—or week? We are not immune from trying to keep a class hour or term going even though neither we nor the students can think of any question to which we want to find the answer.

In short, teachers in custodial institutions of education—i.e., most teachers—have a problem. Not only do their students not want to be there, the teachers don't want very much to be there—certainly not there as baby-sitters. Bamboozling, then—of self and of others—is the solution to this problem. The best way to handle the situation is to call things by the wrong name. So we allow ourselves to imply we are more fully allies of the students than we are. We don't allow the exercise of authority to show, if we can possibly help it, but cover it with an appearance of rationality. We allow ourselves to seem more committed to learning and rationality than we really are.

But most teachers are not good at *conscious* deception, especially those teachers who want to be open, enlightened, and help-ful to students. They are just trying to do the best they can and have the least conflict. So they don't call things by the wrong name on purpose. They simply allow things to be fuzzy in their own minds. And so both students and teachers are bamboozled.

Here's what I think it feels like to be bamboozled: you feel lots of good teachers are on your side, they've been helping you as hard and as sincerely as they can to fulfill your human poten-tial. You still can't figure out what you want to do, except that you know you don't want to do something that someone else wants you to do; you feel oppressed but you can't decide who is oppressing you; you feel unfree but you can't think of anything reasonable you *couldn't* do if you really put your mind to it; you feel sort of mad, but you don't quite know who you are mad at, except yourself; or else you are just sort of depressed and with-out energy, and you can't really tell the difference between your real intention and your idea of what you would like your inten-tion to be, though perhaps the problem is that you don't know what a real intention feels like, it's been so long since you've had a good healthy one.

What shall we conclude? One conclusion is that we need to have more people giving the sort of education that Freire de-scribes. We have very little pedagogy truly designed to liberate, and we need more. But in all truth we must admit to ourselves that few of us, because of our temperaments and because of our institutional setting, are in a position to offer it. It is no acci-dent that what Freire describes is so far from most institutional education. Institutional education grew up through society's need to bring its young into its own culture. The activity I know which *does* resemble Freire's activity is something that has re-cently grown up for the sake of liberating people from society's culture: consciousness-raising groups. In such groups, as I know them, someone may or may not have some leadership role, but there is usually genuine collaboration (or at least that is the idea); the subject matter to study is the lives of the members; the goal, however, is not just to change perceptions or aware-ness—not even just to change those lives—but to change objective, external reality; and usually rationality and critical thinking are felt as essential and valuable. (Sensitivity-training groups and therapy are similar to what Freire describes; but in T-groups and therapy, the concern is usually not with changing the world, only the members, and often critical thinking and rationality take a back seat.)

But though it is not feasible for most institutional teachers to follow the model laid down by Freire, there is something else we can do. We can examine scrupulously the nature of our teaching, and if it doesn't fit all four principles we can stop pretending, through words or implications, that we are engaged in an education to help people be free. For we are not. In short, we can start, this Monday morning, to refrain from bamboozling students. For most of us this would involve making statements such as the following:

- "This is a course I am giving. I have chosen the materials and procedures without consulting you, making my own decision on the basis of my experience and judgment."
- "I'll try to be fair, but remember that decisions about grades and credit are unilaterally mine."
- "We are not studying your lives here. You may or may not find something here which you can apply to yourselves."
- "We are not trying to change the world here. Our enterprise consists of manipulating spoken and written symbols; perhaps some laboratory or 'practice' kinds of physical action. Group interaction may also be important."
- "This is not education designed to make you free. This is education designed to make you smarter, more perceptive, more sensitive. We will try to call things by their right names here. I also hope it will make you more competent in making transactions between your own perceptions and your thinking. I cannot here help you liberate yourself. By and large that is something you have to do yourself."

But many teachers will say these statements don't fit their teaching. Their teaching is much more open than that. They share a great portion of the decision-making with their students. Perhaps half or even more. And they even follow the good advice of making scrupulously clear to the students which areas are for group decision and which things the teacher himself is deciding. But even here, with these open teachers, there is one more statement they should make: "The decision as to which parts are for you to decide and which parts are not is *my* decision and mine alone. And if something unforeseen happens I can always revoke my decision and change the ground rules." Unless the teacher is one of the very rare persons for whom this statement does not hold, he should make this statement openly.

Statements like all of these grate on the ears of most teachers and students. Yet they very often apply accurately to the teaching situation. If we were more courageous about making them, many students would say, "I guess I don't really want this," and they would leave and start attending and swelling some of the few institutions where something more like Freire's model is possible. I am thinking of institutions like Campus Free College and "open university" and "adult degree" sorts of colleges (e.g., Empire State College) where credit can be given by someone other than the teacher and where education need not be separated from action in the world. These kinds of institutions will grow more quickly through the migration of students than orthodox institutions will change through the attempts of faculty and administrators to change them.

Besides, even if all teachers *could* do what Freire is talking about, I would still want to put in a plea for something very different. There are other goals for education than to make people free. Freire's way of talking about education serves to reinforce only one model of teaching and learning.

In effect, he implies a cognitive dissonance model. It centers on contradiction. Everyone has cognitive dissonances, contradictions between various elements of what he or she knows or perceives. We have problems even we don't know about. The teacher's function is essentially to heighten the student's awareness of these dissonances—to overcome the human tendency to let sleeping contradictions lie. The teacher is, perhaps, more a "facilitator" than a teacher in that he doesn't make the student learn things: the force that makes the student learn things is his own itch, his own dissatisfaction, his own problem. The facilitator simply tries to heighten the itch. Socrates is the paradigm teacher of this sort: he kept asking people questions till he uncovered the fact that the person believed two or more things that didn't make sense together; then he left the person to his own itch (he wasn't even a "resource person").

I believe in this kind of teaching and learning. But I wish to put in a word for a different, perhaps opposite model of teaching and learning. It is old and traditional, but (therefore?) it may be neglected, at least by those teachers interested in Freire.

Socrates turns out to be the *locus classicus* for this other model, too: it could be called the emulation or participation model of teaching and learning. Or the falling-in-love model. It is Platonic or Freudian. Or perhaps infectious. You find yourself in contact with someone you like and perhaps admire. The more you are with him, the more you want to be like him. You want to know what he knows, feel what he feels, have the opinions he has. You probably adopt many of his mannerisms. Or hers. Teacher as "role-model"—though that term seems to be a pale defensive abstraction trying to guard against the emotional truth we sometimes actually feel: he or she is someone you want to eat or someone you want to eat you—to love or be loved. In effect you want to be inside or actually *be* this person. The force that drives this kind of learning is not the itch of a problem or contradiction but the itch for the person who is teacher.

Freire is very negative about this kind of thing. He talks about how terrible it is when "to be" equals "to be like." He wants the student to be autonomous, self-motivated, to have only his own intentions and to take full responsibility for them. Education as emulation or participation involves imitation, dependency, and not taking full responsibility. Freire (after Fromm) calls emotional dependency "necrophiliac."

As I see it, these are not just two random styles of learning but the two main processes involved in human growth which Piaget calls *assimilation* and *accommodation*. Freire's education-as-cognitive-dissonance is assimilation: the organism brings what is outside into itself on its own terms; it eats the world and digests it and makes the eaten portion of the world take on the shape of the organism; the organism keeps its own shape, identity, autonomy. In contrast, education-as-emulation or participation is Piaget's accommodation: the organism grows by letting its guard down, letting its outlines and identity become fuzzy; it participates in other people or things; allows itself to be swallowed by what is different from the self—to merge or expand into what is different.

As Piaget recognizes, these two aspects of growth are dialectically or developmentally linked. You can't have one without the other. A deficiency in one inhibits the other. Thus, though perhaps Freire is right to advocate only the autonomy-centered learning for adults in South America, we are crazy if we do the same with middle-class adolescents in this country.

So many parents and teachers fear allowing a student to have an acknowledged dependency. We reward children and students for being autonomous and separated—unmerged with authority figures—from the earliest possible age. In this way too, we bamboozle them and prevent them from growing: make them think their problem is lack of courage to be autonomous and self-actualized. They are all doing push-ups trying to develop the "courage to be free," when what so many of them lack is the courage to be dependent, the courage to be unfree.

There is a fear among many students of any kind of emotional dependence, childishness, lack of autonomy. Especially students who identify with experimental or anti-authoritarian styles. There is an extreme need to live the cool values: exist for the moment; take complete responsibility for self; no dependency; short-term relationships with no demands on the other party; everyone do his or her "own thing"; never "lay your trip" on someone else; try to live up to what Fritz Perls, Carl Rogers, and others prescribe, be self-actualized. Interestingly it's not just negative expectations that are tyrannical. The expectation that everyone deep down is healthy and loving and giving and mature—and will start being that way when you give him or her a chance—this too can be oppressive.

So many students are going through the motions of being independent, autonomous, even anti-authoritarian. But actually they are doing so in a primitive and "broken record" sort of way. Trying harder and harder but getting no growth, fulfillment, or gratification from it. They are hungering for the opposite kind of relationship. Or else they are actually enmeshed in childish and dependent relationships but in a covert, unacknowledged, and therefore unproductive way (a transference relationship with your "facilitator").

Teaching at M.I.T. up through last year I was continually struck with the need for the kind of learning and teaching that Freire emphasizes. At a traditionally structured institution the primary need seems to be to clear a space so that the student can make some real choices. In a sense clearing a bit of space for free choice takes precedence over trying to teach. In such a situation teaching by "facilitation" of cognitive dissonance—getting the student to teach himself—seems the best answer. But this year at Evergreen, a much more open institution, I feel more need to answer this question: What can a teacher do when there already *is* significant space and choice and the student doesn't feel so trapped in the institution or the classroom? This situation brings to mind the other model, the other half of the dialectic of growth.

In trying to come to grips with Freire's book and my reactions to it, I am made to discover a contradiction at the heart of our culture which I hadn't focused on before. A psychological contradiction, not an economic or political one. We preach freedom, but we don't really practice it. The need I sense now is to work on changing not so much the practice as the preaching. Part of the youth culture *is* an attempt to repudiate our compulsive worship of freedom: the "back to nature" and Eastern mysticism movements involve a hunger for merging and letting down the borders of the self, relief from autonomy and doing your own thing. What is called for is, on the one hand, to try to safeguard better the basic freedoms in the *political and economic* realm (if we had more modest objective goals for freedom, we might attain them), but, on the other hand, to cease trying for *psychological* freedom all day every day. We could try, in short, for a culture in which people have *free choice,* yes, in almost any important decision, but also a culture that says it's all right at times to choose modes of relating that are dependent and non-autonomous. We are held back from maturity and autonomy by a compulsive refusal to satisfy the less acceptable hunger for participation and merging.

CHAPTER 6

✿✿✿

In the essay that follows I explore the effects on teaching that flow from using a competence-based approach to education. (The essay grows out of working for three years as a member of a research team investigating a dozen or so experiments in competence-based higher education.)*

What seemed at first a very specialized enterprise—a study of competence-based education—turned out to be remarkably helpful in leading me to see much I'd not seen before about the teaching process, the authority of the teacher, and the role of "professor."

The distinguishing mark of competence-based education is that "ends" or "outcomes" are always specified. To write about this approach, then, is to write about the relationship between means and ends in teaching. I started off my three-year investigations with a temperamental resistance to the idea that we should always spell out the "outcomes" of our teaching. To do so violated my own intuitive habits of learning and teaching, and also seemed to work against the precious noninstrumental tradition in higher education—namely, that learning is best when it is for its own sake rather than for goals or ends. Even before I started I had glimpsed here and there thoughtless teachers and administrators sometimes becoming extremely foolish in talking about "learning objectives" or "behavioral objectives."

I try to make my reflections more concrete by including excerpts from my field notes about particular people in particular institutions.

---

* I was recruited for this research project on the basis of a long essay not reprinted here: "Shall We Teach or Give Credit: A Model for Higher Education." For our report, I wrote two essays: a case study of "my" site—a competence-based management program at Seattle Central Community College—and the essay here.

※※※

Trying to Teach
While Thinking About the End

A student knocks on the office door. He enters and says, "I wanted to talk to you about the paper you handed back today in class. You gave me a B minus. I don't really see from your comments what's the matter with it. I really worked hard on it. It really answers the questions. It's carefully done. You don't really point out anything seriously wrong with it."

The teacher looks at the paper and tries to remember what he was thinking when he graded it. He leans back and looks out the window. Sighing wearily and wishing he hadn't, he begins to talk about things being a bit vague here and there, about missed opportunities. He contemplates saying, "Yes, it's true you don't really say anything wrong, and I'm not just grading on style, but there's something missing. The paper doesn't measure up. And it's not just a matter of my own prejudice or pleasure. I have a definite sense of an external standard for an A paper, and this doesn't make it. But I can't tell you exactly what you should have done. There are many things you might have done." But he knows from experience that this kind of candor only makes things worse. He settles for pointing out some ambiguity of thought, some poor writing, and some specific points he can learnedly rebut.

Is there anyone who has not experienced this kind of scene? The account can be shaped to suit one's prejudices: either into the story of a virtuous student victimized by a bumbling, incompetent teacher or into the story of a teacher with a sense of the best that humankind has thought and done, heroically trying to preserve civilization against the insidious erosion of callow youth.

But either way, I see that student in my mind's eye, going on to major in engineering or education, then going on to graduate school, all the while muttering, "There's no excuse for asking students to do something if you can't specify exactly what constitutes a good job," and finally growing up to invent competence-based education.

In this essay I attempt to explore the effects on college-level teaching of a competence-based approach. I start by describing the most direct and straightforward effects of a competence approach upon teaching, and then I explore some of its paradoxical effects—paradoxes I see in the spirit of the competence approach itself. Finally I address the question that has perplexed me most during our study, that is, whether a competence approach rules out or inhibits certain styles or temperaments in teaching.

Since competence-based education tells you to start by determining the competencies you want students to attain—the outcomes—and only then to plan your teaching to fit them, its effects on teaching would seem to depend almost entirely on what those competencies are. But there is little agreement within the movement about the nature of competencies. That is, they can be oriented toward *performance* or *knowing how to* (for example, play the following musical pieces up to a certain standard, or solve this particular problem); or they can be oriented toward *knowledge* or *knowing that* (for example, explain the difference between the baroque and classical styles; or describe the theory of problem-solving). In addition, competencies can be oriented toward disciplines (for example, the department of music at Florida State University has competencies entirely within that discipline); or they can be what are called *generic competencies* that cut across disciplines (for example, "communicating" or "critical thinking" at Alverno College in Milwaukee—where students work on attaining these generic competencies through course work in different disciplines). And finally, competencies can simply be small or big: there are scores of competencies a student must attain in only one nursing course at Mt. Hood Community College, in Gresham, Oregon, while at Alverno there are only eight competencies required for the bachelor's degree. (Of course, each of the eight Alverno competencies is broken down into six levels and conversely the myriad Mt. Hood nursing outcomes are clumped—even across courses—into large categories, for example, "asepsis" or "patient comfort." Still, some programs feel crowded and some feel expansive because of a tendency to think in terms of small competencies or big competencies.)

In the end, however, the most interesting and important effects of the competence approach on teaching seem to me to transcend these variations among competencies and to result from the basic competence situation itself in which outcomes—and often assessments—are devised and made public in advance, and teaching is planned to fit them.

Direct Effects

Foremost among the effects of competence-based education on teaching is that it breaks up the role of the college teacher into many different parts. I never thought the organization of conventional higher education was simple until I had to think about competence-based education. But it is. Just divide knowledge into areas, handing the big areas to departments and the small ones to individual teachers. Let the students sign up, give everyone your blessing, and ask for grades at the end of the quarter (making sure, however, to collect payment at the beginning of the quarter). I get great pleasure from seeing this simplicity, but as with so many innocent pleasures, it is experienced primarily in retrospect. Where I used to see just a college teacher teaching, now I often see an array of distinct functions:

1. Devising the competencies: writing out in advance the knowledge and skills a student must have to get credit.
2. Validating the competencies: going to the outside world to determine whether these are the competencies people really need for certain jobs or studies or tasks, or whether these are the competencies people really want for whatever goals they might have. (Strict constructionists insist that the educational institution has no right to decide by itself what should be taught.)
3. Designing the instruction: figuring out what subject matter, activities, and materials should be used to help students get these competencies.
4. Early diagnostic testing: finding out whether students are

suited for this instruction or need special help or perhaps
already have the competencies.
5. The teaching itself.
6. Late diagnostic testing: determining whether students are
ready for certification, for example, giving a "practice final";
this also tells teachers which parts of their teaching worked
and which parts did not work.
7. Certifying: making up and giving tests to see who gets credit.
8. Advising: not just helping students clarify their own goals
and find their way through the complexities of the institution
and its regulations, but also helping students figure out the
best ways to do these things.

Of course we didn't see different people performing each one
of these functions, but the competence approach, with the opening wedge of asking you to specify outcomes and assessments in
advance, invites you to distinguish among all these tasks that
used to be simply the overall job of the college teacher. This tendency to distinguish functions helps explain why these programs
are so expensive in time and dollars. Theoretically, of course, the
mere conceptualization of different functions shouldn't cost more
time or trouble, but once you begin to separate functions, you
tend to increase the amount of work.

Imagine, for example, two teachers from the same or overlap-
ping disciplines who have decided to collaborate in an outcome-
oriented fashion. Each figures out the competencies that the students must have by the end of the course and puts these in
writing. Each agrees to assess the other's students at the end.
Even though there is no time spent on validating the competencies, on extra advising, on alternate learning paths or on
committee meetings, nevertheless this proto-competence program
would cost both teachers additional time: to figure out and write
down their competencies clearly enough so that the other could
test for their presence or absence in students; to work out assessments; and to *do* assessments carefully enough to trust them with
students they hadn't worked with for fifteen weeks.

*Second, competence-based education attacks the role of "pro-
fessor."* The higher the status of the college or the university, the
more likely that its teachers are called professors and that they

have complete jurisdiction over all teaching functions. In particular, they would feel affronted if someone started telling them what they should cover in their courses or how they should grade their students. ("Are *you* trying to tell *me* who gets credit in *my* course?") In effect, society hands students to the professor and says, 'Teach them what you will; then decide whether they learned it and deserve credit. You don't have to tell what the component parts of your course are or what your criteria are for giving credit." That, really, is the entire educational transaction, apart from counseling, registration, and administration. Of course, departments supposedly ensure to society that professors are responsible and competent. But being nothing but groups of professors, departments are in a ticklish position for this regulatory function. Although they can be decisive in refusing tenure to a member for lack of good research and publication, they seldom ensure that teachers teach competently.

But competence-based programs are apt to take some of these functions out of professors' hands: faculty in these programs seldom have unilateral power over what the outcomes should be—and sometimes no power at all—and often they will be partially or wholly unconnected with the assessment function. It is no accident, then, that competence programs are not usually found at high-status colleges. Many of them are at places where the faculty members are not called professor and where—before the program was instituted—the faculty had little autonomy or sovereignty compared to what is taken for granted at high-status colleges and universities.

Though a competence program can be a vehicle for a faculty to renew and reorganize its collegial control over the curriculum (see Chapter 5 of Grant and Associates), the competence-based approach invites lessened faculty control. There is often a distinct animus against "professors" among people in the movement—an animus I also sensed in some of the staff at the Fund for the Improvement of Post-Secondary Education (FIPSE)—and in many of these programs, faculty do not feel their usual control over the curriculum. As one dissatisfied faculty member said, "We don't own the curriculum anymore. The administration does." Sometimes it is indeed the administration, but more often, in fact, it is a matter of new groupings of faculty working

out the curriculum together; when these groups are not organized along departmental lines, some faculty members experience a loss of control.

In addition, if there is to be a real process of validating the
competencies—going outside the academy to see what others think
ought to be taught—then clearly the faculty's sole responsibility
for deciding what should be taught is diminished. Many legislatures are getting into the competence-based act and specifying
the things that ought to be taught. Many college teachers are
content to let legislatures specify what should be taught in primary or secondary schools, but are very offended if they specify
what colleges or universities should teach. (The Supreme Court,
too, has ruled that primary and secondary school teachers are not
entitled to the academic freedom enjoyed by college professors.)

Specificity of outcomes, separation of functions, and alternate
learning packages make manifest something that has always been
true but which conventional curriculums mask—namely, that
students can learn without teachers but teachers cannot teach
without students. In some programs there is significant investment in auto-instructional packages, and some use of them by
students. But what I see as a more decided trend than the elimi-
nation of teachers is the use of such adjunct persons as undergraduate tutors and nonprofessional counselors, helpers, and
mentors.

There is also a special kind of teaching in competence-based
education programs that perhaps is not so much teaching as it is
high-level advising, that is, helping a person learn things which
you don't happen to know much about yourself. It is not surprising that these programs make heavy use of words like "men-
tor" and "facilitator" for people in quasi-teacher roles who do
things that are hard to describe clearly. The skills required of
these people are not the traditional ones asked of college professors—namely, a profound knowledge of what is to be learned—
but rather a sensitivity to and sympathy with the student, as well
as a special feeling for styles and modes of learning.

In competence-based programs of professional training, there
is a widespread tendency to hire yet another kind of nonprofessional teacher, that is, "practitioners" or people who actually
work at the jobs or do the things for which the students are pre-

paring. Practitioners help in validating competencies—in making
sure that the learning is indeed preparation for the real thing.
What these teachers lack in teaching experience they are supposed to make up for by bringing into the classroom an emphasis on actual performance and the standards of the "real world."
They are to help students see a connection between the classroom and the work they may do later in life.

In most cases it is cheaper and less troublesome to hire these
nonregular teachers for part-time positions with no fringe benefits. They need not be involved in meetings or in policy decisions
and they often must accept conditions of employment that regular teachers would find unacceptable.

There is an obvious reason why competence-based programs
can use these teachers: it is easier for nonexperts to teach a subject when they are provided with an explicit statement of teaching outcomes—sometimes even with a lesson plan or full outline
for the course—and when they don't have to design or adminis-
ter any exams. (It is especially helpful if the program has built
alternate learning paths: opportunities for dissatisfied or disgruntled students to learn in some other way instead of staying
around and disrupting the class.)

Another potential loss of professionalism and perhaps status
for professors involves the important word *accountability*. If you
separate the instructional function from the assessment function,
you have a way to measure the productivity of the teacher—or at
least to seem to measure it—that seems more accurate than the
present method of just counting how many students take a
teacher's course or pass the examination.

I think of College IV at Grand Valley where adjunct part-time
teachers are paid per mastered credit; that is, they do not get paid
unless the student passes. (The student gets three tries.)

But a story from Mars Hill College in North Carolina shows why
you cannot measure teacher "output" unless you also measure "input." Three sections of introductory calculus were taught by three
teachers. One of the sections, taught by a new teacher, did poorly;
the next quarter this section was taught by someone who was acknowledged to be an excellent teacher, and it still did just as poorly.
The original teacher was vindicated. (How many of us can be so

fortunate in having our deepest feelings corroborated: "I know they're not learning much, but my students are a bad lot.")

Different schools have handled this potential dethroning of the professor in different ways. Florida State University had professors at the start and has tried to keep them in the competence setting. Seattle Central Community College opted for part-time practitioners, yet the regular faculty are not seen by many as "professor types" (that is, few have Ph.D. degrees and they are not expected to do research). Justin Morrill College at Michigan State University offers the ultimate insult and forgoes teachers altogether, but given their university context, they probably had to choose either full-fledged professors or none at all. Alverno has the most viable solution to the problem of teacher-dignity and teacher-role. The English teacher, for example, still chooses what plays or stories to teach in her course, and she doesn't have to change from English teacher to teacher of, say, "values" or "critical thinking"; yet she has an added responsibility to be on a competence committee and to teach those plays or stories in such a way as to help students pass assessments in certain competences such as critical thinking or valuing.

Third, competence-based education usually forces teachers to rethink what they teach. In some of the competence-based programs, teachers end up teaching subject matter that is new to them. But usually it is a matter of reorganizing what they teach—and in doing so, reconceptualizing it. For example, someone might say to me, "To teach with a competence approach, you have to know precisely what you teach," and I might reply, "I do know precisely what I teach. Chaucer." But he would then go on to say, "But that isn't what I mean. What does this 'Chaucer' look like when it occurs in a student—that is, what changes do you hope will occur in your student from studying Chaucer with you?" Now I might answer, "I expect the student to change to the extent that he will be able to write the following correct answers to the following questions about Chaucer." (And I would pass muster with the behavioral objectives people if I had specified those questions and answers with the right kinds of precision.) But most of the people at the colleges our team visited wouldn't be satisfied with that answer. They are looking

for something bigger. They are indeed idealists, and I might pro-
test that they want me to delude myself into having grander objectives than a teacher of Chaucer has any right to have. But
these idealists would not be deterred. They would reply, "Yes,
but by studying Chaucer, what new or better ways of understanding texts, looking at the world, or managing the self do you hope
to produce in those students?"

I think of Terry Anderson at Antioch Law School in Washington,
D.C., who used a consultant to help him in an interesting empirical
approach to competence teaching. He was teaching constitutional
law, but what was he really teaching and testing for? Knowledge of
cases? If so, what kinds of cases? Analytical thinking of a certain
sort? A certain conception of "the law"? Lucidity of prose? Creativity? Finally, how well did his testing match his teaching? He had
the consultant observe his teaching, assignment giving, test making,
and test grading to help him answer these questions. He did not set
out with the grandiose plan of restructuring his whole curriculum
or teaching something brand-new. He simply wanted to determine
what he was actually doing. But learning more clearly what he was
actually doing led him to make some changes—none really earth-
shaking—which nevertheless made a big difference to him and his
students. In short, he still teaches for the most part what he was
teaching, but he now has greater control and intentionality in his
teaching.

His empirical approach strikes me as wise. Like most teachers, I
would probably give a stupider answer to the question, "What
should a student get from studying, say, Chaucer?" than the answer
you could get if you watched my teaching behavior and extrapo-
lated from the *best* parts of it. My answer to the big fat abstract
question would likely be naive and dominated by my favorite theories and hobbyhorses, and it would lack the sophistication and
shrewdness that have probably developed in my behavior over the
years. Yet, on the other hand, much of my teaching behavior may
well be blind or misguided or ineffective—or simply aimed at goals
that I don't approve of when I see them in the plain light of day.
When I am thus confronted with all the answers that can be extrap-
olated from my behavior, I can get the benefit of conscious concep-
ual thought without having to put up with its shortsighted naiveté.

*Fourth, competence-based education helps teachers get more
taught.* A competence-based program gives you better grounds

for refusing credit in a course, but most programs simply cannot survive—either with the administration or with their constituency—if they flunk too many students. And since you can't just give C's or D's to those students who sort of have a kind of general picture but don't really have mastery (as you can in a regular curriculum), you are in a sense "struck." You really do know they lack genuine mastery, and you now have the means to help them attain it; that is, you can allow them to take more time and use different routes to learning. In short, the competence structure increases the likelihood of having to bring more students to the point of mastery. And it is precisely those students who have difficulty learning the material in the normal length of time and by the normal methods of teaching-and-learning—those students who usually get a C or a D—who are the most difficult to teach.

> I think of two students in music at Florida State University. One joined the program because she was in a hurry to finish college, and it would give her the chance to move ahead more quickly. She soon saw that she wouldn't go faster, but that she would learn more and better. The other student said that she joined because, having asked an older, regular student about a problem with which she needed help, she was told, "Oh, I don't know, I took that last year." This made her decide to join a program where she would really know what she learned.

The teachers that thrive in these programs often seem to have been bothered in the past by the large number of students who passed courses without really attaining the given knowledge or competence. They are exhilarated at finally having an approach which ensures that their students really will learn. I talked to a whole range of teachers who were initially very skeptical about a competence approach, but when they finally saw the results on the learning of their own students, they became enthusiastic supporters.

This feeling is especially strong among teachers with poorly prepared students. One teacher described the competence approach primarily as a way for the teacher to maintain high standards when she has a classroom full of such students. It is easy for teachers with poorly prepared students in non-competence-based curricula to become completely demoralized. The low level of success among the students causes teachers to become cynical and tired. Sometimes they try to teach the few students in each class that they think can grasp the material and sometimes they just go through the motions. This leads to what I think is a common mood in teachers: a feeling that students are clods, that culture and civilization are crumbling, that there's nothing to do but make cynical, sarcastic jokes. It is a mood of failed hope—of the very hope combined with idealism that made them go into teaching in the first place. Since it is not politically possible to flunk all the students, teachers end up giving passing grades for performances that they really think are worthless. Thus that smell of sour idealism. The competence approach seems to help teachers get out of this swamp by allowing them to *demand* more.

But if the competence approach usually helps teachers raise C, D, and F performances up to what we might call a B or B minus level, does it invite A performances to sink to mere B minus—to mere mastery? I didn't hear any teachers make this complaint. Besides, many of these programs retained conventional grades along with the competence approach.

Fifth, the competence approach is liable to make the teacher feel more exposed. Teachers must submit their teaching to external review of various sorts. Before the course begins, the outcomes and the assessment procedures—often the tests themselves— must be published to students and to colleagues. This is very different from merely publishing a course description. Often outcomes and assessments must be judged by colleagues to see whether the course will fit with generic college-wide competencies. For example, at Alverno the English teacher must write a module to show how her teaching of the short story will really help students pass a certain assessment level in, say, critical thinking.

I think of my visit to Cynthia Stevens' class at Alverno when she showed me her course outline for the whole semester: a huge and impressive lesson plan spread over two sides of legal-size paper, containing not just headings but well-thought-through, concrete topics and activities. Then I sat down with some students and they happened to open their notebooks. I was surprised to see the same two sheets of paper. I realized that I had simply assumed, without thinking, that the teacher would not hand out this plan to her students.

Of course, the competence teacher's teaching is even more nakedly exposed when, at the end of the semester, it is revealed how many students passed an assessment administered by someone else. If a large number of students don't pass, it is threatening to the teacher.

I think of a teacher at the College for Human Services in New York City during a meeting of an assessment committee that was on the brink of failing a student. He gave many reasons why this decision didn't seem fair: it was partly the college's fault, partly the fault of the internship setting which was a poor learning situation. But he finally blurted out, "It's not fair to punish her for *my* shortcomings as a teacher."

Sixth, competence-based education invites the separation of the teacher from what is taught and invites a collaborative relationship between teacher and student. Traditional college professors are invited by their central role in the educational transaction to be an embodiment of what is taught. They are by definition experts in the subject. They contain the thing to be learned inside them and hence are invited to become people who profess, people who stand up in front of students and say, in effect. "Get what is inside me inside you. Look at me; listen to me; be like me. I am important." It follows, of course, that professors are gatekeepers who contain within themselves criteria for judging whether the student knows the subject. They are not obliged to publish those criteria or have them validated by someone else. They may indeed conclude that those criteria in their purity cannot be explicitly or publicly articulated—or at least not in such a way that they can be understood by any but the few other experts who also possess this knowledge.

A competence-based program, on the other hand, since it requires the specification and publication in advance of outcomes and assessment procedures, invites the separation of the teaching and the assessment functions. Someone other than the teacher may be the gatekeeper or wielder of standards for the subject.

Our team saw different persons teaching and assessing in roughly half the cases that we observed. I believe that this separation has important consequences because of the different psychological stance toward the student implied in the teaching role and the assessing role. If you want to increase your chances of success in the teaching role, you will take a stance that communicates to students in one way or another that you believe they can learn the material and that you are not deterred by words or behavior on their part protesting that they are incapable. But if you want to increase your success as an assessor in smoking out facile work that doesn't really represent mastery, you must adopt the opposite stance and assume that students don't know the material; you must be as critical as possible and refuse to be influenced by confident or impressive appearances.

When teachers and assessors are different persons, teachers have a kind of "coach" or "ally" role: they are helping the student pass a test given by someone else. They are rewarded by adopting the hypothesis that the student can learn. The student needn't be afraid to reveal weakness or ignorance to the teacher since the teacher isn't the certifier. The student can get better help from the teacher and thereby increase chances of passing the test by being open and honest with the teacher.*

I was impressed by the numbers of competency teachers who were allies with their students and avoided the difficulties that arise in the conventional arrangement, where the student is apt to look upon the teacher as the enemy who must be conned, psyched out, or evaded. Because these teachers haven't so much authority vested in them as gatekeepers of their subject matter, they are more approachable. A more collaborative relationship

---

* I am not asserting a simpleminded resemblance between a teacher's actual style in the flesh and the role of teacher or assessor. That is, someone may be particularly good as an assessor and therefore shrewdly critical in detecting hidden shortcomings in student answers and yet nevertheless be warm and cordial in manner. On the other hand, someone particularly skilled in the teacher role may use a negative tone of voice for positive expectations, saying, in effect, "OK you bastards, I'm going to *make* you learn this stuff and I don't care how much it hurts!" This may seem a nasty snarl from a mean teacher, but it can be a manifesto that all can learn. Such a teacher is not the certifier who refuses credit but rather, as it were, the marine sergeant marshaling his rigors to help his platoon win the prize.

can spring up. These teachers aren't forced into the role of keeping the purity and integrity of their subject matter from being defiled by the unwashed. They are not so likely to be hurt or insulted if students hate "their" area or are dismal at it.

I think of Wes Collins, who teaches music at Florida State University. He was actually pleased that the assessment committee for his wind students was likely to have people of different persuasions about embouchure or lip position. Although he had always tried to cover the subject matter well, he knew he had tended to teach his view and think in terms of it. Now he had to make sure his students could defend any point of view to a hostile assessor.

Even when the instruction and assessment are done by the same person—as we saw in many cases—the competence approach helps teachers deal better with these conflicting roles and hence have a better relationship with students. When the assessment instruments are spelled out publicly in advance, teachers can be more explicit about judgments, using clearly specified criteria that neither they nor the students are so apt to confuse with the teacher's own person.

In a non-competence-based situation, on the other hand, where assessments are seldom spelled out clearly in advance, and where the teacher must therefore try to embody both the teaching and the assessing roles, the path of least resistance is simply to lean more toward one or the other, and hence be better as teacher or assessor. Thus teachers tend to drift into being (as students like to say) "hard" or "easy." Until my visits to competence programs, I had never seen so many teachers who manage to be both hard and easy—both very demanding in their standards and yet very supportive and positive as teachers. I think the separation of teaching and assessment functions helps make this possible.

I asked John Millay, sociology teacher at College IV of Grand Valley, whether he ever had difficulties switching from the teaching to the assessing role with the same students. He said that since he had started teaching in an outcome-oriented fashion, he had never had a difference of opinion with a student—or even bad feelings—about an assessment decision. This is a result, he said, of the fact that the competence approach forces him to publish to students at the be-

ginning not only the outcomes for the course, but specifically what
the assessment will be. In effect, he must say, "Here's the final exam.
The course will try to teach you to give good answers to the following questions. Here are the criteria I'm going to use to decide what's
a good answer and what isn't."

*Seventh, competence-based education invites collaboration
among teachers.* A college ought by definition to be collegial, but
college teachers seldom have to agree with each other. College
teaching is the vocation for individualists. In most competence-
based programs we observed, however, faculty members had to
work out collectively the competencies and the criteria for successful performance. This process almost always involved struggle at first but in the end usually produced more cooperation
and understanding. It was seldom a matter of a simple tug of war
between pre-existing positions. Usually brand new conceptualizations had to be forged. Most faculty members appreciated improved collegiality and the resulting new insights into subject
matter.

*Eighth, competence-based education invites collaboration
among students.* I think of the biology students at Florida State
University spending a lot of time together in a lounge, talking
and helping each other out. The competence approach means
that such students are not competing against each other for
grades on a curve in a zero-sum game (if he scores higher, I necessarily score lower). All are simply working for mastery. There
is usually less time spent in class, and students are more on their
own. Many of them find peer collaboration to be an enjoyable
and effective method of learning. Where programs provide space
and suitable conditions for this kind of collaboration, it seems to
occur (except when the students are working adults).

There is another link between the competence approach and
student collaboration. When I first noticed that many teachers
broke their classes down into small groups, I just assumed this
was a matter of temperament—which no doubt it was. But then
I looked more closely at the tasks that they were setting for their
students. I realized that a competence approach pushes a teacher
to articulate what is to be learned in such a way that there are
clearer criteria for determining whether a given answer is satisfactory or not. A competence setting, that is, would tend to dis-

courage such tasks as "Discuss the poem," and would instead encourage such ones as "How is the mood of the poem or the response of the reader affected by specific images? Be sure to discuss three of them." Given this second task, a group of students on its own can certainly be expected to collaborate in distinguishing strong and weak responses and coming up collectively with its best answer. With the global task, "Discuss the poem," on the other hand, a teacherless group is more apt to flounder unproductively and slide into the thoughtless morass of. "Well, that's your opinion, and this is my opinion." When all questions are like "Discuss the poem" or "Discuss the influence of Russia on global politics," the only thing students can do with their answers is hand them in to the authority and wait for the verdict. And because it is so often a verdict based on unstated criteria, the student is likely to quarrel with it or fail to understand it.

I hadn't realized before how possible it is to take complex issues, work out criteria, and get students to engage in collaborative learning.

I think of the College for Human Services. It first decided that to be a good human services worker involves, among other things, the ability to establish a professional relationship on the job. Only then did it try to decide what a professional relationship is characterized by. (Their students are apt to be rejected as nonprofessionals at agencies.) Having defined the characteristics of a professional relationship, students can more competently discuss a fuzzy issue, such as whether a person is behaving professionally with colleagues, and can come to agreement with assessors as to their verdict.

I think also of the following observations by Zelda Gamson, of our project team, about Allan Wurtzdorf's class at Alverno:

The class I observed was just beginning to work on competency two, level three, which attempts to get students to analyze the relationship between environmental settings and behavior. The twenty-one students were divided into five groups. They were quietly talking about the settings, usually single rooms, which they had been asked to observe. Each student was first to describe her setting to the other members of the group in great detail and then go on to identify the potential psychological impacts of that setting. An interesting discussion started in the group I observed about one of the younger student's dormitory room. Two older women in the group began drawing out information about how the young student and her roommate used the room, and it became very clear that the room was primarily a social space and not a study space. The older women asked whether the young student or her roommate used the desk (the answer was no), where they studied (the answer was on their beds), what they kept on their desks (the answer was knick-knacks and various things they dumped when they came into the room). The older women were beginning to develop hypotheses about why the younger women did not use the desks as study spaces and about the impact of the design of the dormitory room and the larger dormitory setting on students living there. An altogether intelligent discussion. I only had a few fleeting minutes with Allan Wurtzdorf, who circulated from group to group. He did say to me that he loved teaching this way and had enjoyed developing the module for the environmental psychology course. He noted that since "everything is laid out, you don't have to justify what you are doing and students know what is expected of them." I found it an interesting exercise and an enviably focused way of dealing with what could be either very fuzzy or, at the other extreme, very technical material.

Ninth, competence-based education encourages students to be less passive and to take more responsibility for their own learning. At first I wondered whether spelling out everything so clearly might not reduce students to obedient followers of orders. When I didn't see that happening, I began to realize that it can be liberating for students to have everything spelled out and that the most common cause of student passivity is leaving things unspecified. When a teacher publishes only a brief course description and doesn't spell out on opening day how things will work, he is in effect saying to the student, "Just follow me, just trust me, don't ask questions. I will take charge of all decisions."

I think that learning depends on personal investment more than on anything else. I thought that to spell everything out might diminish investment, but I saw students investing themselves more in competence programs than I usually see them do in traditional curriculums. I finally realized the source of my confusion: leaving things open and unspecified adds to *my* investment as a teacher. It gives me room for choice and adventure and excitement. I can do things on the spur of the moment, change directions three weeks into the course because of a new thought. But it is seldom that I or many other college teachers are willing to share fully this choice over options with students. Therefore, leaving things open gives me more options, but it tends to give students less sense of choice and control.

There are a number of what might be called *negative* measures of the initiative and responsibility required of students by competence-based programs. In virtually every program that allows flexible timing, students procrastinate in coming to take their tests and get credit. The pipelines get clogged. Credit or FTEs are not generated as quickly as in a normal program. I saw many programs resort to this or that device to get students moving along—for example, compulsory appointments with advisors at certain intervals. Teachers were often having to hunt down students and say, "Look, you know it well enough; come on in for the assessment on this unit so you can start working on the next."

What is the problem? Are the students in flexibly paced programs just wasting time? This didn't seem to be the case. Many students, it is true, didn't know how to organize and budget their time. This problem was most serious with adolescents and disadvantaged students; middle-class adults did better. But the main factor here is a major psychological change when students have any choice over scheduling their assessments. In normal curriculums, students sign up, work as hard as they want, probably harder just before the exam, and then take the exam because they have to; it is the appointed day. In the time-flexible format students must *do* something: they must go to the test, not just wait for the test to come to them. When a student makes this act and says, "I want to be tested now," his or her whole relationship to learning becomes very different. That student has taken much more responsibility and is thrust into being much more adult. At times I even found myself wondering whether this responsibility might not be too much of a burden, especially for young or disadvantaged students. That feeling grew when a teacher told me, in a guiltily relieved tone: "They don't blame the teacher anymore; they blame themselves."

This need for student initiative and responsibility seems widespread in the programs, though none, as I recall, specify these qualities as competencies. Not all students, of course, demonstrate responsibility. To handle this problem, some programs simply set up procedures so that less initiative is needed, at least at first, while others simply allow those who don't develop initiative to drop out. Dropout rates are high in many programs, and I think this is the main reason.

Finally, competence-based education invites the individualization of learning. The competence movement, of course, does not have a monopoly on individualized learning. Methods like the Keller Plan have gone far in adapting it even to completely traditional curriculums. Nevertheless, the impulse to individualize learning seems unusually strong in many competence programs. Many of the teachers feel that one of the main purposes of putting learning into a competence format is so that people can learn at their own speed and in their own style. In most of the programs that our team observed, the teacher sat down individually which each student at least once, even if the format was primarily a group one.

But we also saw many hindrances to individualization. For one thing, most registrars cannot deal with students starting or stopping courses at any time, and most business offices don't know how to make out bills unless people are enrolled for a quarter or a semester. Second, all the individual interactions take a great deal of teacher time—usually more than there is in a week. And on top of everything else, students often *want* to sit in the same room with others as part of the learning process. This may be just the persistence of the old Adam—"it doesn't feel like school without *class*"—but I believe that people often need the support, encouragement, and solidarity they get from groups. Some programs that started out with the emphasis entirely on individual, one-to-one interactions found it necessary to institute some kind of group meetings.

Paradoxical Effects

How does competence-based education relate to intellectuality? On the one hand we see in these programs the grand old American pragmatic and anti-intellectual tradition that says talking isn't real, only doing is real. Performance is stressed. Outcomes are usually roles, jobs, tasks—not just knowledge, and certainly not just knowledge for its own sake. There is an animus against what is merely "academic"; against teachers who just teach theories, ideas, and words; against students who can pass tests with good writing and fancy language but may not be "really competent." The spirit of the competence movement is anti-baloney—and baloney is usually seen as something verbal and conceptual.

Yet on the other hand I am struck by how central and pervasive in the competence-based movement is a certain kind of intellectuality: an emphasis upon—almost a preoccupation with—analytic self-consciousness. You are always supposed to know what you are doing and why you are doing it. You must have chosen your outcomes or goals, you must have some awareness of how and why you arrived at them, you must figure out how to break them down into parts so that you can measure progress toward them, and you must figure out criteria for demonstrating when you have attained them. In short, the movement is anti-intuitive. It attracts people who enjoy analysis and classification.

> I think of Sister Joel Read, President of Alverno, saying that there are two kinds of people in the world: those who understand the historical process and group process and insist on clarity and organization of ideas; and the "intuitives." It took me a minute to realize that "intuitive" could be a bad word. Especially—*mea culpa*—from a woman.

> I also think of Diana Dean, architect of the nursing program at Mt. Hood, saying that teachers must have heightened self-consciousness, must analyze; it's not good enough for them just to know the larger outcomes—they have to know all the specific behaviors that make up the larger outcome.

College teachers traditionally lack such self-consciousness about the process of teaching. It is traditionally felt that attention is better given to the subject matter than to pedagogy. Teaching is seen as something inherently mysterious. Metaphors for teaching are apt to come from realms judged inimical to analysis or self-conscious scrutiny: teaching is like a delicate human encounter, like love, like sex. You destroy it if you try to shine a bright light upon it. People in the competence-based movement have little patience with this kind of thinking. To them, if something is important, it's worth analyzing.

And it is true enough that college teachers are characteristically unclear about their goals. Many haven't even decided what *kind* of things their goals are; that is, they haven't made it clear to themselves to what extent their goals consist of: effects upon student behavior, thinking, or character; or effects upon their own behavior or knowledge; or effects upon published knowledge. If you don't know what your goals are, you can hardly know whether you are attaining them. You are liable to be blown about by the conflicting cues of popularity, scholarly eminence, success in "winning discussions," or simply feeling good as you walk out to the parking lot at the end of the day. Teachers traditionally deal in what is fuzzy, unseen, mysterious, inner—in what seems indistinguishable from baloney.

Some of the mystery is no doubt inherent in teaching. Certainly, if you think of teaching in any lofty sense—trying to influence character, trying to influence or improve society (and who, really, ever became a teacher without harboring deep down some goals such as these?)—you are usually in the dark about the effectiveness of your teaching. How can you possibly have a clear sense at the end of the day, of the year, even of the decade, whether you are making progress? (Thus, there is the same fantasy in the collective unconscious of all teachers: the great hero drops in and says, "I owe it all to you and your teaching many years ago. I hated it then, but now I want to *thank* you for making me do all those things.")

But the intellectual tendency in competence teachers won't let you off the hook just because your ideals are whoppers and in a sense unrealizable. These people will insist on analytic self-consciousness and say, "I see. Yes. So you want to create 'better people'? Fine. Now tell me what these better people might look like or things they might do that would distinguish them from ordinary people." And before you know it, they will have you specifying some outcomes that you could actually try to attain— and not only that, but begin to measure your success—and not only that, but all this while engaged in teaching Chaucer or physics or accounting.

Competence teachers often have a special anger against those who actually take pride in being intuitive, who say they can't state their goals and criteria or that it would destroy their human integrity or academic freedom to do so; who say no one else could assess the students in their course or assess them as teachers because no one else is competent in exactly these standards or criteria.

Our own project team, as visitors and observers of competence-based programs, received some of this resentment and anger. If you believe in making goals and criteria explicit, you could scarcely help but be suspicious of our team since we hadn't formulated—much less published—any explicit goals or criteria for our investigations beyond agreeing to write case studies of the evolution of these programs. You could experience us as unprofessionals simply fooling around.

Certain things follow from this heightened self-consciousness. One is an increased analytical self-consciousness about subject matter. And when teacher achieve this kind of self-consciousness, they tend to become excited about their discovery and want to pass it on to their students. Thus, many programs don't merely ask that a student do something or know something. They want meta-knowledge or second-stage learning too: knowing *what* you are doing; knowing *about* your knowing. Merely getting the task done is not good enough, and hence all the self-evaluations in these programs. I couldn't figure out the connection at first. I associate student self-evaluation with the kind of "old-fashioned" personalistic non-outcome-oriented experimentalism of places like Antioch or Goddard. But I soon realized that this analytic self-consciousness in teachers makes them try to foster it in students too. It is also true, however, that teachers are not always successful in passing on this enthusiasm for analytic self-consciousness; in fact, some students are intimidated or drop out.

A final consequence of the analytic self-consciousness in competence programs is a high emphasis on planning. I had never before seen so many teachers who planned so much. One would often see teachers who worked out lesson plans for the whole term, and these seldom seemed to be the kind of fake lesson plans that some public school teachers make because their supervisors require them to.

In all these ways, then, I sense a highly analytic self-consciousness alongside the mood of anti-intellectuality.

❀

*Is the spirit of competence-based education egalitarian and
anti-elitist?* On the one hand, it is certainly anti-elitist in the
common sense of the word. There is a spirit in the competence-
based movement that says anyone can learn and that, except for
diagnosis, it is immoral to have assessment at the entrance to
educational institutions. Hard-nosed, door-closing assessment only
belongs at the exits or conclusions of the educational experience.
People in the movement are very aware that no elite colleges are
involved in competence-based education and participants tend
to view elite colleges as the enemy. They see elite colleges as
rooted in norm-referenced assessment and rank-ordering—engaged in using education as an enterprise to distinguish superior
people from the rest. For there *is* a spirit in elite higher education that says, "Education is not really teaching people to know
or do things. Yes, of course, we do that, but that's not the point.
The point is to find out who has a first-class mind. That takes
time—as long as three or four years. People can look good after
only a year or two but turn out to lack real quality. What they
know doesn't matter; indeed it's better if their minds are not
too cluttered up with facts and ideas, otherwise they can't really
think straight." The Oxford Greats program is, as it were, the
locus classicus of this spirit. Studying Greek and Latin didn't
make a better governor of India, but it was a good chance to see
who had quality.

A high proportion of the programs that we looked at have a
definite mission to move society in a more democratic, egalitarian
direction. (Sometimes this is stronger in the wording of the grant
proposal than in subsequent behavior, and may be an example
of verbal operant conditioning by FIPSE.) There is a feeling that
elite institutions and elite teachers have unfairly dominated the
very conception of what educational institutions and teachers are
supposed to be like, that this situation has operated to the disadvantage of the majority of citizens, and that competence-based
programs are going to start changing things around.

Yet on the other hand, the competence-based approach, with

its insistence on complete learning or mastery, reflects a kind of puritanism that is itself elitist. It's quality they are after. The "real thing." The teachers set extremely high standards and demand from the student large amounts of self-management, initiative, and—perhaps at the root of all such qualities—confidence that one *can* make it. But it is precisely these qualities that are often in short supply in the disadvantaged students whom these anti-elite programs sometimes specifically seek.

I think here of the nursing program at Seattle Central (specifically designed for students who couldn't get into other nursing programs), which a few years ago became self-paced. Almost none of the students finished. I think too of my conversation with a black teacher at Florida State University who was weighing the pros and cons of a merger between the university and a nearby black college. She noted that an outcome-oriented curriculum seemed to be just what disadvantaged black students need: they wouldn't then have to be the "dumb" ones in the back of the class, get lower grades, or hold the class back since all students can learn at their own speed. Yet her own experience teaching in such curriculums made her realize that it is precisely the disadvantaged students who are the first to drop out of these programs. And they drop out quietly; a competence-based program never has to fail anybody. These students just don't have the self-confidence to persist, especially when they must work very independently. This becomes a comfortable situation for an institution or a teacher who doesn't really want to deal with disadvantaged students. It reminds me again of the teacher who said, "They don't blame the teacher anymore; they just blame themselves."

Since competence-based institutions are raising standards at the same time as they are opening doors wider, they can make their egalitarianism really functional only if they are terribly shrewd, tireless, and well-planned in giving extra help and support to underprivileged students. For, really, the competence approach fits elite students best, that is, it fits confident, well-prepared students who can say, "Just tell me what I need to know and don't bother me with your classes and lectures. I'll tell you when I'm ready. Now get out of my way, I'm in a hurry." And, it is the highly elite institution, really, that is naturally closest to the competence approach. It is of the essence at Har-

vard and Oxford, for example, not to care whether students go
to classes or lectures, not to care anything about process but only
about outcomes: papers and exams. The difference is that elite
schools, with their goal of trying to identify the most talented—
and their tacit equation of talent with the ability to deal with
the unexpected—tend to leave outcomes unstated; in an elite
school, it would seem against nature to hand out the final exam
on the opening day as so many competence teachers do in one
form or another.

Somewhere between elite, confident students for whom the
competence approach is natural, and underprivileged, poorly
prepared students who must struggle to find the confidence and
self-management skills necessary, there is a third population:
adults who are already functioning in society. The competence
approach seems just right for these autonomous and functioning,
but not necessarily middle-class, students. They can set their own
schedules; they know how to take charge of themselves because as
functioning adults they've learned that no one will do it for
them; and also—because they are adults—they are in a hurry and
don't want to waste time.

Is competence-based education teacher-centered? It is clearly
hostile to professors and professing: standing up there and putting yourself at the center of the stage, asking students to look at
you and listen to you, in a sense even to ingest you or fall in love
with you. Many good teachers do this kind of professing, and
many people learn best and fastest from such teachers. As Socrates pointed out, we fall in love with beautiful or wise persons
more easily than with beauty and wisdom. But this kind of
teaching can just as easily be described in hostile terms: ego trip-
ping, limelighting, narcissism. Whatever way you describe it,
however, competence people are against it. Here is a typical
comment: "I could no longer give myself up to the process of
doing what I enjoyed doing in my teaching. I had gotten too
self-conscious about outcomes." She discovered that doing what
she enjoyed doing, was used to doing, and felt good doing, didn't
in fact bring the outcomes she desired.

Competence teachers insist on taking themselves out of the
center and focusing instead on the student and the things the
student has to master. They are likely to characterize traditional

and elite colleges as places where teachers just go into classrooms and talk about whatever interests them in an ego-centered way. I found competence teachers as good as their prejudice. That is, they didn't let themselves be in the limelight. They were often mentors, helpers, facilitators—people who helped students manage their own learning. And I began to reflect—being myself something of a teacher-centered teacher—that this is asking a great deal. Yes, it may be good for students, but can one really sustain a whole teaching career on such a selfless stance? After all, students don't have to be in our classrooms very long but we do. Even if we don't deserve the satisfaction that comes from being in center stage, can we teach with passion and intensity for very long with no direct ego gratification? The dynamic competence teachers that I saw teaching with passion and intensity— the many good ones—can they really keep it up for five years? Ten? Twenty? Aren't the involvement and intensity consequences of the newness? Aren't most teachers who sustain themselves as passionate teachers really engaged in a kind of narcissism? I suspect they are.

Nevertheless, I found it necessary to think further about this issue, and about what these teachers had told me. I began to suspect that although they aren't professing in that limelighting way, they are engaged in something equally arrogant and, in a sense, self-centered. And they admit it openly. That is, all these impressive teachers said to me in one way or another that they were committed to the new approach because it permitted them to have more of an impact on the student than conventional teaching did. It permitted them to shape or change the student more.

I think of Milton Ford in College IV at Grand Valley sending a student home with a module on literary criticism. After only three or four hours of work but in accordance with certain strict guidelines, the student comes in to discuss the reading and the written responses. Milton remembers saying to himself with amazement, "I've *done* something to that student's mind." He never had a sense of making this much impact in conventional teaching.

I think of Cynthia Stevens at Alverno saying, "Competence-based education is a radical infringement on the right of teachers to manipulate students." But later in the same conversation she admitted that she does indeed have a strong personality, that she wants students to feel even her personal impact, and most of all that she feels she can have a bigger impact on students through her competence-based teaching. Admittedly the kind of impact she wants to have is for them to become more independent, autonomous, critical people—people who figure things out for themselves. Yet this laudable goal cannot be called anything less than an attempt to mold personality to her own specifications.

These teachers are thus willing to give up professing from center stage but, for many of them, only in the interest of greater effectiveness in *shaping* students—if not to their own image, at least to their own consciously chosen specifications. If you lob them a kind of classic liberal question, "Do you really think it's right or valid or honest for teachers to play with people's minds like that and try to change people's character and behavior?" you will find them ready at the net to smash it home: "All teachers are engaged in playing with people's minds. It's dishonest to pretend otherwise. Your only choices are whether to know what you are doing, and whether to be effective at it." I now realize that this kind of mission, given the success that many of these teachers seem to have, could sustain teachers for a whole career.

Is competence-based teaching student-centered? When I think of student-centered teaching I think of something in the tradition of Antioch and Goddard—personalistic, often loose, sometimes anarchistic. All these qualities are pretty squarely the opposite of what one finds in competence-based programs. Student-centered teachers are often anti-puritan, anti-work ethic, while I find a strong puritan work ethic in these new programs. Student-centered enterprises tend to let students determine their own goals and outcomes, and student-centered teachers are usually oriented away from assessment. By contrast, the spirit in competence programs is for firm criteria set long before the student arrives and never bent for the benefit of some particular student; and all teaching is directed toward tough, bottom-line assessment. The spirit, in short, is very hard-nosed.

Yet competence-based teachers do tend, in the last analysis, to be student-centered in a crucial sense; whatever you teach, you must always state it in terms of *what it would look like embod-*

ied in a student. Thus, no matter how puritan, tough-minded, or assessment-centered the teaching is, an important part of the teacher's attention must always be focused on the student, the student's needs, and how the student will internalize the subject. This is one of the reasons why one-to-one conferences tend to play a bigger role in competence programs than in conventional teaching.

Is competence-based education inimical to learning by immersion? The classic case involves literal immersion: throw 'em in the water so they'll swim. Immersion teaching in higher education is represented by the teacher who deliberately talks over the heads of students and engages in a conversation with a couple of the brightest ones—or with herself—while the other students must flounder and feel lost, and only gradually begin to get a feel for what is going on. Learning by immersion, when it works, tends to produce fast and extensive learning: entire gestalts. Language teachers, for example, have made explicit the principle that if an instructor has to explain everything and get students to understand everything, the class can move only at a snail's pace compared to what is possible if the instructor just forges ahead, doing it "too fast." However, learning by immersion—as with language learning by this method—always entails disorientation and frustration for the learner. And learning by immersion doesn't always work because the learner is liable to give up. Also, it is tinged with a kind of elitist flavor since, in a sense, that's just what it is: just throw them in the water, let the cream rise to the top, and let the others disappear. It tends to be elite college teachers who prefer talk-over-their-heads pedagogy.

The mood of analytic self-consciousness in the competence movement produces an understandable prejudice against the chaos and elitism of the immersion style. The competence procedure asks teachers to figure out exactly what they want to teach, and this process tends to inspire them to work out the component parts of a course and the best incremental and rational order for presenting them. I sensed a prejudice against just plunging into the thick of things.

But if it were to be demonstrated that such a method does work in achieving certain outcomes, competence-based teachers would certainly go along. Indeed they wouldn't settle for "just plunging in"; they would try to analyze what kinds of plunging in work best for what kinds of teaching. In addition, competence-based education stresses learning through life experience, job experience, and simulation, and these tend to be experiences of learning by immersion, with all of the advantages and disadvantages: speed; having to wait in disorientation for the new gestalt; and failure for the timid and nonpersistent.

Does Competence-Based Teaching Exclude Certain Teaching Styles and Temperaments

This question, I realize finally, is what drew me deeper and deeper into a fruitful perplexity during the three years of our study. The tongue returns to the aching tooth. I can answer Yes quickly enough: I do see a slight narrowing in the range of styles of teaching in the programs I visited. But from almost the beginning I had an intuitive sense that this question can also be answered No. Now I think that my intuition was also right.

Let me start by posing the question in its most extreme or biased form—a form, however, that reflects the real fears of many thoughtful teachers: Does competence-based education reduce the teacher to a coach merely drilling people to pass exams? Does the competence approach kill all true education or deeper thinking? If outcomes are trivial and teachers lazy or unimaginative, and if assessment procedures are stupidly mechanistic and inappropriately precise, these fears would be realized. But we did not see outcomes or teachers or assessments of that sort, nor did we see those dismal results.

But what if we move to a more moderate form of the question: Does competence-based education lead students and teachers to be predominantly pragmatic? Not simpleminded or trivial or blindly mechanical, mind you, but does it lead to a slight narrowing in the range of human styles, away from creativity, intution, play, humor, and purely disinterested curiosity? Is the spirit of competence teaching, in short, the spirit of instrumentalism?

I do think, in fact, that the spirit of instrumentalism predominates in the programs we saw. The movement attracts pragmatic, no-nonsense people: "If you can't justify everything in advance, you are falling down on the job and you are unprofessional. You must always know what you are doing. If you haven't figured out your goals and outcomes and planned your activities on the basis of them, you are irresponsible." There is a puritan prejudice against intuition, play, irony, and humor. And certainly the path of least resistance in a competence-based program is simply to teach to the examination.

But competence-based teaching needn't be dominated by a spirit of instrumentalism or pragmatism; its full range of possibilities has not been exploited in what I saw. For one thing, historical factors have played a large role in creating the present instrumental spirit. The approach appeals most obviously to schools of professional training where the instrumental spirit, understandably, is already strong. Teachers of nursing, even of law, have always tended to have outcomes in mind since they can so easily imagine how the student will have to perform in the hospital or in the practice of law. And even when teachers in professional schools try to put these pictures to one side and teach more toward disinterested inquiry, students tend to wrench pragmatic goals back to center stage. We saw very few liberal arts colleges with competence-based programs, and it will probably take much longer for such colleges and for teachers opposed to instrumentalism to see that a competence approach might be helpful.

In addition, the competence-based movement is clearly reacting against elite higher education with its tendency to proclaim, after Aristotle, that learning for some purpose is always inferior to learning for its own sake. If more liberal arts colleges and more colleges of higher status were to try out a competence-based approach—a huge "if," I admit—I believe that the spirit of competence-based teaching would be considerably expanded. I believe, in fact, that every kind of teaching would be fostered.

I base this view partly upon some of the teaching I actually saw, and partly upon analysis of what seems to me possible.

The only liberal arts college I saw using a competence approach was Alverno. Although the teachers there tended somewhat toward the instrumental in their neglect of the intuitive and creative dimension when working out the competencies that characterize a liberally educated person, nevertheless they articulated deeply intelligent outcomes which seemed to permit and invite all kinds of teaching. For example, the assignment mentioned earlier in which students were asked to describe a room in terms of its effect on users was an instrumental teaching procedure, perhaps, but also one that invites the intuitive and the unexpected.

I also saw how the very instrumentalism of a competence program can paradoxically permit a teacher to be shoddily noninstrumental. I am thinking of a lecture I heard at one of our sites. It was a boring, rambling, poorly organized, and badly presented performance. There was no sense of outcomes, direction, or planning. Such lectures are not uncommon in higher education, but what seemed new was seeing how students were able to get considerable value out of this poor performance because of the competence-based curriculum it was part of. From talking to some of them afterward, I discovered that though they didn't like the lecture, they knew what they needed, what to look for in the chaos. I could see that they weren't just tuning it out with those obvious manifestations of boredom or anger—slumped bodies and glazed eyes—which are so familiar in traditional college lecture halls, where students don't really know what they need to know. The students I saw were able to take a more active, shaping role in getting what they needed out of an unshaped performance.

Also, because the competence approach helps teachers specify goals, it thereby helps teachers figure out their own private agendas better, and, as a result, some teachers seem to expand and enlarge the kinds of goals they work for.

I saw many small examples of this, but I think particularly of Arlene Fingeret teaching adults basic competencies in math and reading. As a result of her analysis of the students, she adopted the following competencies in addition to basic math and reading: (1) knowing more specifically when you are stuck by recognizing the signs—from a feeling in your stomach to the way you clench your fist to a special kind of drowsiness; (2) having a whole repertoire of conscious options you can choose among when you are stuck—from various plans or algorithms for attacking the problem, to more intuitive plans for sneaking up on the problem, to being able to ask for help, all the way to having the choice of saying, "The heck with it, I quit"; (3) having the confidence in a school setting to take risks and follow hunches and not feel that you must always know how to do a task correctly the first time; (4) gaining a political and cultural

understanding of schools in our society so that you don't blame
yourself as incompetent and helpless if you have not yet learned to
read or do math. Fingeret worked very hard on these supplementary
competencies in addition to the math and reading—harder in fact
than the students were comfortable with. Yet the students all passed
the assessments on math and reading and achieved higher scores
than were usually achieved by concentrating on those subjects alone.

I see Fingeret as a teacher who refused to be restricted by the
official or assigned competencies (not that she by any means
scorned teaching basic math and reading): an emphasis on outcomes helped her become more conscious and explicit than she
would otherwise have been about a very different set of outcomes. Obviously she had already developed an interest in these
goals in her previous teaching, but she had not worked them out
so clearly or taught with them in mind so explicitly before. The
official goals forced her into a dialectic process that in turn
allowed her to be clearer about her own special agenda as a
teacher and how to realize it. At one point in our conversation, I
referred to the competencies she had added as "subsidiary"—they
helped lead the students to do a better job at the stated ones.
She bristled. "They're *more* important," she said.

As I think about this woman who, on the one hand, teaches
competencies much more practical and pedestrian than most college teachers feel they should have to stoop to, but who, on the
other hand, teaches more than most college teachers try for,
namely, a basic change of consciousness, I recall a sentence from
James Chapman: "The old distinction between what is practical
and what is theoretical tends to disappear. Precisely the same
element of information may be theoretical if given at one time
and essentially practical if given at another." (408).

Perhaps, for the sake of argument and at the risk of selling
her short, we can see Fingeret as representing the spirit of enlightened and flexible instrumentalism. But the additional question that interests me is: How *far* can one go in a competence-
based format away from instrumentalism? I have, to be frank, a
certain personal stake in behavior that is not goal oriented—
even in nonsense. I structure my exploration around three
pointed questions:

First, in a competence-based program, can I teach a course in a new area or on a question I cannot answer or around a book I wish to explore for the first time? That is, can I teach toward goals but not know how to get there? Can I make my teaching a journey of exploration for me as well as for the students? I recently taught a course in Shakespeare, and that is not my main field; I am about to teach a course in peace studies, an area not even in my discipline; Gerald Grant, who headed our research project, taught a seminar in assessment as a way to learn about it. Would these enterprises be possible in a competence-based format?

The answer seems to depend on the nature of the outcomes. If they were *in* the new subject matter, I wouldn't know enough about that subject matter to specify the outcomes in advance. The last thing I would figure out at the end of the semester—if I were lucky—would be what is really important. But if, on the other hand, the competencies were not *in* the subject matter but were more generic, then I think I could set out on my exploration and have my adventure in a competence-based setting. That is, I could teach Shakespeare in such a way as to help students attain competence in, say, critical thinking or literary explication or how to get literature and their own experience to interact. These would be fruitful interactions between generic competencies specified clearly in advance and new and different subject matter looked at in terms of them. Some of the most powerful teaching we saw was a result of this kind of interaction.

Second, in a competence setting, can I teach toward no goal? Can I teach for purely disinterested inquiry? Can I have learning entirely for its own sake? Surely this refusal to consider ends goes squarely against the competence approach. But here again, the competence approach itself forces me to think more clearly about what I mean by my question. First, is it the student or the teacher I am asking about? If I want students to engage in disinterested inquiry and become better at it, I don't see any reason why this cannot be taken as an educational goal, an outcome, a competence. Frankly, I am not impressed with the ability of most colleges and universities to foster the love of disinterested inquiry in students. I think faculty members might do better if they actually specified this kind of inquiry as a competence and planned teaching and learning situations specifically for the sake of fostering it. There is nothing logically inconsistent or empirically impossible about getting students to take as a goal the ability to engage in behavior that is not oriented toward a goal. I suspect that most higher education does not suffer from too much concern for distinterested inquiry but rather from too little—pieties to the contrary notwithstanding.

But what if my goal is for *me,* as a teacher, to engage in purely disinterested inquiry. Can I be purely noninstrumental as a teacher in a competence-based format? Can I, that is, teach without having a clue where I'm going. Without even knowing what the real question or problem is? This, after all, describes where one often finds onself in any serious inquiry. Here again we stumble upon another sense of the word "professor" that seems diametrically opposed to the spirit of competence-based education. That is, the "professor," in traditional lore, is a comically impractical chap, hopeless at getting where he wants to go, always forgetting where he set out for in the first place, always digressing, always forgetting the point: "Let's see now. What was I talking about?"

If I do this purely exploratory teaching in such a way that students actually learn competencies stated somewhere in advance, it would be appropriate although it may require a certain benevolent stage managing by someone else—for example, discreet notices posted somewhere that say, "Elbow thinks he's teaching Chaucer, but really he's teaching writing or epistemology." Or perhaps I am teaching Chaucer but in a very peculiar way. A competence system can be especially useful here because it enables students to study and get credit in Chaucer (or in some particular competence) without having to endure the teaching of the "Chaucer person." In conventional curriculums, there are many students who don't take subjects because, though they wish to pursue the subject, they don't want to work with the teacher involved. Often a class is ruined by being half-filled with students who cannot or will not benefit from the teacher's approach or style, yet to get credit they have to undergo this person's instruction. Without that disgruntled half, the teacher and the remaining students might flourish.

But what if I really don't help students toward stated outcomes with my teaching? Or what if I cannot get a producer or stage manager to make my performance available to the right students at the right time? Then I'm in trouble in a competence-based program. I may be thrashing around in the dark in a wonderful way—producing all kinds of growth for me and even producing outcomes in students that are grand but not called for in the curriculum. Presumably that is not enough. The astringent spirit of the competence approach would give an uncompromising answer: "Yes, creative drifting is important, but you'll have to do it after class or at home or as part of your research. While you are teaching, you'll have to find some way to help students toward the stated outcomes—unless you can persuade us to adopt your new outcomes."

But I venture to suggest that many of us who say that our teaching is a journey of disinterested inquiry into the unknown are not really behaving as unpredictably as we like to believe. For just as the absentminded professor is likely in fact to be quite predictable—he is engaging in instrumental behavior designed to produce specific outcomes in a process which his wife or students can describe clearly even if he cannot—so too we may very sincerely say at the beginning of the semester, "I don't know where this course is going to end up; we'll just have to follow the process of reasoned inquiry where it leads us," yet the student who took a course from us last semester is likely to know just where we will end up. In short, many of us who say we engage in disinterested inquiry have intentions and goals that for some reason we prefer to know incompletely or not at all. The competence-based people would say that we have a duty to become more aware of our goals and take more responsibility for our intentions.

Third, are certain goals or outcomes unsuitable for a competence approach? Are the "deep" goals of "true" education—as opposed to those of training and professional education—unattainable by the very act of choosing or stating them as outcomes? Does instrumental consciousness prevent us from arriving at certain destinations? Are there butterflies we cannot grasp with goal-oriented fists? Aristotle says that we cannot teach metaphorical ability. Socrates suspects that we cannot teach virtue. Others say we cannot teach growth or tolerance for ambiguity or lovemaking or how to empty your mind.

In short, I wish to explore as directly as possible the suspicion that a goal-oriented approach is inherently limiting—at least in certain realms. This suspicion is quite widespread; otherwise the word *methodical* wouldn't so often connote *dumb*. I admit to the suspicion myself. For one thing, it seems to me that people who care too desperately about knowing exactly what they are doing and why, what the goal is, and how terms are defined, often have a tendency to run away from ambiguity, uncertainty, and contrary voices from within and without—a tendency which leads to behavior that is dogmatic, inflexible, and sometimes just plain stupid. If people listen only to voices they understand or proceed only according to plan, they cut themselves off from half their intelligence. In many situations, nothing is more likely to *preclude* good thinking than defining terms at the start. For another thing, certain kinds of learning seem to take place only if people remove their shoulders from the harness of a goal for a while and engage in noninstrumental behavior. Most wise teachers have a sense of the paradoxes involved in learning: how the hardest things are often learned only when students stop trying or stop practicing. I can think of a whole range of non-goal-oriented activities that lead to deep learning: play, exercises for learning how to meditate, free association in psychoanalysis, freewriting. Many of these are exercises in learning to not-try, to unclench, to remove the shoulder from the harness.

But my reflections on competence-based teaching have helped me finally to realize that, even though these may be instances of not trying and even of removing the goal entirely from mind, it is incorrect to call them instances of *not having a goal*. Most of them are activities worked out, in fact, to help people achieve particular goals, but to help *by means of* removing a counterproductive consciousness of the goal. The techniques often involve learning to take loops, detours, or roundabout paths. I end up suspecting, then, that there is nothing one cannot adopt as an educational goal or outcome, but that certain goals must be worked toward with great tact and intelligence, and others with a wise indirection. I suspect that the slippery, tricky goals all involve organic development or personal growth.

If, for example, one were to adopt, as outcomes for teaching, the stages of moral development enumerated by Kohlberg or the stages of cognitive development set forth by Perry, one would have to be wise and subtle. I can well imagine ineffective, perverse, or even harmful teaching toward these outcomes. But that doesn't mean the attempt is wrong or doomed to failure; witness the many successful examples of people who do indeed intentionally help others attain growth or other subtle developmental goals. Admittedly these people are often called "parents" or "counselors" or even "employers" rather than "educators." But the mere fact that they are not formal educators doesn't mean they don't sometimes adopt these goals quite consciously.

I think, at this point, of Outward Bound, one of the many institutions arising in our culture which can variously be described as providing education or therapy or simply intimacy—institutions lying somewhere between school and family. Outward Bound programs adopt and announce such goals as courage, confidence, the ability to give and receive support from a group, and even maturity. They do amazingly well at attaining such goals. But they do a characteristic dance with respect to outcomes, that is, they shuffle around what is focal and what is subsidiary—what you have your eye on and what you don't. (See Polanyi, 1958.) They arrange things so that the student's attention gets fully occupied with what could in a sense be called "subsidiary goals"— getting to the top of the mountain, getting something to eat, or not getting killed. At the time, it might seem odd to call these goals "subsidiary," but that is the whole point: they are pressing enough to take your mind off the tricky developmental goals— which is just what is needed with tricky goals. But taking your mind off a goal is not the same as not having it for a goal. And teachers in Outward Bound do not take their eyes off the developmental goals.

If anything can be taught, can anything be assessed? That is a more difficult question to answer. It may well be that part of the wisdom and subtlety required for the teaching of developmental goals involves refraining from direct or blatant assessment of them or at least of assessment at certain points in the learning process. An Outward Bound experience could be called all teaching and no assessment; that is, if students make it through the "course," they automatically pass the "final." Or perhaps we should call it all assessment and no teaching; that is, if students make it through the final, they can skip the course. A somewhat similar ambiguity about teaching and assessment emerges in some competence programs. Ostensibly they are interested in separating teaching and assessment, but their very exploration of new forms of assessment and instruction often serves to muddy the distinction. Many of the assessment procedures at Alverno and the College for Human Services—the places that set outcomes most closely connected with human growth and development—are clearly functioning as learning procedures.

We can finally be clearer, then, about the paradoxical answer to the question for this section; namely, does competence-based education exclude certain *styles* or *temperaments* in teaching? But we must first distinguish between two dichotomies that are similar and easily confused. To start with, there is the dichotomy between two *temperamental styles:* a pragmatic, no-nonsense style of always keeping your shoulder to the wheel, always knowing exactly what you are doing and why, never fooling around, and never leaving anything ambiguous; versus the contrasting style of inviting intuition, ambiguity, play, and some thrashing around in the dark. But that dichotomy between temperamental styles is different from a dichotomy between two *strategies:* a strategy of formulating your goals and priorities as clearly as you can, and trying to think clearly and awarely about how to attain them, versus a strategy of simply going along by instinct or intuition or tradition or habit, without examining assumptions, and of seeing where you come out.

Now obviously, people who have a goal-oriented temperament are more likely to choose a goal-oriented strategy. And that is what we see now in the competence-based movement. But the strategy and the style don't have to match. In my own case, for example, I realize that I can adopt a more goal-oriented strategy without changing my more non-goal-oriented temperament or giving up some of my favorite non-goal-oriented learning activities, such as games or freewriting or interludes of unstructuredness. Indeed, because I have begun to adopt a more goal-oriented strategy for attaining some of my subtler educational goals, such as growth, creativity, and metaphorical thinking, I am beginning to be more conscious and intentional in my use of non-goal-oriented teaching activities. I conclude, then, that competence-based education, though it is a goal-oriented strategy, need not foster only goal-oriented styles and pragmatic temperaments in teachers.

Conclusions

1. For teaching in a competence program, much depends on the outcomes and assessments. Indeed a competence-based program *is* the outcomes and assessments. You can teach however you want as long as you succeed in preparing the students for the assessments. If the outcomes are trivial or the assessments blindly mechanistic, you can still teach how you want, but you will have to swim against the tide of trivialization or bad faith.

2. But although you can teach any *way* you want in a competence-based program, you probably cannot teach *what* you want as freely as most faculty members can at high-status colleges. The competence approach is a vehicle for allowing new constituencies—administrators, colleagues, and legislators, for example—to have a share in deciding what will be taught. (Perhaps having to put up with these new constituencies led the programs we saw to exclude almost entirely the most obvious new constituency for helping decide what should be taught, namely, students.)

3. We did not often see the competence-based approach used stupidly or in bad faith, but it is probably true to say that the system lends itself to such uses. For the competence approach represents, among other things, a more unified, integrated, and tightly organized way of putting together an entire curriculum. If stupidity or malevolence were in the saddle, they could be more pervasive and damaging in their effects than in traditional colleges and universities, which are organized around departments and thus have the not inconsiderable benefits of anarchy: parts of the organism are blessedly immune from influence by other parts.

4. But even though we did not see competence-based education narrowed to a vehicle for triviality or bad faith, I at least did not see it broadened out as much as it could be into a vehicle for the fullest spectrum of styles and temperaments in teaching. This will not happen until the approach is used by a wider range

of people and institutions. For the competence approach is understandably most attractive to people with a goal-oriented temperament and to institutions of professional training where there is already an obvious outcome: a job or profession. The competence approach is indeed helpful for such persons and institutions, but I judge it particularly helpful for those people and institutions who are most likely to be suspicious of it: people with a non-goal-oriented temperament, and colleges of liberal arts where there is woeful disagreement as to the purposes of education.

5. Even though competence-based education has more to do with outcomes and assessments than with what kind of teaching is used, the teachers played a central role in the programs we saw. When teachers get involved in competence programs, they tend to become enthusiastic. But why do they become enthusiastic over programs that take so much out of their hides? I think it is because the approach helps them to teach better and thereby to feel more sense of accomplishment. It both forces and helps teachers to figure out more clearly what they have been trying to do, to become more aware of their latent assumptions and premises, and often to go through this process collaboratively with colleagues. The result tends to be teaching that is more intentional, effective, and energized.

6. Nevertheless, I don't see how it could be anything but scary to contemplate teaching in a competence-based program for any teacher in higher education who, like myself, has never taught in one. In any program, I would look for assurance: (1) that faculty members will have a major role in determining the outcomes and assessment procedures; (2) that the outcomes will be broad and deeply intelligent and not neglect the larger dimensions of human growth nor the special dimensions of intuition and creativity; and (3) that a feedback loop will operate in *both* directions. It will not just use assessment to provide feedback on the effectiveness of teaching, but it will use the experience of teaching to provide feedback on the validity of the outcomes and assessments. To put it bluntly, if my students fail the assessments, we will not just ask what's wrong with my teaching. We will also ask whether the students are perhaps not ready or able to attain these outcomes; whether perhaps the outcomes are desir-

able but very lofty (for example, if the outcome sought is a change of consciousness, only 10 percent success might be cause for celebration); and whether perhaps I had instinctively veered in my teaching toward new and better outcomes which we should adopt instead of the present ones.

Such assurances are no doubt hard to secure, but without them, I doubt whether many faculty members in colleges and universities can be induced voluntarily to try a competence approach, despite what I hope I have shown to be its obvious benefits.

CHAPTER 7

❀❀❀

This essay makes a claim that is obvious to any honest observer of teaching (despite the syntactic tangle): good teaching is impossible, but *some* teachers teach well; but these teachers do it in completely different ways; and yet there must be some stateable principles we can find. In short, I am trying to work out a dialectical solution to the paradox of authority that has occupied the essays of this part.

In my study of Chaucer I'd seen that wise *understanding* tends to consist of the ability to see and affirm the truth of contrary *points of view*—the ability to keep one view from "winning" or undermining the other. (See Chapter 11.) In my subsequent work in writing, I'd come to see that wise *performance* tends also to consist of the ability to engage in contrary *behaviors*—the ability to keep one subperformance from winning or crowding out the other.

Embracing Contraries in the Teaching Process

My argument is that good teaching seems a struggle because it calls on skills or mentalities that are actually contrary to each other and thus tend to interfere with each other. It was my exploration of writing that led me to look for contraries in difficult or complex processes. I concluded that good writing requires on the one hand the ability to conceive copiously of many possibilities, an ability which is enhanced by a spirit of open, accepting generativity; but on the other hand good writing also requires an ability to criticize and reject everything but the best, a very different ability which is enhanced by a tough-minded critical spirit. I end up seeing in good writers the ability somehow to be extremely creative and extremely critical, without letting one mentality prosper at the expense of the other or being half-hearted in both. (For more about this see my *Writing With Power*, especially Chapter 1.)

In this frame of mind I began to see a paradoxical coherence in teaching where formerly I was perplexed. I think the two conflicting mentalities needed for good teaching stem from the two conflicting obligations inherent in the job: we have an obligation to students but we also have an obligation to knowledge and society. Surely we are incomplete as teachers if we are committed only to what we are teaching but not to our students, or only to our students but not to what we are teaching, or half-hearted in our commitment to both.

We like to think that these two commitments coincide, and often they do. It happens often enough, for example, that our commitment to standards leads us to give a low grade or tough comment, and it is just what the student needs to hear. But just as often we see that a student needs praise and support rather than a tough grade, even for her weak performance, if she is really to prosper as a student and a person—if we are really to nurture her fragile investment in her studies. Perhaps we can finesse this conflict between a "hard" and "soft" stance if it is early in the semester or we are only dealing with a rough draft; for the time being we can give the praise and support we sense is humanly appropriate and hold off strict judgment and standards till later. But what about when it is the end of the course or a final draft needs a grade? It is comforting to take as our paradigm that first situation where the tough grade was just right, and to consider the trickier situation as somehow anomalous, and thus to assume that we always serve students best by serving knowledge, and vice versa. But I now think I can throw more light on the nature of teaching by taking our conflicting loyalties as paradigmatic.

Our loyalty to students asks us to be their allies and hosts as we instruct and share: to invite all students to enter in and join us as members of a learning community—even if they have difficulty. Our commitment to students asks us to assume they are all smart and capable of learning, to see things through their eyes, to help bring out their best rather than their worst when it comes to tests and grades. By taking this inviting stance we will help more of them learn.

But our commitment to knowledge and society asks us to be guardians or bouncers: we must discriminate, evaluate, test, grade, certify. We are invited to stay true to the inherent standards of what we teach, whether or not that stance fits the particular students before us. We have a responsibility to society— that is, to our discipline, our college or university, and to other learning communities of which we are members—to see that the students we certify really understand or can do what we teach, to see that the grades and credits and degrees we give really have the meaning or currency they are supposed to have.*

---

* I lump "knowledge and society" together in one phrase but I acknowledge the importance of the potential conflict. For example, we may feel *society* asking us to adapt our students to it, while we feel *knowledge*—our vision of the truth—asking us to unfit our students for that society. Socrates was convicted

A pause for scruples. Can we give up so easily the paradigm of teaching as harmonious? Isn't there something misguided in the very idea that these loyalties are conflicting? After all, if we think we are being loyal to students by being extreme in our solicitude for them, won't we undermine the integrity of the subject matter or the currency of the credit and thereby drain value from the very thing we are supposedly giving them? And if we think we are being loyal to society by being extreme in our ferocity—keeping out *any* student with substantial misunderstanding—won't we deprive subject matter and society of the vitality and reconceptualizations they need to survive and grow? Knowledge and society only exist embodied—that is, flawed.

This sounds plausible. But even if we choose a middle course and go only so far as fairness toward subject matter and society, the very fact that we grade and certify at all—the very fact that we must sometimes flunk students—tempts many of them to behave defensively with us. Our mere fairness to subject matter and society tempts students to try to hide weaknesses from us, "psych us out," or "con us." It is as though we are doctors trying to treat patients who hide their symptoms from us for fear we will put them in the hospital.

Student defensiveness makes our teaching harder. We say, "Don't be afraid to ask questions," or even, "It's a sign of intelligence to be willing to ask naive questions." But when we are testers and graders, students too often fear to ask. Toward examiners they must play it safe, drive defensively, not risk themselves. This stunts learning. When they trust the teacher to be wholly an ally, students are more willing to take risks, connect the self to the material, and experiment. Here is the source not just of learning but also of genuine development or growth.

Let me bring this conflict closer to home. A department chair or dean who talks with us about our teaching and who sits in on our classes is our ally insofar as she is trying to help us teach better; and we can get more help from her to the degree that we

---

of corrupting the youth. To take a more homely example, I may feel institutions asking me to teach students one kind of writing and yet feel impelled by my understanding of writing to teach them another kind. Thus where this paper paints a picture of teachers pulled in two directions, sometimes we may indeed be pulled in three.

openly share with her our fears, difficulties, and failures. Yet insofar as she makes promotion or tenure decisions about us or even participates in those decisions, we will be tempted not to reveal our weaknesses and failures. If we want the best help for our shortcomings, someone who is merely fair is not enough. We need an ally, not a fair judge.

Thus we can take a merely judicious, compromise position toward our students only if we are willing to settle for being *sort of* committed to students and *sort of* committed to subject matter and society. This middling or fair stance, in fact, is characteristic of many teachers who lack investment in teaching or who have lost it. Most invested teachers, on the other hand, tend to be a bit passionate about supporting students or else passionate about serving and protecting the subject matter they love—and thus they tend to live more on one side or the other of some allegedly golden mean.

But supposing you reply, "Yes, I agree that a compromise is not right. Just middling. Muddling. Not excellence or passion in either direction. But that's not what I'm after. My scruple had to do with your very notion of *two directions*. There is only one direction. Excellence. Quality. The very conception of conflict between loyalties is wrong. An inch of progress in one direction, whether toward knowledge or toward students, is always an inch in the direction of the other. The needs of students and of knowledge or society are in essential harmony."

To assert this harmony is, in a sense, to agree with what I am getting at in this paper. But it is no good just asserting it. It is like asserting, "Someday you'll thank me for this," or, "This is going to hurt me worse than it hurts you." I may say to students, "My fierce grading and extreme loyalty to subject matter and society are really in your interests," but students will still tend to experience me as adversary and undermine much of my teaching. I may say to knowledge and society. "My extreme support and loyalty to all students is really in your interests," but society will tend to view me as a soft teacher who lets standards down.

It is the burden of this paper to say that a contradictory stance is possible—not just in theory but in practice—but not by pretending there is no tension or conflict. And certainly not by

affirming only one version of the paradox, the "paternal" version, which is to stick up for standards and firmness by insisting
that to do so is good for students in the long run, forgetting the
"maternal" version which is to stick up for students by insisting
that to do so is good for knowledge and society in the long run.
There is a genuine paradox here. The positions are conflicting
and they are true.

Let me turn this structural analysis into a narrative about the
two basic urges at the root of teaching. We often think best by
telling stories. I am reading a novel and I interrupt my wife to
say, "Listen to this, isn't this wonderful!" and I read a passage
out loud. Or we are walking in the woods and I say to her, "Look
at that tree!" I am enacting the pervasive human itch to share.
It feels lonely, painful, or incomplete to appreciate something
and not share it with others.*

But this urge can lead to its contrary. Suppose I say, "Listen
to this passage," and my wife yawns or says, "Don't interrupt
me." Suppose I say, "Look at that beautiful sunset on the lake,"
and she laughs at me for being so sentimental and reminds me
that Detroit is right there just below the horizon—creating half
the beauty with its pollution. Suppose I say, "Listen to this delicate irony," and she can't see it and thinks I am neurotic to enjoy such bloodless stuff. What happens then? I end up *not* wanting to share it with her. I hug it to myself. I become a lone con-
noisseur. Here is the equally deep human urge to protect what
I appreciate from harm. Perhaps I share what I love with a few
select others—but only after I find a way somehow to extract
from them beforehand assurance that they will understand and
appreciate what I appreciate. And with them I can even sneer at
worldly ones who lack our taste or intelligence or sensibility.

Many of us went into teaching out of just such an urge to
share things with others, but we find students turn us down or
ignore us in our efforts to give gifts. Sometimes they even laugh
at us for our very enthusiasm in sharing. We try to show them

---

* Late in life, I realize I must apologize and pay my respects to that form of
literary criticism that I learned in college to scorn in callow fashion as the
"Ah lovely!" school: criticism which tries frankly to share a perception and
appreciation of the work rather than insist that there is some problem to
solve or some complexity to analyze.

what we understand and love, but they yawn and turn away. They put their feet up on our delicate structures; they chew bubble gum during the slow movement; they listen to hard rock while reading *Lear* and say, "What's so great about Shakespeare?"

Sometimes even success in sharing can be a problem. We manage to share with students what we know and appreciate, and they love it and eagerly grasp it. But their hands are dirty or their fingers are rough. We overhear them saying, "Listen to this neat thing I learned," yet we cringe because they got it all wrong. Best not to share.

I think of the medieval doctrine of poetry that likens it to a nut with a tough husk protecting a sweet kernel. The function of the poem is not to disclose but rather to conceal the kernel from the many, the unworthy, and to disclose it only to the few worthy (D. W. Robertson, 61ff.). I have caught myself more than a few times explaining something I know or love with a kind of complexity or irony such that only those who have the right sensibility will hear what I have to say—others will not understand at all. Surely this is the source of much obscurity in learned discourse. We would rather have readers miss entirely what we say or turn away in boredom or frustration than reply, "Oh, I see what you mean. How ridiculous!" or, "How naive!" It is marvelous, actually, that we can make one utterance do so many things: communicate with the right people, stymie the wrong people, and thereby help us decide who *are* the right and the wrong people.

I have drifted into an unflattering portrait of the urge to protect one's subject, a defensive urge that stems from hurt. Surely much bad teaching and academic foolishness derive from this immature reaction to students or colleagues who will not accept a gift we tried generously to give (generously, but sometimes ineffectually or condescendingly or autocratically). Surely I must learn not to pout just because I can't get a bunch of adolescents as excited as I am about late Henry James. Late Henry James may be pearls, but when students yawn, that doesn't make them swine.

But it is not immature to protect the integrity of my subject in a positive way, to uphold standards, to insist that students stretch themselves till they can do justice to the material. Surely these impulses are at the root of much good teaching. And there is nothing wrong with these impulses in themselves—only *by themselves*. That is, there is nothing wrong with the impulse to guard or protect the purity of what we cherish so long as that act is redeemed by the presence of the opposite impulse also to give it away.

In Piaget's terms, learning involves both assimilation and accommodation. Part of the job is to get the subject matter to bend and deform so that it fits inside the learner (that is, so it can fit or relate to the learner's experiences). But that's only half the job. Just as important is the necessity for the learner to bend and deform himself so that he can fit himself around the subject without doing violence to it. Good learning is not a matter of finding a happy medium where both parties are transformed as little as possible. Rather both parties must be maximally transformed—in a sense deformed. There is violence in learning. We cannot learn something without eating it, yet we cannot really learn it either without being chewed up.

Look at Socrates and Christ as archetypal good teachers—archetypal in being so paradoxical. They are extreme on the one hand in their impulse to share with everyone and to support all learners, in their sense that everyone can take and get what they are offering; but they are extreme on the other hand in their fierce high standards for what will pass muster. They did not teach gut courses, they flunked "gentleman C" performances, they insisted that only "too much" was sufficient in their protectiveness toward their "subject matter." I am struck also with how much they both relied on irony, parable, myth, and other forms of subtle utterance that hide while they communicate. These two teachers were willing in some respects to bend and disfigure and in the eyes of many to profane what they taught, yet on the other hand they were equally extreme in their insistence that learners bend or transform themselves in order to become fit receptacles.

It is as though Christ, by stressing the extreme of sharing and being an ally—saying "suffer the little children to come unto me" and praising the widow with her mite—could be more extreme in his sternness: "unless you sell all you have," and, "I speak to them in parables, because seeing they do not see and hearing they do not hear, nor do they understand" (saying in effect, "I am making this a tough course *because* so many of you are poor students"). Christ embeds the two themes of giving away and guarding—commitment to "students" and to "subject matter"— in the one wedding feast story: the host invites in guests from the highways and byways, anybody—but then angrily ejects one into outer darkness because he lacks the proper garment.

❀

Let me sum up the conflict in two lists of teaching skills. If on the one hand we want to help more students learn more, I submit we should behave in the following four ways:

1. We should see our students as smart and capable. We should assume that they *can* learn what we teach—all of them. We should look *through* their mistakes or ignorance to the intelligence that lies behind. There is ample documentation that this "teacher expectation" increases student learning (Robert Rosenthal 33–60).

2. We should show students that we are on their side. This means, for example, showing them that the perplexity or ignorance they reveal to us will not be used against them in tests, grading, or certifying. If they hide their questions or guard against us they undermine our efforts to teach them.

3. Indeed, so far from letting their revelations hurt them in grading, we should be, as it were, lawyers for the defense, explicitly trying to help students do better against the judge and prosecuting attorney when it comes to the "trial" of testing and grading. ("I may be able to get you off this charge but only if you tell me what you really were doing that night.") If we take this advocate stance students can learn more from us, even if they are guilty of the worst crimes in the book: not having done the homework, not having learned last semester, not *wanting* to learn. And by learning more—even if not learning perfectly—they will perform better, which in turn will usually lead to even better learning in the future.

4. Rather than try to be perfectly fair and perfectly in command of what we teach—as good examiners ought to be—we should reveal our own position, particularly our doubts, ambiva-

lences, and biases. We should show we are still learning, still willing to look at things in new ways, still sometimes uncertain or even stuck, still willing to ask naive questions, still engaged in the interminable process of working out the relationship between what we teach and the rest of our lives. Even though we are not wholly peer with our students, we can still be peer in this crucial sense of also being engaged in learning, seeking, and being incomplete. Significant learning requires change, inner readjustments, willingness to let go. We can increase the chances of our students being willing to undergo the necessary anxiety involved in change if they see we are also willing to undergo it.

Yet if, on the other hand, we want to increase our chances of success in serving knowledge, culture, and institutions I submit that we need skill at behaving in four very different ways:

1. We should insist on standards that are high—in the sense of standards that are absolute. That is, we should take what is almost a kind of Platonic position that there exists a "real world" of truth, of good reasoning, of good writing, of knowledge of biology, whatever—and insist that anything less than the real thing is not good enough.

2. We should be critical-minded and look at students and student performances with a skeptical eye. We should assume that some students cannot learn and others will not, even if they can. This attitude will increase our chances of detecting baloney and surface skill masquerading as competence or understanding.

3. We should not get attached to students or take their part or share their view of things; otherwise we will find it hard to exercise the critical spirit needed to say, "No, you do not pass," "No, you cannot enter in with the rest of us," "Out you go into the weeping and gnashing of teeth."

4. Thus we should identify ourselves primarily with knowledge or subject matter and care more about the survival of culture and institutions than about individual students—even when that means students are rejected who are basically smart or who tried as hard as they could. We should keep our minds

on the harm that can come to knowledge and society if standards break down or if someone is certified who is not competent, rather than on the harm that comes to individual students by hard treatment.

Because of this need for conflicting mentalities I think I see a distinctive distribution of success in teaching. At one extreme we see a few master or genius teachers, but they are striking for how differently they go about it and how variously and sometimes surprisingly they explain what they do. At the other extreme are people who teach very badly, or who have given up trying, or who quit teaching altogether: they are debilitated by the conflict between trying to be an ally as they teach and an adversary as they grade. Between these two extremes teachers find the three natural ways of making peace between contraries: there are "hard" teachers in whom loyalty to knowledge or society has won out; "soft" teachers in whom loyalty to students has won out; and middling, mostly dispirited teachers who are sort of loyal to students and sort of loyal to knowledge or society. (A few of this last group are not dispirited at all but live on a kind of knife edge of almost palpable tension as they insist on trying to be scrupulously fair both to students and to what they teach.)

This need for conflicting mentalities is also reflected in what is actually the most traditional and venerable structure in education: a complete separation between teaching and official assessment. We see it in the Oxford and Cambridge structure that makes the tutor wholly an ally to help the student prepare for exams set and graded by independent examiners. We see something of the same arrangement in many European university lecture-and-exam systems which are sometimes mimicked by American Ph.D. examinations. The separation of teaching and examining is found in many licensing systems and also in some new competence-based programs.

Even in conventional university curricula we see various attempts to strengthen assessment and improve the relationship between teacher and student by making the teacher more of an ally and coach. In large courses with many sections, teachers often give a common exam and grade each others' students. Occasionally, when two teachers teach different courses within each other's field of competence, they divide their roles and act as "outside examiner" for the other's students. (This approach, by the way, tends to help teachers clarify what they are trying to accomplish in a course since they must communicate their goals clearly to the examiner if there is to be any decent fit between the teaching and examining.) In writing centers, tutors commonly help students improve a piece of writing which another teacher will assess. We even see a hint of this separation of roles when teachers stress collaborative learning: they emphasize the students' role as mutual teachers and thereby emphasize their own pedagogic role as examiner and standard setter.

But though the complete separation of teacher and evaluator is hallowed and useful, I am interested here in ways for teachers to take on both roles better. It is not just that most teachers are stuck with both; in addition I believe that opposite mentalities or processes can enhance each other rather than interfere with each other if we engage in them in the right spirit.

How can we manage to do contrary things? Christ said, "Be ye perfect," but I don't think it is good advice to try being immensely supportive and fierce in the same instant, as he and Socrates somehow managed to be. In writing, too, it doesn't usually help to try being immensely generative and critical-minded in the same instant as some great writers are—and as the rest of us sometimes are at moments of blessed inspiration. This is the way of transcendence and genius, but for most of us most of the time there is too much interference or paralysis when we try to do opposites at once.

But it is possible to make peace between opposites by alternating between them so that you are never trying to do contrary things at any one moment. One opposite leads naturally to the other; indeed, extremity in one enhances extremity in the other in a positive, reinforcing fashion. In the case of my own writing I find I can generate more and better when I consciously hold off critical-minded revising till later. Not only does it help to go whole hog with one mentality, but I am not afraid to make a fool of myself since I know I will soon be just as wholeheartedly critical. Similarly, I can be more fierce and discriminating in my critical revising because I have more and better material to work with through my earlier surrender to uncensored generating.

What would such an alternating approach look like in teaching? I will give a rough picture, but I do so hesitantly because if I am right about my theory of paradox, there will be widely different ways of putting it into practice.

In teaching we traditionally end with the critical or gatekeeper function: papers, exams, grades, or less institutionalized forms of looking back, taking stock, and evaluating. It is also traditional to start with the gatekeeper role: to begin a course by spelling out all the requirements and criteria as clearly as possible. We often begin a course by carefully explaining exactly what it will take to get an A, B, C, etc.

I used to be reluctant to start off on this foot. It felt so vulgar to start by emphasizing grades, and thus seemingly to reinforce a pragmatic preoccuption I want to squelch. But I have gradually changed by mind, and my present oppositional theory tells me I should exaggerate, or at least take more seriously than I often do, my gatekeeper functions rather than run away from them. The more I try to soft-pedal assessment, the more mysterious it will seem to students and the more likely they will be preoccupied and superstitious about it. The more I can make it clear to myself and to my students that I do have a commitment to knowledge and institutions, and the more I can make it specifically clear how I am going to fulfill that commitment, the easier it is for me to turn around and make a dialectical change of role into being an extreme ally to students.

Thus I start by trying to spell out requirements and criteria as clearly and concretely as possible. If I am going to use a midterm and final exam, it would help to pass out samples of these at the beginning of the course. Perhaps not a copy of precisely the test I will use but something close. And why not the real thing? If it feels as though I will ruin the effectiveness of my exam to "give it away" at the start, that means I must have a pretty poor exam—a simple-minded task that can be crammed for and that does not really test what is important. If the exam gets at the central substance of the course then surely it will help me if students see it right at the start. They will be more likely to learn what I want them to learn. It might be a matter of content: "Summarize the three main theories in this course and discuss their strengths and weaknesses by applying them to material we did not discuss." Or perhaps I am more interested in a process or skill: "Write an argumentative essay on this (new) topic." Or, "Show how the formal characteristics of this (new) poem do and do not reinforce the theme." I might want to give room for lots of choice and initiative: "Write a dialogue between the three main people we have studied that illustrates what you think are the most important things about their work." Passing out the exam at the start—and perhaps even samples of strong and weak answers—is an invitation to make a tougher exam that goes more to the heart of what the course is trying to teach. If I don't use an exam, then it is even more crucial that I say how I will determine the grade—even if I base it heavily on slippery factors: e.g., "I will count half your grade on my impression of how well you motivate and invest yourself," or "how well you work collaboratively with your peers." Of course this kind of announcement makes for a tricky situation, but if these are my goals, surely I want my students to wrestle with them all term—in all their slipperiness and even if it means arguments about how unfair it is to grade on such matters—rather than just think about them at the end.

When I assign papers I should similarly start by advertising my gatekeeper role, by clearly communicating standards and criteria. That means not just talking theoretically about what I am looking for in an A paper and what drags a paper down to B or C or F, but rather passing out a couple of samples of each grade and talking concretely about what makes me give each one the grade I give it. Examples help because our actual grading sometimes reflects criteria we do not talk about, perhaps even that we are not aware of. (For example, I have finally come to admit that, for me, neatness counts.) Even if our practice fits our preaching, sometimes students do not really understand preaching without examples. Terms like "coherent" and even "specific" are notoriously hard for students to grasp because they do not read stacks of student writing. Students often learn more about well-connected and poorly-connected paragraphs or specificity or the lack of it in examples from the writing of each other than they learn from instruction alone, or from examples of published writing.

I suspect there is something particularly valuable here about embodying our commitment to knowledge and society in the form of documents or handouts: words on palpable sheets of paper rather than just spoken words-in-the-air. Documents heighten the sense that I do indeed take responsibility for these standards; writing them forces me to try to make them as concrete, explicit, and objective as possible (if not necessarily fair). But most of all, having put all this on paper I can more easily go on to separate myself from them in some way—leave them standing—and turn around and schizophrenically start being a complete ally of students. I have been wholehearted and enthusiastic in making tough standards, but now I can say, "Those are the specific criteria I will use in grading; that's what you are up against, that's really me. But now we have most of the semester for me to help you attain those standards, do well on those tests and papers. They are high standards but I suspect all of you can attain them if you work hard. I will function as your ally. I'll be a kind of lawyer for the defense, helping you bring out your best in your battles with the other me, the prosecuting-attorney me when he emerges at the end. And if you really think you are too poorly prepared to do well in one semester, I can help you decide whether to trust that negative judgment and decide now whether to drop the course or stay and learn what you can."

What is pleasing about this alternating approach is the way it naturally leads a teacher to higher standards yet greater supportiveness. That is, I feel better about being really tough if I know I am going to turn around and be more on the student's side than usual. And contrarily I do not have to hold back from being an ally of students when I know I have set really high standards. Having done so, there is now no such thing as being "too soft," supportive, helpful, or sympathetic—no reason to hold back from seeing things entirely from their side, worrying about their problems. I can't be "cheated" or taken advantage of.

In addition, the more clearly I can say what I want them to know or be able to do, the better I can figure out what I must provide to help them attain those goals. As I make progress in this cycle, it means I can set my goals even higher—ask for the deep knowledge and skills that are really at the center of the enterprise.

But how, concretely, can we best function as allies? One of the best ways is to be a kind of coach. One has set up the hurdle for practice jumping, one has described the strengths and tactics of the enemy, one has warned them about what the prosecuting attorney will probably do: now the coach can prepare them for these rigors. Being an ally is probably more a matter of stance and relationship than of specific behaviors. Where a professor of jumping might say, in effect, "I will explain the principles of jumping," a jumping coach might say, in effect, "Let's work on actually jumping over those hurdles; in doing so I'll explain the principles of jumping." If we try to make these changes in stance, I sense we will discover some of the resistances, annoyances, and angers that make us indeed reluctant genuinely to be on the student's side. How can we be teachers for long without piling up resentment at having been misunderstood and taken advantage of? But the dialectical need to be in addition an extreme adversary of students will give us a legitimate medium for this hunger to dig in one's heels even in a kind of anger.

This stance provides a refreshingly blunt but supportive way to talk to students about weaknesses. "You're strong here, you're weak there, and over here you are really out of it. We've got to find ways to work on these things so you can succeed on these essays or exams." And this stance helps reward students for volunteering weaknesses. The teacher can ask, "What don't you understand? What skills are hard for you? I need to decide how to spend our time here and I want it to be the most useful for your learning."

One of the best ways to function as ally or coach is to role-play the enemy in a supportive setting. For example, one can give practice tests where the grade doesn't count, or give feedback on papers which the student can revise before they count for credit. This gets us out of the typically counterproductive situation where much of our commentary on papers and exams is really justification for the grade—or is seen that way. Our attempt to help is experienced by students as a slap on the wrist by an adversary for what they have done wrong. No wonder students so often fail to heed or learn from our commentary. But when we comment on practice tests or revisable papers we are not saying, "Here's why you got this grade." We are saying, "Here's how you can get a better grade." When later we read final versions as evaluator we can read faster and not bother with much commentary.*

It is the spirit or principle of serving contraries that I want to emphasize here, not any particular fleshing out in practice such as above. For one of the main attractions of this theory is that it helps explain why people are able to be terrific teachers in such diverse ways. If someone is managing to do two things that conflict with each other, he is probably doing something mysterious: it's altogether natural if his success involves slipperiness, irony, or paradox. For example, some good teachers look like they are nothing but fierce gatekeepers, cultural bouncers, and yet in some mysterious way—perhaps ironically or subliminally—they are supportive. I think of the ferocious Marine sergeant who is always cussing out the troops but who somehow shows them he is on their side and believes in their ability. Other good teachers look like creampuffs and yet in some equally subtle way they embody the highest standards of excellence and manage to make students exert and stretch themselves as never before.

For it is one's spirit or stance that is at issue here, not the mechanics of how to organize a course in semester units or how to deal in tests, grading, or credits. I do not mean to suggest that the best way to serve knowledge and society is by having tough exams or hard grading—or even by having exams or grades at all. Some teachers do it just by talking, whether in lectures or discus-

---

* Since it takes more time for us to read drafts and final versions too, no matter how quickly we read final versions, it is reasonable to conserve time in other ways—indeed I see independent merits. Don't require students to revise every draft. This permits you to grade students on their best work and thus again to have higher standards, and it is easier for students to invest themselves in revising if it is on a piece they care more about. And in giving feedback on drafts, wait till you have two drafts in hand and thus give feedback only half as often. When I have only one paper in hand I often feel, "Oh dear, everything is weak here; nothing works right; where can I start?" When I have two drafts in hand I can easily say, "This one is better for the following reasons; it's the one I'd choose to revise; see if you can fix the following problems." With two drafts it is easier to find genuine strengths and point to them and help students consolidate or gain control over them. Yet I can make a positive utterance out of talking about what *didn't* work in the better draft and how to improve it.

sions or conversation. Even though there is no evaluation or grading, the teacher can still demonstrate her ability to be whole-hearted in her commitment to what she teaches and wholehearted also in her commitment to her students. Thus her talk itself might in fact alternate between attention to the needs of students and flights where she forgets entirely about students and talks over their head, to truth, to her wisest colleagues, to herself.*

The teacher who is really in love with Yeats or with poetry will push harder, and yet be more tolerant of students' difficulties because his love provides the serenity he needs in teaching: he knows that students cannot hurt Yeats or his relationship with Yeats. It is a different story when we are ambivalent about Yeats or poetry. The piano teacher who mean-spiritedly raps the fingers of pupils who play wrong notes usually harbors some inner ambivalence in his love of music or some disappointment about his own talent.

In short, there is obviously no one right way to teach, yet I argue that in order to teach well we must find *some* way to be loyal both to students and to knowledge or society. Any way we can pull it off is fine. But if we are teaching less well than we should, we might be suffering from the natural tendency for these two loyalties to conflict with each other. In such a case we can usually improve matters by making what might seem an artificial separation of focus so as to give each loyalty and its attendant skills and mentality more room in which to flourish. That is, we can spend part of our teaching time saying in some fashion or other, "Now I'm being a tough-minded gatekeeper, standing up for high critical standards in my loyalty to what I teach"; and part of our time giving a contrary message: "Now my attention is wholeheartedly on trying to be your ally and to help you

* Though my argument does not imply that we need to use grades at all, surely it implies that if we do use them we should learn to improve the way we do so. I used to think that conventional grading reflected too much concern with standards for knowledge and society, but now I think it reflects too little. Conventional grading reflects such a single-minded hunger to *rank* people along a single scale or dimension that it is willing to forego any communication of what the student really knows or can do. The competence-based movement, whatever its problems, represents a genuine attempt to make grades and credits do justice to knowledge and society. (See Gerald Grant et al.)

learn, and I am not worrying about the purity of standards or grades or the need of society or institutions."

It is not that this approach makes things simple. It confuses students at first because they are accustomed to teachers being either "hard" or "soft" or in the middle—not both. The approach does not take away any of the conflict between trying to fulfill two conflicting functions. It merely gives a context and suggests a structure for doing so. Most of all it helps me understand better the demands on me and helps me stop feeling as though there is something wrong with me for feeling pulled in two directions at once.

I have more confidence that this conscious alternation or separation of mentalities makes sense because I think I see the same strategy to be effective with writing. Here too there is obviously no one right way to write, but it seems as though any good writer must find some way to be both abundantly inventive yet tough-mindedly critical. Again, any way we can pull it off is fine, but if we are not writing as well as we should—if our writing is weak in generativity or weak in tough-minded scrutiny (not to mention downright dismal or blocked)—it may well be that we are hampered by a conflict between the accepting mentality needed for abundant invention and the rejecting mentality needed for tough-minded criticism. In such a case too, it helps to move back and forth between sustained stretches of wholehearted, uncensored generating and wholehearted critical revising to allow each mentality and set of skills to flourish unimpeded.

In the end, I do not think I am just talking about how to serve students and serve knowledge or society. I am also talking about developing opposite and complementary sides of our character or personality: the supportive and nurturant side and the tough, demanding side. I submit that we all have instincts and needs of both sorts. The gentlest, softest, and most flexible among us really need a chance to stick up for our latent high standards, and the most hawk-eyed, critical-minded bouncers at the bar of civilization among us really need a chance to use our nurturant and supportive muscles instead of always being adversary.

PART III

⚙⚙⚙

THE EVALUATION PROCESS

Evaluation is a tar-baby. To kick at it is to become stuck fast. My preoccupation with *teaching* has inadvertently caught me up in a preoccupation with what I thought was its contrary, evaluation. My present job of directing a writing program must take some of the blame, but to be a writing teacher is to have your nose rubbed in the complications of evaluation. How can we not reflect on observations like the following?

- The profession has no accepted definitions or criteria for what "good writing" really consists of.
- The process of grading and commenting is necessarily subjective since our individual tastes, our moods, and our feelings about the individual personalities of our students cannot help but play a role in our judgments.
- And even apart from accuracy of judgment, it's not clear what kind of commenting actually helps the student to write better next time. Recent research throws doubt on the efficacy of much teacher commentary.

Yet to be a writing teacher is also to be like a soldier who has lost an arm in a war. Most writing teachers spend more time "grading papers" than on any other task. How can we dispassionately question the worth of something to which we have given so much of ourselves?

Writing teachers are liable to feel jealous of teachers in other fields where evaluation seems less vexed. But once sensitized to the problems of evaluation we see that they are everywhere. Even in something as seemingly precise as an "objective" physics exam, it becomes clear that any student's grade is strongly affected by which questions the teacher chooses to ask and how they are worded. The grade is not necessarily a trustworthy measure of how much physics the student knows or how well she can do physics outside an exam setting. And putting aside the question of measuring past learning, what kind of evaluation or response will most increase future learning? The answers are not clear, yet many teachers seem insufficiently perplexed.

I began my wrestling at M.I.T.—trying, in effect, to build a better evaluation mousetrap. (See Chapter 8 and its introduction—which follow next.) Then in Writing Without Teachers I tried to move away from evaluation. There were two paths away from it. First, the most obvious relief from evaluation came from giving no comment or response at all to student writing. That is, I was overwhelmed by the enormous benefits that come from showing students how to use freewriting and journal writing—words that are completely private and never shown to anyone. A relief for the teacher, but also a relief for the students—and as a result this kind of writing tends to give students (and the rest of us) a burst of investment, pleasure, and fluency in writing.

Oddly enough, I also found relief from evaluation in giving students more responses on certain pieces of writing than they usually get. I began to notice how little a student learns from a grade and a short comment from one reader. I got interested in trying to provide my students with an account of what was going on in my mind as I was reading—trying to give as honest and accurate a picture as possible of the effects of their words in my head. And also provide them with other readers' accounts ("movies of readers' minds"), not just mine. Students can give such responses to each other with only a little training. The writer gets much more information about the effectiveness of her writing.

By being able to provide students more responses, I could finesse many of the problems of evaluation by moving from value judgments to empiricism: instead of trying to provide the student with God's true verdict on her essay, I tried to give her at least four reader's accounts of what her words made happen in their heads. Of course some of these "movies" were highly evaluative ("I got madder and madder at what you wrote") but often such judgments contradicted one another. Thus the student was put in a most valuable position—not just having to follow a teacher's suggestions but having to think: having to examine empirical evidence as to what her words *did* to different readers, and then having to make up her own mind about what revision, if any, she wants to make.

In addition, it turns out that there is an enormous wealth of reader responses that are purposely *non*evaluative yet which are usually more helpful than most value judgments. (For example answers to questions like these: "What is the main idea you hear in this piece? What are the main supporting ideas? Which words and phrases stick in your mind? Describe the writer's voice here. What do you want to hear more about?")

Although these attempts to walk away from evaluation were enormously useful (we evaluate more than we need to in teaching), they also heightened my awareness of how ubiquitous and inevitable evaluation is—and at times even desirable.

All these ruminations were then fertilized by nine years' teaching at The Evergreen State College. It turns out that for institutions too—not just for individuals—a wholehearted commitment to teaching often entangles you in a greater and more self-conscious involvement in evaluation. That is, Evergreen's decision to use narrative evaluations instead of grades led to an academic calendar where every term ends with "evaluation week": teaching of *new* material stops, but in many ways the most powerful teaching of the term goes on. Each student writes a self-evaluation, each teacher writes a student evaluation, and the student and teacher sit down to a lengthy individual conference to discuss these two documents in draft form—before they are revised to become the student's official transcript. In short, once you decide to say something more accurate and helpful than "B—" you are stuck trying to find words for what the student actually learned—and how. (Of course this kind of evaluation depends on a curricular experiment to get more student-faculty contact within the same budgetary constraints: Evergreen teachers have fewer students than in most colleges but see more of them and are responsible for more credit.)

My three years studying competence-based education also heightened my sense that there is no way for teachers to get away from the problems of evaluation. Yes, we can separate teaching from *formal* (or "summative") evaluation, but evaluation is inevitable.

The premise of this section, then, is that although there may be many opportunities to evaluate *less* (e.g., it's not obvious why weekly assignments need *grades* rather than just comments), nevertheless we cannot avoid evaluation. Therefore, we better start learning to do it more accurately, fairly, and helpfully than we usually do. Our evaluative behavior in higher education lags way behind our *psychological* knowledge of how people learn and our *disciplinary* knowledge of the nature of what we evaluate—namely, behavior and texts. (Two seminal books here: *Frames of Mind: The Theory of Multiple Intelligences* by Howard Gardner and *Pygmalion in the Classroom: Teacher Expectation and Pupils' Intellectual Development* by Robert Rosenthal and Lenore Jacobson.)

CHAPTER 8

❀❀❀

M.I.T. in the 1960s was an interesting place to begin wrestling with the complexities of evaluation. On the one hand, of course, the institution lives by numbers. The students and faculty take for granted the quantification of everything—not just evaluation but geography: every building is designated by a number rather than a name (and thus every broom closet has a numerical designation which tells its building, floor, and location. Few students could get into M.I.T. without taking grades very seriously indeed.

On the other hand, the Institute seems so secure in its faith in quantification as to be more casual than most other institutions about dispensing with it. M.I.T. continues its practice (begun in the 1960s) of insisting that all freshmen take all courses pass/fail. They persist in this remarkable policy to make freshmen *less* preoccupied with grades. Carrying that principle even further, they continue a remarkable program I was involved with from its birth: the Experimental Study Group. Those freshmen who join it are freed from taking any courses at all. They are simply given a year's credit and left free to spend their time as they wish. They are provided with the use of a lounge where they meet with others in the program, and a few faculty members are "laid on" a certain number of hours a week and tend to conduct some (noncredit) discussion groups. The program is small but does not choose students on the basis of their academic records. The founder, Professor George Valley (physics), believed he could increase the number of future Nobel Prize winners by getting students less concerned with grades and prescribed courses of study.

When I wrote this next essay, then, I was working in a community where people valued quantitative evaluation more than usual, yet they were also more than usually willing to see its limitations. My instinct was pragmatic but I think sound: we probably cannot get away from numbers when we engage in evaluation in an orthodox institution of higher education, but we can at least try to be a bit more sophisticated with our numbers. If we try to be more accurate about what we're measuring and more realistic about the degree of precision that is possible, we can tell a little more of the truth. In doing so, it turns out that we can avoid pretending that a student's whole performance or intelligence can be summed up in one number. After many years, I end up convinced that a scheme such as this is possible and necessary.

❀❀❀

Evaluating Students More Accurately

It's not a question of whether we like evaluation. When a teacher sees student work he almost invariably has an evaluative reaction. Even if he doesn't, the student almost invariably infers one. Even tone of voice and facial expression play a role here. Besides, we couldn't learn without feedback. Therefore, the only real question is what sort of evaluation to have. We decide best if we figure out what evaluation ought to do.

There are two purposes. The first is to provide the audience with an accurate evaluation of the student's performance. If the student or some other justifiable reader gets an inaccurate impression, the evaluation has failed.

The second function of evaluation is to help the student to the condition where he can evaluate his own performance accurately: teacher grades should wither away in importance if not in fact. We haven't fully taught someone to do something or know something unless he can determine on his own whether he has done it or knows it. A student who remains dependent on the teacher's grades for evaluation is defectively taught in a simple, functional sense: he cannot, strictly speaking, do what he was supposedly taught to do because he cannot do it alone; without help, he cannot tell whether he did it right.

We see here that the agenda for grading reflects what seems to be the agenda in many cognitive activities: the organism must learn to make internal and autonomous an activity that originates as interaction with something outside itself.

The best hope for teaching trustworthy self-evaluation is to give a more accurate and explicit message of evaluation than traditional grades contain. Grades can only wither away in importance when they cease to be ambiguous and magical. The present system too often allows the student to feel them as judgments based on hidden criteria, judgments which he cannot understand and has little power over. If he is rewarded he feels he did the right things, but if the reward fails he never knows which step in the rain dance he missed.

Both functions of grading can only be served if we confront the central question: What constitutes good student performance? Other moot issues—Are grades necessary? Do they harm? Should the student see them? Should they be quantitative? How much should they count?—are really ways of avoiding this question.

We can make headway on this question if we begin a catalogue of components of good student performance which teachers actually imply in their grades—the various messages or definitions of student performance that various teachers consciously or unconsciously imply:

- Command of course information.
- Memory.
- Understanding of the central concepts of the course. (A student may do well here without producing a lot of information or seeming to have a good memory.)
- Logical, conceptual intelligence.
- Application of the central concepts of the course to new instances, seeing the concepts from new and creative points of view, seeing new implications. (This capacity does not necessarily imply the earlier ones: it can accompany a bad memory and serious misconceptions.)
- Creativity, imagination, intuitive insight.
- Effectiveness in speaking.
- Effectiveness in writing.
- Effectiveness in thinking: How well does he come to grips with the question or formulate the question behind the question? Does he see to the heart of the real issue and deal with it persuasively? (Needless to say, the distinction between verbal and thought strategy is rough and problematical.)
- Curiosity.
- Permanence of learning.

- Integration of course matter with what he already knows.
- Growth or improvement.
- Potentiality for further development.
- Judgment.
- Diligence, effort.
- Moral trustworthiness.
- Likableness.
- Enjoyment of learning.

There is an easier way to go about categorizing student performance: performance on papers, in laboratories, on examinations; attendance; preparation for class; participation in class; work on time in acceptable form. But these categories beg the question of what good student performance is.

If a teacher scorns some of my earlier entries, let him investigate more fully the grading behavior of some of his colleagues—or his own. He will discover my list more parsimonious than wild. It would not be difficult, for example, to show that even in college some teachers include dress, appearance, and carriage in their grading, and not merely as accidental corollaries of other factors (not to mention gender and race).

In addition to the terrific diversity of components that a grade is likely to imply in the hands of different teachers, the meaning of grades is further complicated by the fact that the same teacher is apt to treat a component differently at different ends of the A-to-F continuum—for example, to allow diligence, memory, or improvement to operate at the lower end of the scale and not at the upper end.

A slightly different affective logic is not uncommon: A and F are for performances causing acute pleasure or pain, a powerful jolt for the teacher one way or the other of surprise, insight, excitement, or anger, disappointment, disgust; B and D are for performances yielding definite satisfaction or disappointment; C is for the affectless middle. Anyone who pretends to be shocked that grades should measure the affective response of the teacher ought to direct his energies instead to what is more problematic: that it is so seldom admitted. What we need are methods either for preventing the activity or for letting it be clearly admitted and explained, thus sharpening the effectiveness of a tool which undoubtedly can be far more perceptive and acute than purely cognitive discrimination.

This partial analysis of messages implied in grades will serve to suggest more theoretical questions: Is the grade a measure of a particular performance or is it a statement about the characteristics of a person; that is, does it mean, "He remembered X quantity of material today," or, "He has a memory of X quality?" The former can be called the only warranted message. But it can also be called evasive.

Also: are grades a measure of past performance or a prediction of future performance? Since inferences about future performance are bound to be made, the operational question is who should properly make them. It can be argued that certainly the teacher should not; it is beyond his province and hence unfair. But it can also be argued that since someone is going to do it, he should, since he knows more about the student and the testing.

Furthermore, there is the question of what the individual student performance is to be measured against. The class? The school? The nation? The student's potential best? Or is there some standard implicit in the subject matter itself?

Needless to say, these questions do not admit of easy answer. But if asked, they admit a few tentative agreements and many shared and articulated disagreements. Unasked, they admit only hidden ambiguity, inaccuracy, and misunderstanding. If this central and difficult question of what is being evaluated can be squarely faced and dealt with, even if not neatly solved, most other issues about grading can be satisfactorily worked out.

The crucial conclusion is obvious: there is no need to have only one factor in a grade. There is no reason why a university, a division, or a department cannot come to agree on a grid of five to ten factors among which any teacher may choose. To illustrate the proposal, here is a grading grid with a conceivable set of factors. I am not proposing them, nor suggesting that the previous catalogue suffices as a list to choose from.

The value of such a system would be in its flexibility. (One of the categories could even be the traditional A-through-F continuum if some teachers felt they could not accept a different system.) Any teacher could use as few or as many factors as he thought proper. Perhaps one teacher thinks the first factor is the

	(weak)		(strong)	
Name: _____			Pass ☐	Fail ☐

	(weak)		(strong)	
1.	☐	☐	☐	Memory of course information
2.	☐	☐	☐	Understanding of central ideas
3.	☐	☐	☐	Imaginative and creative use of subject matter
4.	☐	☐	☐	Effectiveness of writing
5.	☐	☐	☐	Effectiveness of speaking
6.	☐	☐	☐	Conscientiousness, diligence
7.	☐	☐	☐	Improvement over semester

only proper one. Fine. But let him admit it, and also permit his colleagues to communicate what *their* grades mean. There is no reason why a teacher shouldn't use different factors for different courses, or for different students in one course. A student might happen to display a particular quality (or absence of it), such as diligence, and thus be evaluated on it (if the teacher thought it important). Yet it would be wrong for the teacher to evaluate his other students on diligence unless he actually builds in procedures to test it. Otherwise he simply won't know whether most of his students are diligent or not.

Probably most teachers will have two or three factors they feel are crucial, and will evaluate every student on the basis of them: papers and examinations will be designed to test them. Some of these teachers will feel it is wrong ever to check any other categories. Others will feel it is right to use additional categories when appropriate to a particular student. Some teachers, however, will not call any factors indispensable, but will merely use whichever seem most appropriate to each student's relationship to the particular subject matter. In short, the system's flexibility would allow evaluation to be more closely functional with the measuring instrument (the teacher and his course material) and the things measured (the individual student performance). To the degree that evaluation departs from those two things it is false and untrustworthy.

Notice that there would be no need to assume that all factors utilized had equal weight. The teacher will have his idea of what the relative importance of each should be, but why should he force this judgment upon readers of his grades? If he decides the student should fail, his reasons are likely to be clear, certainly more clear than with conventional grades. And if the student passes, who cares (in this context) whether the teacher thinks creativity is more important than memory or the other way around? The whole point of this system is to let the teacher provide substantive information and allow interpreters to assign their own values.

But how could a department, much less a university, ever come to agree on a slate of five to ten factors? Again a solution suggests itself if we ask the central question, namely, should the slate be the factors teachers *do* use or the ones they *should* use?

The two principles can productively interact. First, an experimental semester. A committee would poll its colleagues and its ingenuity to make an exhaustive list of factors that actually are implied by teachers. This list, phrased concisely, could fit on one sheet of paper. For the experimental semester, teachers would use this long list for grading, with complete freedom to use as few or as many factors as seemed right. But the object would be for everyone to try to feel out all the factors and see which ones seemed valid and meaningful—to try out reality in terms of various schemes for conceptualizing it. (The process would probably suggest new categories or groupings which could be added.) Conventional grades might be given that term for official use.

On the basis of this experiment, a faculty could decide on a list of less than ten. A particularly empirical-minded community might be content simply to subject the results to factor-analysis to see which were most used and where the cut-off fell most naturally. But probably it would be better to start with the results simply as evidence, and on the basis of this and of everyone's experience in trying out categories, consciously debate and decide which factors ought to be used. Ingenious rephrasings and judicious amalgamations of categories would be appropriate in this process. The goal is to achieve the most economical set of terms for the richest disagreement. The debate would be heated, but it is the sort of debate that enlightens. It would force greater communication between disciplines and improve the spirit of teaching.

Grading during the experimental semester would be a bit more trouble, though someone would be sure to call down a shower of soft money for the pains. But the new system that emerged would be less trouble than the present one. It is the present system's indeterminacy and ambiguity that cause agony and long periods of indecision in figuring out a grade. Surely it would be less trouble, and even quicker with practice, to make clearly differentiated and defined judgments than endure the present headache of always having to subtract apples from pears to arrive at one quantitative result. Also it would suffice in the new system to have only three or four points on the continuum for each factor, instead of the conventional five of A through E (or twelve, counting pluses and minuses).

Nor is the plan unworkable. We can simply ask the defenders of traditional grades why there is any necessity for summing up student performance on one scale so that the student body can be ranked quantitatively along one dimension. Even Selective Service no longer cares. Is there any reason why universities must satisfy the conditioned desires of various outside groups—employers, government agencies, and other universities—to know where a student ranks along one dimension? Particularly when that one dimension is specious? Under the new model, on the other hand, the university would be able to satisfy the more defensible desires of such organizations—the desire to know the strengths and weaknesses of a student's academic performance. The interpreter would have to make up his own mind about which qualities he is looking for. And if he is looking for some factor which the teacher didn't use, perhaps creativity or diligence, that would be a far better state of affairs than the present one in which conventional grades are used and the interpreter is likely to infer erroneously that creativity or diligence is measured. Perhaps the system would cause a bit more trouble to admissions committees of graduate departments, but every teacher knows, because of the growing need for letters of recommendation, that there is little real trust in the meaning of present grades and class rankings. (Letters of recommendation are often vague and difficult to assess. The discriminations that would turn up on the proposed system are just the sort needed in such letters.)

On the other hand, we can ask the attackers of traditional grades whether it would really be so bad to make quantitative discriminations between students with respect to one factor or another, so long as the process does not involve the mistake of summing up a student's whole performance on one scale and pretending you can measure all student performances on it. And if a student's whole performance is not summed up in one quantity, he is much less liable, indeed less able, to make the mistake of grounding his sense of worth in the teacher's evaluation. The evils ascribed to quantification would be minimized. "Hey! What did Jones give you in Nineteenth Century?" The question becomes considerably more complex. It could no longer be shouted on the run. A grade would be less often confused with a gift.

Even the registrar could handle this system. A student's four-year career could still fit on a single sheet of paper—thirty-two or forty little checked grids and a key. (All kinds of complex computations could be made on the basis of the various factors checked. Most of the results would be untrustworthy, but far less so than the computations on the basis of present grades.)

Some will say the system might work in the case of a small class where the teacher knows the student well, but not otherwise. But consider the opposite conditions: a university which asks a graduate student to determine an unknown student's grade on the basis of only one paper and one examination. It is in just such cases that the traditional system is most unsatisfactory and the proposed one most necessary. The less data there are for making an evaluation and the more crude the instrument, the more necessary it is that the factors being evaluated be precisely defined (even if it means checking only one box).

A young, inexperienced graduate student is likely to be best at teaching and worst at evaluating. Good evaluation most requires experience and perspective and these are what the graduate student is apt to lack. On the other hand, the senior professor is likely to be best at evaluation and—at times, unfortunately—worst at teaching. Thus the profound badness of some bad courses: everyone is awarded his worst role.

I hear a mathematics teacher saying, "Why all these categories? I teach mathematics! The grades I give are the sum of clear and unambiguous tests on mathematics!" Such a teacher could easily use the one category that fits best, perhaps "understanding of central concepts" or "effectiveness on examinations." But one could fairly say to him that if he cannot distinguish between the different cognitive or heuristic ingredients of his examinations, he proves he is no teacher of mathematics, however skillful he may be at computing correct answers.

I hear a tough talker saying, "I refuse to let my university prostitute itself by officially sanctioning 'effort' as a meaningful educational category for college students!" But the important point here is that the present system does just what he objects to. It gives official sanction to whatever category blows across the fancy of every teacher, without the slightest need to make it conscious or articulate, much less justify it. Thus the proposed model should really offend not so much the tough as the tender—who celebrates the present system because it allows total freedom and total diversity of categories. For the proposal does indeed limit freedom and diversity, but only to bring them within the limits of communicability. Celebrating the flexibility of the present grading system is like celebrating the flexibility of a radically impoverished language, such as a very limited slang: it feels perfect because it means every nuance you intend—but only to you, not to your audience.

It will be objected finally, and most damningly, that what I propose as an experiment is really a regression. The troops in the vanguard are conquering under the banner of Less Grading—note all the pass-fail experiments in progress—and here I come proposing in effect More Grading. But this brings us back to the functions of grading. I certainly want to be up front with the swingers, but I would try to clarify the inscription on the banner: Less Grading is only valid if it really signifies the gradual transfer of effective evaluation from the teacher to the student. Pass-fail systems can potentially serve as a giant step in that direction; no grading, perhaps even more so. But self-evaluation is not easy, and unless it can be assured that teachers will talk regularly with all their students and comment copiously on their papers, at least in a student's first year or two, it seems important to provide models and processes to help students learn to evaluate their work accurately.

This proposal for grading might lead some colleges or universities to other experiments.* But I would leave the emphasis not on specific details or possible variations but rather on the generative process itself—a faculty confronting the three problems in grading: (1) What constitutes good student performance? (2) How do you communicate evaluation? (3) How do you produce in the student the ability to evaluate his own work? If a faculty will sit down together to this task in good faith and with the sense that a solution is actually possible, then whatever plan it produces should be right for it. In addition, of course, the process will profoundly renew the spirit of the university as an institution for teaching.

---

* First, a faculty which takes majoring particularly seriously and which is confident of its stature in the academic world might adopt the following plan: each department or division makes its own grading grid; the student receives the results of such grading for every course he takes, but his permanent record retains these results only for courses in his major or division; all other courses are either blank or pass/fail.

Second, students might be asked to evaluate their own performances for the last two or three years of college. Teacher evaluation in terms of clearly defined factors would prepare them to do this responsibly and accurately.

Third, perhaps students should play an important role in determining what categories should be used in grading.

Fourth, sustained attention to the question of what is good performance will make many teachers wonder about the validity of "pass" and "fail" as categories: whether or not they are substantively meaningful once there is more than one dimension to the grade. Some colleges with faith in the worth of their instruction and their students will dispense with these categories.

Fifth, the system might serve for some colleges with small classes as a transition to the use of only written—totally nonquantitative—grading.

CHAPTER 9

❀❀❀

In 1975 I was invited by the Danforth Foundation to apply for a "mini-grant" of $20,000 for faculty development. I met with a small group of colleagues and we started with the premise that there was no useful way to spend any amount of money if it involved meetings. We came up with a plan for one-to-one work among ourselves: one faculty member each quarter would be freed from teaching to be a "Danforth Visitor" and spend each week visiting a faculty member who had volunteered to be visited. The visitor became a kind of fulltime companion or buddy to a colleague for a week of teaching, conferences, and program-meetings.

By asking for volunteers we got strong teachers requesting to be visited, so there was never any sense that the program was remedial. It was also crucial to the design that the visitor should be simply another fulltime faculty member, not a professional in faculty development or counseling—nor a part of the administration. Since the visitor had to be an ally of the teacher visited, we insisted that the vistor's perceptions could never be allowed to contribute to deliberations on rehiring. (Except by express permission of the teacher visited. Rehiring at three-year intervals was the only important decision because there are no ranks or tenure at Evergreen and salary is fixed and public, based on years of experience.)

In most subsequent years the college has continued to underwrite this collaborative peer evaluation program. It has been endorsed by the faculty, the administration, and the faculty union. Each year more people volunteer than can be accommodated.

During the first year of our experiment, we three visitors took extensive notes and wrote up our experiences and reflections in a long manuscript published only locally by the college. What follows are three excerpts from what I wrote in that manuscript.

Section 9A, *Visiting Pete Sinclair*, consists of some long excerpts from what I wrote during the first or second week of that first quarter of the program. Pete Sinclair was a colleague in literature. I include some of his responses.

Section 9B, *On Being Visited*, is a portion of what I wrote in response to being visited winter quarter for a week by the second visitor, Margaret Gribskov, a colleague from journalism and education.

Section 9C, *Contraries in Responding*, was written after the experiment was completed as I stood back and tried to reflect on the nature of the different kinds of feedback I gave and could have given.

Collaborative Peer Evaluation by Faculty

9A   Visiting Pete Sinclair

In what follows, I will describe how my visits with one colleague worked for each of us. I was the first visitor, and I will simply speak in the first person about my own experiences. Most of what I say will apply to most subsequent visitors as well, although the personality of the individual visitor created enormous stylistic differences. There have been some structural variations, too; in one experiment, three people were visited over a period of three weeks, rather than one person per week.

Well before the week of visitation, I asked the faculty members whom I was to visit to write informally about what they wanted to work on, the parts of their teaching that pleased or did not please them, the changes that they wanted to produce in students through their teaching, and, more personally, the satisfactions and dissatisfactions that came to them from teaching. I also invited stories about good and bad moments not only as teacher but also as student.

I began each week with a long conversation with the person. At first, I would feel somewhat scared in the middle of this conversation. The person was talking to me so personally, so openly. It was interesting and useful. But was I prying too much? After a few of these conversations, however, I began to realize that I was not pushing people at all. If anything, I was too timid. Instead, it was they who were jumping at the opportunity to talk about teaching on a personal level.

I allowed these long, loose conversations to structure themselves around the concerns of the person to whom I was talking. But I did listen for two things. First, I listened for statements of goals and problems so that I could see what I was being invited to do and the kind of permission that I was being given. I wanted to be saying, in effect, "You set the agenda for my visits and feedback. I will give you only the kind of feedback that you desire. You are the boss." But sometimes it is difficult for teachers to know their own goals. I believe that we sometimes pursue goals unconsciously, and I don't want to prevent intuitive steering. Sometimes after visiting a person's classes, I wanted to bring up a matter that I had not been "given permission" to talk about. Sometimes, I did bring it up, because I sensed that the person would not mind. Sometimes, I asked the person, "Can I bring up something that you didn't ask me to talk about?" Occasionally, I didn't bring it up at all. This, I think, is the trickiest issue of the whole design: the person who is being visited ought to be in charge of setting the agenda, but the visitor should also be able to use perceptions that are not already on that agenda. Theoretically, this is an intractable problem. In practice, however, we seemed to achieve sufficient trust and to exercise sufficient tact and intuition to negotiate these shoals.

The second thing I looked for in these initial conversations was memorabilia, anecdotes, and portraits from the person's memory of teaching and of being a student. I wanted to hear about good moments and bad ones, interesting personalities who seemed important, incidents that somehow stuck in the mind. This was a powerful way for people to find out more about their real goals, not just their professional goals. People often wandered into insights as they told me incidents that somehow stayed in their minds through the years. Later on in the week, I would find myself instinctively drawn toward describing the person's present action in terms of these past stories: "You handled that situation just like you said _____ used to do" or "You refused to give that student just what you said you wished that _____ had given you." These conversations opened important doors. Indeed, the writing might have been even more useful if it had followed the conversations rather than preceded them.

Next, I would observe. That is, I would be a kind of companion for a good part of the week's activities: usually a couple of two- to three-hour seminars (our staple here), a lecture or class, an individual conference or two, and probably also the two- to three-hour faculty seminar, where the small faculty team discussed the week's book for their own edification.

Before the final, long conversation at the end of the week (or
the beginning of the next), where I brought together my most
important perceptions and made my recommendations, if I had
any, I usually sat down a couple of times to play back my perceptions of what had happened in a seminar, class, or conference.

I took extensive notes during the initial conversation and subsequent observations. At first, I wanted only to aid my memory—
and perhaps also to cover my nervousness—but it turned out to
make the process one of mirroring what happened—both in the
room and in me—not one of reaching conclusions. Also, I found
that I had more to say than if I sat back to observe and wait for
wise insights. When I left the note-taking machine on full throttle, perceptions, reactions, nuances of feeling, and even metaphors readily came to mind. In a way, I was freewriting, although I was also leaving out most of the syntax. Certainly I
was free-reacting. In the end, I concluded that this had been the
most important part of my approach. It kept me from sitting
back and watching, diagnosing, prescribing: "Let's see. These
seem to be the problems. Here is my advice. "Instead, I played
back my perceptions and reactions in the mixed form in which
they had occurred, which enabled me to give what I have come
from my teaching of writing to think of· as the most valuable
feedback of all: movies of the mind of the observer.

When the person being visited gave his or her permission, I
also used videotape or audiotape to record the sessions that I
observed. I found that the video was not worth the time, trouble,
or expense, especially when we could learn very nearly as much
from a small cassette tape recorder with built-in mike. However,
even when the electronic process was not a bother, I found it no
more than a supplement, certainly not a mainstay of the process.
I speak, of course, as one unskilled in media technology, but
most of my colleagues who have been visitors have reached a
similar conclusion.

What follows are a couple of passages from my extensive notes.
I have turned them into prose fairly similar to what I would
actually say when I was playing back the notes for the person
whom I had visited. For the most part, I replay them without

censoring. I found that by making them as an almost impersonal, mechanical readout of my notes—the moment-by-moment go-ing-on in my mind—my remarks did not seem like implacable judgments or verdicts even if they were negative.

From My Interview with Pete Sinclair, My First Week of Visiting

Pete is in his early forties. Balding in front, dark hair falls straight from the rest of his head almost to his shoulders. He is an impressively handsome man with confident bearing. He is originally from—where? His undergraduate work, in English, was at Dartmouth and the University of Wyoming. He is finish-ing his Ph.D. in Chaucer at the University of Washington. He taught at the University of Wyoming. He achieved eminence as a mountaineer and rescuer of mountaineers. He is an Evergreen veteran who was a member of the original planning faculty. [I leave uncorrected here some of my grosser errors of fact, as a warning to the reader; in fact, Pete had long finished his Ph.D. and had not been a member of the planning faculty.]

He is teaching in a coordinated study program called "From Homer to Hemingway: The Professor's Favorites." Three faculty members, running all year. Mostly classic literary texts. More use of lectures than in past Evergreen programs. An "experi-ment" for being like a traditional great-books course.

We meet in my office. I wasn't sure that this was a good idea. I'm afraid that I will seem like a shrink. I think Pete said that we would be disturbed if we met in his office—lots of students were liable to knock on his door.

He had done scarcely any writing for me in response to my initial questionnaire. I knew that mine had been a kind of over-kill document, but I did love the questions very much. I was disappointed and, I think, a bit resentful that he had not writ-ten. He had just scrawled two pages—two different beginnings to a response. He was unapologetic. He said something like, "Peter, I didn't really have time to do this. It didn't seem worth it. I just thought we would do better talking." "Sure," I said. But it brought up feelings that I often have as a teacher: on the one hand, annoyance ("I gave an assignment and he didn't do it") and, on the other, foreboding ("This is never going to work; I can't make anything happen; I have no control").

These feelings were complicated by the fact that I was somewhat intimidated by him. An original Evergreener from the first planning year, he predates me by two years. More than that, however, he is very confident—even arrogant—in his manner. He seems always to have everything under control—in a place where I find control virtually impossible to achieve. He always seems successful and satisfied with how things are going in his teaching and in his program. That seems unfair and it annoys me. However, my feelings were not so much those of annoyance as of jealousy, I was to realize over the two weeks.

I don't want to overstate these negative feelings. I already counted him as a good friend, if not an intimate one; I think he would have said the same of me. We trusted each other. We liked to talk about issues related to Evergreen, literature, Chaucer, and writing. We enjoyed hearing each other's views, and we respected them.

Thus, my reply was something on the order of "Sure, let's just talk." That is what we did—for three hours. By the end of that talk, I was confident that this was not just a feasible, useful, survivable thing to do but that it was also very exciting.

He did most of the talking. I asked questions, though I did throw in a few of my own thoughts and reactions, partly for the fun of it, partly to prevent the situation from seeming psychiatric or clinical.

I asked if he minded my taking notes. I experienced it as very pushy of me to take notes while I was talking to someone. After a few weeks, I realized that in almost every case the person did not mind at all. In fact, many were flattered to be heeded so closely.

Pete said that the main thing he wanted out of the project was to learn how to lecture better. That was his agenda for the year. He had planned and set up his program with that in mind. He felt confident about his handling of seminars.

I asked him about the outcomes that he has in mind for students. He says he doesn't think too much about what he wants students to get. He is used to students who do not understand him. He hopes that they will come back later in the term—even

later in life—and tell him that they have finally understood what
he was driving at. Sometimes this has happened, he said.

He does not know why he is so often not understood. He
thinks it may be related to his approach to the humanities. His
approach: a continual assault on impossible-to-answer deep
questions.

How does he get satisfaction? When he comes up with a brilliant insight while he is talking to students. He says that his best
thinking occurs in this kind of interaction.

He feels that his lectures are too tight, that he is overprepared.
He is not able to let his mind just roll. His goal is to learn to have
while lecturing the kind of insight experience that he already has
in conversation or discussion with students. He can also get it
while writing, but not while lecturing. "I assume they're getting
something good if I'm having good thoughts."

He says that at the beginning of a course or program, students
tend to be afraid of him. They think he's mean, forbidding. By
the end of the quarter, this is gone; students are no longer afraid.
He says he's not sure what to think of this. Perhaps it's a good
thing; perhaps it makes them think; it certainly gets their attention. But his immediate feeling is that it is not a good thing:
they seem to worry more about him than about the book, which
is where he wants their energy to go, and it prevents honesty and
openness in their interaction with him.

I thought to myself at the time that he is, indeed, somewhat
intimidating. [I reflect on this now as I transcribe my notes. He
says things with a kind of aggressive confidence that he is correct, and he takes a kind of pleasure, I can see, in saying things
in a somewhat perplexing or enigmatic way. He is looking for
truth, but he feels that truth can often take hidden, oracular,
paradoxical, or parable-like forms. He is not a medievalist for
nothing.]

He doesn't know what makes good things happen in class. He
says he doesn't care. He distrusts analysis. He is an interesting
case of a deeply committed humanist who has become very interested in the uses that he can make of some aspects of social
science (psychoanalysis, dream analysis) but who retains a deep
conviction that they are ancillary to "real stories"—humanities

and literature. I would say now that he loves analysis but distrusts it deeply.

I ask him about his important teachers. When he walked in, he said that he had come to a breakthrough as a result of thinking about who his most important teachers were, and he talked about it in his writing. The fact that it has taken thirty or forty-five minutes to get to this matter in the interview is, I suspect, a result of my timidity. When he told me at the outset that he had been thinking about his teachers, I could have said, "Great, tell me about them." But perhaps because I thought it would lead to depth—perhaps because I thought it might be prying—I tiptoed up to it.

[These past teachers of his provided the meat of the interview. My notes are not very good because there was so much—too much—to write down. We probably spent about two hours on this subject. What follows are the sketchiest of notations.]

The first teacher he mentioned was John Senior. "Super prof." Catholic convert. French symbolist. A kind of preacher. At one point, Peter considered converting. "St. Thomas and I are wrong," Senior once said. Pete quotes this to illustrate the utter seriousness with which Senior takes his own pondering. Looking back, Peter concludes that Senior was indeed wrong; Pete was suspious at the time, but he loved it.

John Matheson. Couldn't lecture. Socratic. The novel. Not comfortable in interchange. Classes often uncomfortable. But he was witty. He worked you over. You paid for your insights. The people sitting around him always felt stupid. Yet people didn't resent it. Eclectic. "I really appreciated him."

Glyn Thomas. A romantic. Genius at getting students to express their thoughts. "Godlike Glyn." Could make people feel competent. Could take a student's inane comment and follow it, play with it until it yielded important insight. I asked how Thomas did this—very eager to know for selfish reasons. [It was, by the way, simply pleasurable—fascinating—to hear someone talk openly about important people in his past. He was simply rambling, but there was great power and resonance and "voice" in what he said.] Thomas simply had faith that the insight was there to be found if one worked at finding it. He stayed with the student and the comment until it yielded its insight. He would hold the floor open for this student—not let the other students come in, and keep pushing and asking. Thomas made Pete change from engineering to philosophy.

What did these people have in common? Pete had realized that they had something in common when he was writing in response to my questionnaire, but he wasn't sure how to pin it down. It was a very interesting period of the interview while he searched for words and emphases.

These people were unusually forthright. They were always the most learned people around. They simply knew a lot. That is why Pete wanted to work with Andrew Hanfman this year: perhaps the most learned, bookish person on the Evergreen faculty.

But while they are bookish and have read a lot, *learned* means much more than merely *dogged* here. Pete is not talking about a bland man who is a walking encyclopedia. The people he named all have some quality of personality or character that shows through the learning—or that the learning is a vehicle for. They are wide-ranging in their learning, and they stick their necks out; they do not specialize in one narrow field where they are safe from attack.

Yet he still keeps coming back to the word *learned*. And the learning always has an important element of background learning, classical underpinning—something going back, something underneath the person's current learning. Roots.

They are all good persons. Virtuous. He almost wants to use the word saintly. He tells me the story of the seemingly arrogant, even negative, Stein, who spent a couple of days hunting down a grad student who had cracked up while preparing for oral exams.

Something here seems important, though I couldn't put my finger on it. There is great force in Pete's talk of the virtue in these men. I sometimes perceive Pete as cynical. He has a characteristic, cynical laugh that seems to say, "Suckers always finish last." He sometimes talks about students as if they mean nothing to him. I am not sure what to make of all this.

He openly characterized his meditation on past teachers as an important new revelation for him. Therefore, I feel comfortable in asking straight out how it will affect his teaching in the future. He is very blunt. He says that he has discovered a simple fact. The people whom he admired are all learned. If he wants to feel okay about himself, he has to be learned. He does not do enough reading. He has lots of excuses for not doing enough reading in the past few years, but he admits that they are all hollow. He has to make some changes. He has to get out of Evergreen politicking. He has to sell his sailboat and use the money to build a little study detached from his house. Pay someone to build it instead of using his own time to build it. He has been putting all his time and money into the sailboat.

But neither can he give up sailing altogether. He can go with others; crew with McCann. He has to have adventure, and *adventure* for him is a more serious word than for most of us. He has always had adventure, either in climbing or sailing. He was a serious miler for six years. He became somewhat famous as a climber and rescuer. He gets the experience of peace from such pursuits, but he thinks of the word *peace* in a special sense, since he told me that it is always accompanied by the experience of fear. Can't have peace without fear. "If you have one real strong objective fear, all the phony ones fall away." He talked about his early childhood and his relation to fear. Something about his interest in the "heroic age," where courage and personality have a premium. No way to fake it. He feels a conflict between his interest in being a scholar and his interest in being an adventurer. But I wonder. It seems that all the talk about fear, adventure, and peace is a metaphor for the quality that he is trying to articulate about those special teachers. All of them seem to have been the kind of scholar who climbs a vertical rock with only ropes and pitons.

From Pete Sinclair's Seminar, One Week Later

Large seminar room. Big pile of fish nets on one side of room. Room must have been used by Pete last year in his program about boats and fishing in the Northwest. Pete and students sitting around. It is not quite 9 A.M. when I come in.

"This is always the worst time. The first meeting," Pete mutters to nobody in particular, rubbing his face in his hands. He engages in some talk with me—sitting across the room from him—

about Evergreen history. A kind of conversation just between the two of us, although others are present. Makes me embarrassed, though I enjoy the sense of friendship and closeness implied in the mutual reminiscing.

At 9:10 he closes the door. Threatens to lock it so that late-comers will not be able to get in. I am struck at the guts of his procedure, but in the end, perhaps because it is the first day, he does not actually lock it.

He plays the "name game": the student on his left tells his or her name, second student tells his or her name and repeats the first student's name, third student tells name and repeats first two, and so on. The list gets harder to repeat as it gets longer. I had never seen this before. Seemed very effective. All the re-peating really forces students to remember names. However, I was looking on in a detached way, just sitting there taking notes; I had not been introduced. When it got one away from me, I suddenly realized that they might expect me to play, and that I hadn't been concentrating. Panic. I did have to play. I limped through it, having to ask about half the names. I felt silly.

There were about twenty people. Pete looks at the list of stu-dents he is supposed to have; a few announcements or some-thing to adjust role. Some uncertainty, this first class, whether students are in the right seminar—there are three teachers in the program. Typical first-day business details.

I am not sure what to make of the fact that he does not intro-duce me. Makes me a bit nervous. But I am not prepared to do anything about it. I keep wondering who the students think I am. I am taking far more notes than anyone. What do they think I am doing?

Student starts to ask Pete a question about his lecture of pre-vious day. He cuts her off. "Don't ask about lectures in these sem-inars. If you have questions, bring them up in the question period at the end of the lecture or at the next lecture. Seminars aren't for that."

This leads him to describe the function of the seminars. "These are *your* time," he says. "Lectures are *our* time." Of course, this does not mean that he isn't committed or interested. Besides, he says, seminar is where he gets to see them perform. This is what he needs in order to evaluate them. It's the only way he can see how they think. It's a chance for them to stand up and be counted. I am taken aback by this approach. It would make me nervous if I were a student.

Nevertheless, he sets out the structure for what will happen. It is their time, but he will decide and determine what will happen. For the first hour, he says, he will be almost entirely quiet. If a silence lasts longer than five minutes, he may say something. One senses that he can hold out that long.

For the second hour, he will ask them to do some writing. It will be personal writing, he says. "If you like what you write, there will be an opportunity for you to volunteer to read it. If you don't like it, you don't have to." Seems straightforward and open in a blunt, friendly way. Then a stinger at the end: "If you are all dull people, the procedure won't work."

I note a slight, ironic smile. Some of it seems directed at me: he and I know each other and can share the irony of what he is about—a kind of openness at being closed, obviously keeping his cards close to his chest. He is just the opposite of me. I want to be seen as an open, nice guy—someone you could never get mad at or hold anything against. I'm struck by Pete's willingness to be inscrutable and scary and the object of anger.

Somehow he manages to begin business by just shutting up and waiting. He had made it clear that what they are supposed to be discussing in seminar is the book. The books are *The Odyssey* and Slocum's book about sailing around the world. Girl brings up a reaction. Rather brave of her to open things. Pete asks her to find a passage in the book that made her have the reaction she just described. I think of this as hard on the person who was brave enough to start the ball rolling, but in fact the way in which he asks her to find a passage is friendly, gentle, fatherly. Conveying both his respect for her as one who dared to start things off and respect for her as an individual: "Yes, I know you weren't expecting me to pounce on you for this task, and it's hard, and you may not be able to find a passage right off [hers was the sort of comment for which it would have been hard to find a passage], but I am sure that you can find it, and I am going to stick with you until you do."

[I ask myself in my notes whether he is being gentler with her than he would be if I were not there. However, as I was writing that, I realized that my comment revealed an assumption on my part that he was mean.]

She takes a long time looking for a passage. Silent. She can't find one. Gets flustered. Tries to give up, to pass. He says, "Wait, try to think for a second: When did you first think the thought that you shared with us?"

Then Pete picks up his book and starts looking through it. Book up in front of his face. Long silence while he looks. I am struck by how this stops all business and makes looking for a passage in the text—in the most concrete physical sense—a central activity for the class. I wonder whether he is doing this consciously, or whether he is only trying to take up time so the girl can stop being flustered and find a passage. [I'm being like the students, always seeing ulterior motive in any random action of an authority person. Probably he was simply trying to find a passage himself.]

The girl, trying to give up: "Oh, I don't know. Someone else say something, please." She doesn't say just that she can't find a passage but that she doesn't know whether her remark makes any sense at all. I note that Pete resists what she's trying to do: he insists on taking her remark seriously. I note that he also could be seen as rewarding the first speaker by taking her very seriously. If so, he succeeds: this girl, and even the thrust of her remark, remain one of the main focuses for the whole three-hour period.

I am struck when Pete closes his eyes at one point in the conversation. Powerful, in a way. He is pursuing some thought in his own head while conversation goes on. Assertive of him. Of course, my unspoken assumption is that the teacher is supposed to follow everything closely. It was disdainful of him to do what he did. I didn't think it was sinful, however. Just intriguing.

From Pete Sinclair's Lecture, Two Weeks Later

"At what point did Penelope know him?" Pause. A student answers from the audience. Wasn't sure whether Pete really wanted someone to answer his question, but it felt good to have someone answer. Establishes a connection between speaker and audience for me.

"She gets gifts. That's her timid action," says Pete. I don't understand at all.

I am moved to reflect on the structure of Pete's lecture: "And then, and then, and then, and then." He's going through the *Odyssey* narrative. But I don't understand why. The effect is to keep us on a string. I look at the students, and I think that they want to get out.

"The focus of the book is on her bed. The suitors, Telemachus, Odysseus." This is the sort of point that I have been missing. I feel energy.

The story is finally over, the *and thens*. "One way of saying it is that there are two levels. She is operating on the conscious and the preconscious levels." At this point he has a different voice. He is looking at them. Until now, he has been talking to the book and to his notes. Only now does he start talking to us.

"That is all I have to say." No summing up, no perspective. That disappoints me. I see now that his last sentence—"He rules the kingdom and house, she rules him"—was the last word of the entire lecture. I feel the brevity as unsatisfying and even hostile to us. Not clear to me what he's saying about the nuclear family. Not clear what he meant by the two examples from the text that he just read. Especially not clear what all those passages from the text early in his lecture had to do with this conclusion.

Finally, he says in effect, here are a few things left over. Ends with a dribble. I feel let down. I sense hostility in his refusal to be completely clear, to spell out what he has to say.

"I believe that Homer has his hands on something basic—that we might go down the tubes like other civilizations, but Homer has something to tell us to cure our problems." [Not sure that these are Pete's actual words.] This could be his main point. I want it to be—it would be satisfying—and perhaps he wants it to be, but it's not, which makes me mad. He's keeping us on a string, refusing to give.

He asks for questions. The first have nothing to do with what he has been saying. I take this as a sign that I was not alone in failing to understand what he was saying.

"Why did he kill the suitors?" someone asks. Pete gives a very witty answer. Right on the spot. Sums up a lot of issues in the book. Example of the depth and wittiness of his mind. Exactly what I felt was lacking in the lecture. Rich and fat and lovely. Element of surprise. Excellent timing. The lecture was long, a bit disappointing, and had no timing or else bad timing.

Kids keep calling you "Pete" in what feels like a familiar way. Trying to be your buddy. It makes me suspicious.

He gets warmed up and talks with more power as he answers questions, talks to the audience, makes real connections, produces quick, off-the-cuff trains of thought that are not backed up with citations from the text. Nevertheless, they have real power and impact. Everyone hears them, considers them, is forced to see the text in terms of them.

Someone disagrees with his characterization of the maids as unjust. He thinks for a moment and says that the *imagery* used for the maids implies that they were unjust, and he quotes some of the imagery from memory. I am impressed. When he is pushed, he comes up with evidence straight from the text instead of repeating his assertion with macho assurance. [Sometimes I sense a macho stance that I don't like.]

He enjoys talking with people—not a lecture. The repartee, the wit, the need for a quick answer—it is a kind of contest; that is what he loves. The question is how to get some of that into a lecture.

Pete Sinclair's Written Reflections to Me, Three Months Later

Dear Peter,

I'm going to resist your social scientific impulses by writing a letter that gives you conclusions instead of data. I really don't believe that a process for helping teachers to learn how to teach can be developed that will be independent of the personalities of the teachers involved. However, I do think that your effort to find such a process is worthwhile.

I have learned more about teaching this quarter than in any other quarter except for my very first. For years, I have been hoping to learn how to lecture. I can conduct a class, and can write a good paper and deliver it—that is, I can make a speech—but I cannot do that in-between thing called the college lecture. I think I will learn how to do it by the end of the year. Right now, I'm hitting about every other one.

It has been rough. For one thing, it takes nothing less than an act of courage to follow Andrew every week. I don't know what would have happened if I hadn't had your help. I suppose I would have come up with something, but right now all I can imagine is a total, humiliating disaster. So you see, I have made a big thing out of this—why?

I was twenty-eight years old when I decided to become a teacher. One thing that I learned from your question about teachers who had been role models was that I had liked several teachers and that I had liked them as a class. They were all powerful men, and their power was knowledge. They had very little power over other men and sometimes even less over students, but they seemed to be in command of their minds. Only now do I see it this way. When I answered the question in October, I said that they were all scholars. This has been an extremely important insight for me. When I am teaching a class or a seminar, I only have to worry about my students' minds. I have always been able to read other people's minds, for psychological reasons that are well known to me. For a class, I have predetermined the intellectual content, but the seminar is the students' ball game, and I just referee. In the case of the delivered paper or speech, the intellectual content is established early on, and most of my energy is rhetorical. (It takes me about eighteen hours to prepare a speech.) So why was I not able to lecture? Because I did not believe in my personal authority. A good lecture reveals a good mind working over a body of material; it reveals the lecturer's mastery of the material. Some good lectures are dramatic performances, but that isn't my style. I have always felt that I didn't know enough, hadn't mastered anything. I know that is true of everybody, but somehow it doesn't make any difference.

Now, you would like to know how you helped me to find this out. First, we both have to admit that you couldn't have helped me if I had not wanted to be helped. If we had been interested in establishing a classification of teaching styles with me as one type, I would not have learned much. I had to admit to having a problem. In fact, that's all that I did do. In September, I probably would have said that the reason why I was not a very good lecturer was that I hadn't had much practice. That was enough, because it implied that I had to do something other than what I had been doing.

Your feedback had two parts: you told me what I said, and you told me how you were feeling. Both of those were crucial. I often discarded your account of why you were feeling what you were feeling, but even so, it was useful. I also ignored most of your suggestions about how to do this differently. Let me give you an example. You said that first you felt stimulated by something that I promised to talk about, then you felt confused because I didn't make clear how what I was saying related to that promise, and finally you were irritated that I did not deliver the goods. You suggested that I repeat my main point several times and that I allow my voice to emphasize the critical points. Two lectures later, I found myself writing four issues critical to my argument on the blackboard and erasing them one by one as I raised them. Repetition by sight is at least as effective as repetition by sound, and it doesn't seem like repetition. When you erase something, the audience involuntarily puts it back in their minds, which is a pretty effective way of getting them to do the emphasizing. Incidentally, this just happened; I didn't plan it ahead of time. Andrew and some students said some nice things about that lecture.

The trick to discovering a psychological pattern is to assume that what is done involuntarily is done deliberately and then to ask why. You told me what I did—both what I said and the effect that it produced in you—and that was all I needed to hear to understand why I did not want to lecture well. In a way, I didn't want to be heard and understood, in case it turned out that I didn't have as good a grasp of the subject as I thought I should. In fact, I usually do have a pretty good grasp of the subject, and this is often revealed in the question period after the lecture. In other words, what your honest and critical feedback proved to me was that I was doing a little trick to conceal myself and that the trick wasn't working.

One final and absolutely essential point. It was very important that, through various conversations and from watching you teach, I had learned to respect you. First of all, I had to feel that I couldn't trick you. More importantly, I couldn't have figured all this out if I hadn't thought that I could do better. This is easier if you also think that I can do better. I believed that you believed that I could do better when you told me honestly what I was not doing well. Thanks.

Pete Sinclair

Pete Sinclair's Response to My Write-Up of My Visits, One Year Later

Peter,

I've had a hard time buckling down to this, because I haven't been able to figure out what to do with two facts: on the one hand, your subjective feedback method worked for me; on the other hand, I don't trust it. To put it another way, for more than a month I have been asking myself, "How can it not matter that Peter made so many mistakes?" Now, I don't mean that your method was only okay or that it helped me some; I mean that it really worked. I got much more out of your working with me than I had hoped. But I haven't been able to get comfortable with the fact that not only do you not verify any of your observations, verification is beside the point. I almost feel that every observation that you make could be theoretically wrong and it would still work. That is almost frightening. It must be immoral. However, under the pressure of your deadline, I have thought of something that seems significant and that enables me to make a few observations.

First, some mistakes that do not matter. I was not on the planning faculty and I finished my Ph.D. six years ago. Those mistakes were fun. They are like jokes that you made at your own expense. I also admired you for letting your projections hang out like that. You didn't know that they were mistakes, but you knew that you had to be making some such mistakes, and I knew that you knew. This is my first important observation: the fact that you subjected your own guesses and assumptions to skeptical analysis and that you did so in conversation as well as in writing provided the model that I, the observed, needed. You led the way into the only critical question: "How am I deceiving myself?" If I had gotten involved in the question, "What do they—meaning you or my colleagues or the deans or my students—think of me?" the whole experience would have been dreadful. That is the key to this whole activity.

The second important observation follows from that. You did the right thing in not getting much from the students. Only certain kinds of self-deception can be worked on. The ways in which I deceive myself about how my students feel about me are not interesting. We more or less dropped the question of why students seem to be afraid of me early in the year. In your written account of the seminar, you provide lots of data that would be helpful in answering that question, but we didn't talk about it. (Incidentally, I no longer find the question interesting.)

Third and last important observation: I am fairly certain that you and I have very fundamentally different goals for ourselves as teachers. In everything you wrote, only one thing really exasperated me—the phrase "setting Steve up as winner." That remark made me feel that we had totally different vocabularies. Everything else brought the day of the seminar back to me clearly, even though we almost never had the same slant on the same incident. That phrase drew a blank. Eventually, I had a hunch. Jones is a great teacher. Senior and Thomas were great teachers. I wonder if you want to be a great teacher. A great teacher does a lot of teaching with his personality. The student learns because of what the teacher is. I found out fairly early that I was either not cut out to be or not interested in being a great teacher. A person who is not a great teacher and who is not going to become one can do things that would be destructive if they were done by a great teacher. For example, I am often rude. Eventually, the students figure out that this doesn't mean anything. My personality has no importance. I think that some such distinction might be useful in your taxonomy. I know that taxonomies are not supposed to be set up teleologically, but in the humanities we get to do almost anything.

As a not-so-great teacher myself, allow me to speculate on the two. It is undoubtedly better to be a great teacher. Only great teachers change human destiny. Great teachers do have to be careful with their "interpersonal relationships," as we say in the pop-psych business, but they can be wrong a lot and it's still okay. Not-so-great teachers have to have interesting ideas, and it's really better if they are right. If they say things that are not true, these things have to be very interesting. Everything that a great teacher says is interesting, and he has to be sure only that the main thing he says is true. A great teacher also has to be there a lot in some sense, if only in his students' fantasies. It doesn't sound like a lot of work to be a character in somebody's fantasy life, but the great teachers I know are made very tired by their students. I used to talk to Senior and Thomas about anything I thought was interesting. So the amount of work is about the same, either way. The thing that I don't know is how one finds out which kind of teacher one is and whether one has any choice about it. Maybe you will have some more thoughts. I would love to talk more about it.

Second best,
Pete Sinclair

I hope that this view over our shoulders as I visited one man's classes will give a sense of what it was like and encourage readers to try an approach that does not require experts or large amounts of money. I have not described my use of what are, perhaps, the two most obvious tools for faculty development; feedback from students and audio- or videotaping. I did use both tools, but not extensively or well, probably because I invested so much of myself in being a companion, observing, taking notes, and sharing perceptions. I might be able to make better use of these two tools if I were to do it again.

What this approach requires is participants who care about teaching and about each other and who are willing to look closely at what they see and to report accurately how they respond. The process is built on trust, but our experience leads us to believe that trust flows naturally from the structure of the procedure—as long as safeguards are observed. In my view, the procedure also rests on a crucial assumption about teaching: namely, that there is no single right or best way to teach and that what is good practice for one teacher may not be so for another. Needless to say, the process is enormously rewarding for the visitors as well.

9B   On Being Visited

Dear Margaret,

I found your week's visit important and valuable. I felt supported and validated and this was crucially helpful to my teaching. Two things were particularly important for me. The first was the meeting at my house where we played a tape of the beginning of one of my seminars. (I have notes of it.) The second was something you said to me: I didn't take any notes, but have thought about it many times in the following months as the main thing that "happened" in your visit to me.

A. The meeting was the first of the spring quarter. My house, 4/21/76. We watched excerpts of a tape of my seminar and of Mark Levensky's seminar. There were seven teachers there (including yourself) and the student who ran the video equipment.

For me it was excruciating.

The tape was of the beginning of my second discussion class of the quarter. I had used the first week of the quarter for workshop-like activities for getting started—a lot of writing and working out of goals—rather than for discussion classes on the subject matter. The program was called Peace and Conflict Studies: it was a one-quarter (ten-week) full-time program for about twenty upperclass students and myself. It was explicitly advertised as a collaborative, exploratory program. I made it clear in the published description that it wasn't in my field of professional training; that I was gearing up to teach a year-long program in it for freshmen (with one or two other faculty); and that I was inviting these upperclass students to help me explore the terrain.

The tape showed the beginning of a three-hour seminar where I had announced to the class that we could take up to 45 minutes to decide on the topic to focus on. We could wander around till we got the topic, but when we decided on it, I would keep our nose to the grindstone. Topics that came up: a couple from student papers that week (a few students wrote papers each week which were read by the whole seminar); where do people get hope or lack of hope for the possibilities of progress in the world? when does healthy aggression become unhealthy? something about the values of people who lived through World War II and those of students who hadn't. I ruled out two topics for some reason I can't remember. Students opted for dropping "hope/no hope." (I acceded even though my own instinct told me that was the right thing to talk about at this point in the quarter.) Everyone diddled on the last two and so I chose one, finally: something about the question of responsibility of the individual to the group or state.

I knew it was too big a subject but I felt stuck: I had said to students that I would not insist on *what* topic we talk about, but that was in return for insisting on a task-oriented way of talking about it. Yet I enjoyed the challenge of trying to think on the spot about how to make progress in just a couple of hours on such a difficult question.

I think that by noon we really did make useful progress. We ended up with two lists on the board: reasons why individuals might decide to feel no obligation to the state; and reasons why people tend to obey or go along with the state.

But people sitting in my living room that afternoon—all of us having rushed away from school sort of tired and out of breath, some people late—none of them saw this class that I've just described (this vision from inside my head of my own class). What they saw was 30 minutes of the old wishy-washy, unclear me: mixed messages ("I think I would prefer to do this, but we can do that . . ."); hemming and hawing; allowing things to drift interminably. It was painful for me to watch. But the worst part was my realization that it was really *much* better than it looked to these colleagues of mine.

For they didn't understand the context that I just explained—the shape of the whole three-hour class and the ground rules. They just saw the opening desultory 30 minutes. And though I could have tried to explain the context to them, I didn't do so for a number of reasons. For one thing, I didn't know how awful it would look when the machine was turned on. (I hadn't looked at the tape: I thought I was ague-proof.) And if I explained the whole thing, it would have felt like apologizing and being defensive: I felt (as director of the faculty peer visiting program) I should set an example of not being defensive. Besides, I often explained to students that if they want the most useful feedback on their writing they shouldn't start out *explaining* their piece: "don't be defensive." So I sat there and squirmed.

Also, I didn't make people give extended or full movies of their minds. They just made short comments. (I think it wasn't clear whether you, Margaret, or I was in charge of this portion of the meeting. By the end of the tape, I wasn't able to muster any assertiveness.) In my notes I recorded only a couple of comments:

—Marilyn said she thought it was better than three years ago (when we had taught together). I left more space for people now. But I didn't really "find the topic"; and didn't let it connect with their experience.

—Mark said I simply picked the wrong topic. I knew the right one and didn't pick it. And that 45 minutes for finding the topic was 40 minutes too long.

—I felt Maxine making fun of me: "Peter, you're just being you: What else would you be?"

—Peggy and Linda said they were flabbergasted by my patience. I felt them trying to be charitable.

I ended up feeling laughable. I felt very unsafe. I felt no one there could see my *strength* as a teacher.

We went on to view some of Mark's seminar. He taught decisively.

I end up with the following conclusions about such meetings:

- The teacher should view the tape or tapes ahead of time and pick out one that he feels comfortable about sharing.
- On the basis of that viewing and decision he may feel moved

to make an opening explanation of context. He should do so, Peter Elbow's macho principles of pure feedback to the contrary notwithstanding.

- People have to watch a long enough piece of tape and try to *enter into* the class: react from inside, not from outside.
- It's *got* to be a safe place. This is probably the main principle. Somehow some kind of trust and support have to be established. (This was the first meeting together of this particular group of people.) There needs to be some kind of social contract. I think people there *did* more or less feel they were there for each other's support and help, but Margaret and I didn't think about laying the groundwork: more time; more entering in. We were all too rushed and not *making enough* of the process. But I'm not sure how it should be done.

❀

B. The main thing I remember about your visit—the thing that I keep mulling over in my mind—was something you said to me during our final interview when you gave me your reactions. Though you don't emphasize it in your description, it was the main transaction for me.

I had been struggling for so long to try to be more task oriented—to try to get more done. You said to me, however, that you were suspicious of these efforts. I seemed to be trying so hard to be something different from what seemed to be my style. And not only is it my style, you insisted, but it also *works*. That is, I *was* kind of bumbling and disorganized and vague, but you insisted that I managed to cause crucial meetings and interchange among the faculty about teaching—something that others had tried and not succeeded in doing. I got results. People may continually criticize me for vagueness or unclearness or lack of decisiveness in various contexts—and it has been a continuing tradition of feedback I get (I think of colleagues telling me that my lectures and speaking voice aren't clear and decisive enough)— but I get things done. And you pointed out that I seem to manage to teach successfully too. I am respected and appreciated by students. Which is true. (Though I need to qualify this if I want to be scrupulous: a certain proportion of students get mad or turned off by my teaching. The ones who most appreciate me seem to me—surprise! surprise!—to be intelligent and perceptive. The ones who go away mad seem to want to be told just what to do and not take initiative—and also not to want to consider ambiguities and difficulties.)

This whole line of thought took me by surprise. My first reaction was disappointment. In effect—though I don't think I put it in these words—I was asking your help to be better at X and you told me, "Don't do X, do Y." But it had just the sort of effect that I think I see myself having upon some of my students when I tell them that some part of their writing has power that they think is yukky. They go away disappointed, perplexed, even annoyed, but a seed has been planted that germinates and sprouts. I've put a pebble in their pocket and they can't help turning it over and over in their hand. So you with me. I just kept thinking about it.

Now, in retrospect I can sum up the whole matter (with maximum generality) as follows. For teaching, I have mostly one *voice,* one *style:* my power is wrapped up in that. If I want power, I've got to use *my* voice. If I want to use some voice or style that I find more pleasing, I'm free to do so, but I can't have power that way. *Yet*—the crucial next step in the notion—I am not trapped for life in one voice or style. I can grow or change. But *not* unless I start out inhabiting my own voice or style. If I do that, then I can grow or change and start to use other voices or styles—slowly. In short, I need to accept myself as I am before I can tap my power or start to grow.

What was intriguing for me was that though I had worked out this formulation with regard to writing—and even generalized it slightly toward growth in general—the fact is that when you took this line with me (and I have no idea what kind of mental set was behind it in your mind) I didn't at first recognize it as something familiar to me. I had exactly the reaction that I have come to notice in some students. I was surprised and perplexed. I didn't want to follow or agree with it. For the fact remains that when I see myself being bumbling or rambling or caught indecisive or vague, I experience it as *awful.* I hate it and hate myself. At first I used to say, "so what?" Or even not believe the feedback. But I've come to get so much feedback of this sort in recent years that I've come to experience my vagueness more and more the way it is experienced by people who hate it or are annoyed by it. So I've become very sensitive: I can detect it when I do it only slightly: I hear my voice start to mumble or trail off when, in the middle of a sentence, I suddenly have the sense that what I'm engaged in saying might be wrong; I see myself start to fade and go silent and look at the ceiling when I need to make a decision in class between X and Y and can't see which one would be better to do; I notice myself starting to pull back into my shell when I notice something annoying is going on (usually some student talking too long or the whole group going off in what seems like an unfruitful direction), but I can't think of how to stop it—I feel paralyzed. Yes, I get more and more sensitive to these behaviors in me, more and more annoyed, but somehow absolutely *no better* at changing them, no matter how hard I try.

As a result of your comments, comments that absolutely contradicted this pattern I'm describing, some things happened—some new perceptions of myself—in the weeks that followed. Not dramatic events but important faint new experiences. I remember three things.

1. A slight loosening of my "set" of how I perceive myself. A profound change even though there were only wisps of it periodically. That is, I remember some moments of simply *re*perceiving my style and voice. Catching myself being my old self, starting to feel the old revulsion, but then saying, "Wait a minute, remember what Margaret said, maybe that's not so bad. I'm not a failure and an incompetent, you know. Remember all the things I've succeeded at. Remember how I've actually got some things happening among faculty—got some people thinking and doing things—that were hard for most people to make happen; remember those students who really appreciated me; I'm *not* such a bad teacher. Remember the effect I've had on some students' writing. That bumbling sound, that indecisiveness, that's not just some hateful incompetence, that's me, and I've done some good things with it. I don't have to hate myself so, I don't have to feel such a sinking feeling in my stomach when I hear that sound, I don't have to feel so hopeless at the fact that my best efforts don't seem to change it all." Obviously, not all those words would go through my head. (Though some would.) But the feelings expressed by those words did definitely occur to me

on a number of occasions. There was a definite re-experience of
self or behavior as not so bad. Not a complete re-experience—just
the beginnings. But it was momentous and very memorable. And
it happened a number of times, and persisted. (Though of course
the negative or revulsive experience of self also persisted, somewhat weakening.)

2. The second thing that happened followed from the first.
Since I found myself more accepting of this tendency in myself,
I began to find myself more open and less apologetic about it.
That is, I had tended to try to change and disguise and get rid
of that tendency to bumble whenever it showed its head. I would
feel, "Uh oh, here it comes again, I've got to stop this in its
tracks, nip this in the bud, I've got to sound decisive, I've got to
take that bumble out of my voice, I've got to keep the students
from knowing that I don't know what to do, don't know which
is the right thing to do at this point, how to get such and such
happening, how to stop this drift into the doldrums." And a
sense of tightness and panic would ensue. But now I found myself starting to allow myself to do traces of something very different: to acknowledge my self, my style, my voice. That is, I found
myself openly saying words to the effect of, "you know, I'm stuck,
I don't know the best way to get from here to there, I don't know
which would be the best thing to do next." Not all the time, but
at certain points. Important things followed from this. The most
noticeable to me was a sense of immense relief. I guess I was
starting to "come out" and no longer be a closet bumbler. The
other effect, however, was that there seemed to be a renewed
power and effectiveness. I began to notice that the effect of
bumbling was no longer so paralyzing and dead-making upon
the atmosphere in the room. It even *helped* get things done. For
the main effect of the other kind of behavior—the panicked attempt to suppress bumbling—was great deadness, fog, heaviness,
dullness palpably filling the air. I suspect there is an important
general principle here: that what is inhibiting to a class is when
the teacher is inhibited or alienated from his own behavior—a
conflict between doing X but wanting or trying to do Y—no matter what the X and Y are. Whereas on the other hand when there
is a congruence between behavior and intention or conviction,
the effect is a loosening, lightening, and freeing of the atmo-

sphere—some fog lifted from everyone's consciousness. And it doesn't so much matter what the particular behaviors are.

Subjectively, then, there was a profoundly different feeling. There was a sense of standing *squarely behind* my behavior such that if someone pushed against it, it did not fade or give way; if someone knocked on it, it gave a solid noise instead of sounding hollow and fake. As a result, it felt as if these very behaviors had some force, some power, some resonance so they could *exert force* or have impact on others. Thus I had the experience of having more power and being more effective by ceasing to struggle to be powerful and effective.

3. In addition, this self-affirming seemed to trigger the possibilities for a slow developmental or growth process. It seemed to me that as I affirmed and stood behind my bumbling voice better, I was freed—on certain occasions when somehow I wanted or felt the need—suddenly to be clearer, more decisive, and more direct.

All this sounds too momentous. I suspect it would have taken a discerning eye to notice any actual changes in my behavior. Perhaps there were *no* outward changes. The old behaviors and feelings persist. But the seeds are sown and a crucial change is started. I feel better; and I think it's a fact that my students are enjoying my teaching better. To be scrupulous again, I could talk about problems and dissatisfactions with my teaching this fall of 1976. However, as I write now, at the end of the fall, I'm thinking that part of my difficulties might have come from not having sufficiently internalized the very insights that I've just been working out on paper for the first time. I think this fall that I reverted a bit to disowning my bumbling, and tried for too much decisiveness. (The problem, of course, is how to do justice to my hunger for task-orientation and my style of bumbling.) For all these insights I've just been writing about have just been sitting in notes all this time—not fully thought-out or written down till now. The reader must understand that all this is thinking that is still in process.

❁❁❁

9C Contraries in Responding

There is nothing like training the evaluative gun on oneself and
one's peers (as opposed to using it only on students) to heighten
one's awareness of the complexity of the process. I end up writing about evaluation in two of its most opposed manifestations:
subjective and objective responses.

Subjective Responses: Movies of the Viewer's Mind

I had originally imagined that I might end up my visitation of
a teacher with some prepared presentation, written or oral, in
which I summed up my perceptions and tried to make helpful
suggestions. It didn't work that way. What I ended up giving the
teacher was simply my attempt to play back my notes and then
to discuss issues as they arose in that situation.

Most of what I've written so far here [in the report—describing
four or five visitations] is an attempt to realize my notes into
more coherent prose—though of course the present version lacks
many details that would have still been in my mind when I "replayed" them. But I don't have notes of the conversations that
ensued as I tried to engage in this responding process.

I usually had at least three replay sessions. In the first one, and
perhaps the second, I would tread somewhat gingerly: I wanted
to get through my notes; I was trying to get a feel for how the
teacher was reacting to my reactions and perceptions; and I tried
to get a feel—from the disgressions and interactions that occurred
as I played back my notes—what issues would be most useful and
acceptable to the teacher.

Toward the end of these sessions I would allow myself to address general issues, give advice, or whatever. In effect I tended to move from "reporter" to "commentator," although the "reporter" made no attempt at objectivity.

If you wanted to take a negative view of my procedure you could call it the product of laziness and cowardice: I didn't force myself to work out clear conclusions and recommendations; and when some occurred to me naturally, I slipped them slyly into mere "replaying of my notes" instead of taking full responsibility for them. The "lazy" part doesn't seem quite fair; I was certainly working hard. The "cowardice" part could stand. And yet I still want to defend this procedure. This is a style of responding that I've slowly developed in trying to deal with writing over the last few years: trying to give students feedback on their writing and also trying to help students give feedback to each other.

I think of it as "empirical feedback"—giving the *facts* of what actually occurred in the observer or reader: those *perceptions* or *reactions* which underlie judgments, conclusions, or advice. It may be true that I devised this procedure because I didn't feel confident enough to say, "This is what's wrong with your writing, and this is what you should do." Writing seems too mysterious and I'm too unsure of my authority about it. Similarly here, I find that teaching is too mysterious and I am too unsure of my authority to give conclusions and recommendations.

But there is something powerful and appealing—and I believe useful—about just telling what happened. It's a relief *not* to give conclusions and recommendations. People are often so defensive about them; there are so many ways to deny them or not hear them. But I just present my view of the events, just tell the story of what actually occurred in me. I've devised the perfect tool for my temperament: a way to be pushy and still timid. What I say in my replays cannot be so easily ignored or disagreed with. For example, it would happen a number of times that I would have some reaction—for example, that I felt intimidated by a teacher's behavior at some moment—and when I told this to the teacher he or she would give all kinds of reasons why my reaction didn't make sense: she was really doing such and such, she knows that students could tell she wasn't trying to be intimidating, she can point to specific behavior of students to show that they are not

intimidated by her, and so on. I tend to say, "yes, yes," sometimes even to start genuinely to be convinced that my response
didn't make sense. But then I would catch myself and say, "but
I did write down that phrase in my notes at that moment in the
class. I really *was* feeling intimidated at that moment." Almost
as though I am saying "yes, I'd like to agree with you, I can see
that you are right, but my troublesome partner who was visiting
your class and taking notes refuses to deny his reaction."

This procedure can be abused. At times people successfully
convinced me I was abusing it. That is, sometimes I really had a
full-fledged conclusion or a recommendation—sometimes I really
thought there was some basic pattern occurring in someone's
teaching and I didn't like it or thought there was a particular
change or direction that the person ought to make; yet sometimes I didn't come right out with my conclusion or recommendation, and instead, timidly, I just hinted around or disguised it
as merely part of my "perceptions of what was going on."

Using empirical feedback wasn't new to me. What I was engaged in learning this year is how to be more straightforward
and honest on the occasions when I really did have a conclusion
and a recommendation. On such occasions I tried to sense whether
the person was willing to listen to my conclusions and recommendations, but even when I wasn't sure he was willing, sometimes,
in order to maintain the honesty of the relationship, I had to
come clean with my conclusions.

The question of how "empirical" and how "prescriptive" to
be is one that differs for different people. I'm at a stage where I
have to learn—for the sake of honesty—to be as prescriptive as I
really am. Many people, however—and I suspect *most* teachers—
don't have any trouble being prescriptive and need to learn to
be more empirical.

Over the course of the fall there was a wide variation between
my perceptions and reactions toward teachers—with respect to
how much I experienced conclusions and recommendations and
how much I just experienced some useful perceptions of classes.
My notes for Pete and Will are pretty typical, though for them
perhaps I had slightly fewer conclusions and recommendations:
small ones here and there; one major conclusion and piece of advice to Pete about lecturing. My reactions to Pete's individual

conference with his writing student [not reported above] were typically ambiguous: I was genuinely troubled by some of what I saw but didn't experience conclusions or advice because I had no clear sense of what was really happening and whether *any-thing* ought to be changed. I could see that Pete wielded a re-markable power and that it worked effectively in his teaching.

In my visits to Bill and Margaret, I clearly did have some pre-scriptive conclusions. With Bill I sensed something that was cen-tral to his teaching, though in fact I had no sense of how to make a change: I merely had a sense of how usefully to *describe* a con-dition that was troublesome (not being able to wrestle with all his strength). In the case of Margaret it was a small detail (the matter of asking rhetorical questions) but it did relate to the whole moral climate of her classroom—which is central to her teaching.*

Over the fall, I can't remember having conclusions or recom-mendations that I stopped myself from giving (because of either my timidity or my sense that the person wasn't able or willing to hear them). To be in the position of visitor was an inspiration to try to achieve bravery and honesty without arrogance.

What was more characteristic was for me to give my conclu-sion and recommendation in the midst of replaying a class. Per-haps it would develop into a little discussion between us. The teacher might find it easy or hard to agree. Usually I would just drop it and go on with replaying my notes. In general I didn't push my conclusions very hard.

---

* From a note to Margaret, 12/76:

I'm struck at how much more negative you experienced my feedback on your lecture than I intended. *Perhaps* I was more critical than I realized. But really I don't think so. What I think now is that you were very dis-satisfied with your lecture, hence no matter what I said, you assumed I was being understatedly kind about a horrible lecture. Since this phe-nomenon would apply both to you and to me, let me elevate it to a gen-eral principle of universal validity: anyone with any tendency to think he or she isn't doing a good enough job, isn't smart enough, isn't talented enough, etc., is very likely to experience *any feedback* as criticism. The moral of the story is that until one is really secure that one is adequate and doing a good job, one cannot hear feedback clearly.

Of course I might have transmitted my feedback unclearly, but for what it's worth at this point, I can still remember how impressed I was with your lecture as a very professional performance.

In one or two cases I pushed. One occasion sticks in my mind.
I had a reaction and conclusion and explicit advice which the
teacher resisted hard. But I kept hammering nevertheless. I was
amazed to see myself doing this. I've often thought about it. I
think there were two reasons. For one thing, I grew to feel close
to this person and felt I was pushing against something that was
a source of serious discomfort for him. In addition, I think I felt
a strong identification: I was objecting to something I find re-
pugnant in myself. In this sense I guess I was saying, "If I can
stamp it out in this person, perhaps I can stamp it out in me."

But what needs stressing is the fact that *most* of the time I
had no conclusions, judgments, or advice. Sometimes this seemed
perplexing to the person I was visiting. Sometimes I even allowed myself to fall into being defensive about it. After all, we
tend to think of feedback as judgments, conclusions, and advice.
To have none—and instead merely to have a string of perceptions
and reactions that don't add up to anything special—that's liable
to feel like coming empty-handed. But the moment I stopped
and thought seriously about it, I was fine again. I feel confident
I'm right in this approach to responding. Judgments, conclusions, and advice are not just elliptical but radically untrustworthy. Usually they are false. Actual perceptions and reactions,
on the other hand, are almost always valuable and trustworthy—
though one can draw incorrect conclusions from them.

Categories for Objective Responses: Things Teachers Do

I had the germ of this scheme in my first week of observing. To
be precise, I started thinking about it during Pete Sinclair's first
seminar. I was experiencing him as extreme in his holding back—
his seeming to do nothing and yet equally strong and overt in
his interventions. It got me to thinking about what it would
mean to do absolutely *nothing;* and then what are the various
"somethings" that you might add to nothing. I made only the
beginnings of a scheme then. I thought about it periodically, but
didn't carry it further till this summer. I offer it here as the beginnings of a scheme that might be useful not only to an observer but to a teacher who was trying consciously to decide what
stance or style to take in a discussion class, that is, what kinds of

interventions he wants to try to make and what kinds to try to avoid. I offer it somewhat apprehensively since others, like Bales and Flanders, have worked more professionally at such classification systems.

A teacher's interventions can be grouped into three general categories: he might steer or add control; he might add "presence" (adding energy, safety, and support); and he might add perceptions and information.

1. Adding control or steering

(a) Not at all. Just be there. Permit anything.

(b) Negative steering, e.g., saying, "You can do anything at all *except* X, Y, and Z." Pete, for example, implied at one point, "You can do anything at all but talk about the nature and function of seminars themselves."

(c) Steer to a *general* area, e.g., "We can discuss anything, so long as it has *something* to do with the book assigned for homework."

(d) Steer to a specific area, e.g., "We must stick to *this* particular issue or question."

(e) Steer not to a particular content area but to a particular mode, e.g., "People must come up with a particular task and work on it, but I don't care what the task is"; or "We can discuss anything so long as the majority stay involved"; or "You must cite a passage from the text for everything you say."

2. Adding presence—Energy, safety, support

(a) Brute safety. Many teachers or leaders who take a no-steering role say either implicitly or explicitly, "Anything can happen here, but I will prevent people from ganging up cruelly on one person."

(b) Implicit caring and human concern. Some teachers and leaders—even when they are completely silent—communicate with their presence that they care about the people there, care what happens, and believe that the process really is beneficial. (Conversely, I think students can feel it when a leader or teacher is in bad faith, that is, doesn't really care about the people or the process or feels the whole thing is a shuck. E.g., "It's all a lot of bull, but if they want to keep coming, I don't mind being here and getting paid.")

(c) Explicit caring and concern. Overtly expressing things like "You're doing fine; this class is trying hard, is doing well; I like you"; even (given the right tone) "You are wrong; you're not trying hard enough."

(d) Individualized caring and concern. Supporting or protecting or somehow bringing along a specific student—one that probably needs special support.

(e) Being a good cop/MC/host/facilitator. Adding pure sociability. Keeping people from interrupting or dominating things. Yukking it up, making for jokes and laughter and greater friendliness. Getting people to introduce themselves.

(f) Jumping in yourself and adding your own energy. Sharing your own curiosity and hunger for the right answer and fun at the enterprise. Getting mad because you aren't getting the satisfaction you have a right to expect.

3. Adding perceptions and information

(a) Just interpreting *group* process. Most people who supposedly take a no-steering role usually add not just some safety and sanction; they also usually add interpretive comments. In a sense such teachers do "nothing at all," but by occasionally interpreting what the *students* have done, they considerably influence what students get out of it.

(b) Just interpreting *intellectual* process. That is, not determining what is discussed, not adding to it, but simply pointing out implications, premises, contradictions, or separating issues that get tangled. E.g., "Notice the implications between what you are now saying and what everyone agreed on at the beginning." Or "Aren't you really considering two questions at once here, tangled up in each other?" Or "How does your conclusion here relate to what the book says?"

(c) Joining in the effort yourself. Instead of merely standing back and helping *them*, actually engaging yourself in trying to figure things out: "I just noticed that if we consider such and such and consider such and such, it follows that . . ." These two

categories—interpreting and joining in—may seem to overlap.
After all, the process of interpreting is a crucial ingredient in
trying to join in and figure something out. But the distinction I
have in mind is clear when you think in terms of the teacher's
stance as a person toward the group. There's a big difference between, on the one hand, not really wrestling *along with* the students and instead being a kind of referee or helper trying to help
them play better; and on the other hand, joining in and playing
along with them. It's often a matter of holding back vs. not holding back—keeping a kind of perspective vs. entering in such that
you might lose perspective. There's a special pleasure for most
teachers that comes from really joining in, wrestling, and playing
for oneself. (And certain students at certain times cannot abide
the "artificiality" of a teacher who isn't joining in.) But if you
are teaching beginning students in an area of your professional
expertise, it's almost impossible really to join in: from the first
moment of class, you know what the "answer" is or where you
are trying to go. Evergreen offers more opportunities for joining in since we so often teach in interdisciplinary programs and
deal with areas outside our professional expertise. I suspect the
reason university teachers traditionally prefer to teach graduate
students is because they can join in more with graduate students—not have to hold back.

It is useful here to distinguish whether the question you are
joining in on has emerged from the students or whether it's a
question you yourself have set, that is, is it "their business" or
"your business" you are joining in on?

(d) Simply adding information: being a learned reference
book or data bank or dictionary for the class.

✿

In using a classification like this to determine your stance as a
teacher, you could take a theoretical, *a priori* approach: simply
decide which modes of action you want to use and try to shape
your behavior accordingly. Or you could use an empirical approach which I think would be richer: first get help in observing
your actual behavior; then look at the results and decide which
behaviors seem better and which ones worse. (Not forgetting to
ask whether the "better ones" are in fact coherent or reconcilable.)

In this way—trying to take advantage of the tacit knowledge that shows up in one's actual behavior—you could slowly work toward a conclusion about what stance or approach is preferable, and as a consequence what changes if any you need to try for. I can imagine a teacher going through this latter empirical approach and ending up not making any overt changes in behavior at all (perhaps even retaining some things that seem conflicting), but by seeing and affirming better what she is doing, ending up much more effective and comfortable.

It is obvious that I did not, in giving responses to my colleagues, make much use of these objective categories or of any organized taxonomy of teaching behavior, nor try much in general for purely objective feedback—though I tried to get as much accuracy and detail as I could into my observing, note-taking, and replaying. In a sense I tried to force any subjective reactions as much as possible to grow out of or be embodied in accurately observed detail.

Nevertheless I have the impulse to learn to use this sort of thing and think I should do so: not as a substitute for movies of my mind but as an opposite modality that would lend more richness and weight to the whole feedback enterprise. Especially, it would serve as a kind of antidote where pure subjectivity got out of hand. And in the case of dispute, such a taxonomy could permit the observer and teacher more easily to agree about what was actually happening, and in this way increase the accuracy of their perceptions (though of course a single behavior might well fit more than one function).

CHAPTER 10

❀❀❀

Needless to say, I *like* giving movies of my mind. I like it for the good information it gives to the person being "evaluated" (whether it's a teacher being observed or a writer getting responses), but it also teaches the *responder*. I am bemused, then, to see how much my present job has involved me—and finally *interested* me—in a kind of evaluation I hate to perform: pure judgment, ranking, or measurement.

As early as 1969, when I wrote the essay that is Chapter 8 here (and also a 1971 essay, "Shall We Teach or Give Credit"), I'd thought seriously about the "responsibilities of the institution" for making evaluative judgments. The classic example is society's need for the licensing of, say, doctors or pilots. The state sets up institutions to perform that task. But never till now (as director of a writing program) have I been drawn so far into literally *identifying* with the educational institution. When I came I inherited a mass testing procedure where we gave at least 3,000 proficiency exams a year. In effect, it was my responsibility to *measure* the writing proficiency of every undergraduate. (We've since abandoned that exam for a system of measurement-by-portfolio that I believe is more accurate.)

I find myself responsible for sixty or so sections of writing each semester. Because these are taught largely by graduate assistants, every grade given is, by some dismal legal technicality of the university, to some extent *my* grade. My nose (and theirs) is rubbed in this fact by my having to sign every change-of-grade form as well as every recommendation that a graduate student might write for a student. In a sense, then—and I cannot help sometimes experiencing this sense in the middle of the night—I give 1,300–1,500 course grades a semester. And those proficiency exam verdicts are legally *my* verdicts. (Whenever there is any danger of my forgetting all this, I am jolted back to awareness by the characteristic impulse of the dissatisfied Long Island student to say, "I'll have to see my attorney about this exam grade.")

And so the absurdity of it emerges more than occasionally. It's not so hard to step back a few paces and smile at myself as I get sucked into more acquiescence in *measurement* than society needs for its protection, than an institution needs for good teaching, and than students need for good learning. We are not after all licensing pilots. Does the student need a *grade* on a paper every week for fifteen weeks in order to make the course-grade fair? Does a grade on a paper make a student learn more or read the commentary more carefully?

These questions, then—combined with a heightened perplexity in the literary and philosophical world about what might constitute validity in simply deciding what any text *means*—have drawn me into being more curious than is probably good for me about trustworthiness in measurement. Thus these final reflections.

⚘⚘⚘

Trustworthiness in Evaluation

Problems in evaluation get harder and harder to ignore. This is especially true now in the academy with our heightened interest in hermeneutical issues—in the problematic nature of interpretation and perception. That is, if two of us differ about the meaning of a text or an utterance or a piece of behavior, I can go on arguing for my interpretation, and my colleague can go on arguing for hers, and no one in the academy—neither philosophers nor social scientists of any ilk—can bring to bear any generally accepted criteria for deciding which of us is right. Yet virtually all grades represent interpretations and evaluations of what someone said, wrote, or did. And we continue to let grades determine very weighty consequences for students, such as scholarship money and acceptance into other programs and schools. Thus we go on giving grades as though we had some consensus about the nature and trustworthiness of interpretations, especially the interpretations and evaluations of single observers—when we do not.*

Obviously we cannot make our evaluations absolutely trustworthy, but there is something disturbing about sailing serenely along with our present practices—particularly at a time when students seem driven to take grades more and more seriously. Therefore I want to suggest three general strategies for increasing the trustworthiness of our grades and comments: breaking

---

* I write here of a general issue, "trustworthiness," because the more precise issues, "validity" and "reliability," tend to be hopelessly tangled up together in the normal and inevitably crude activity I treat in this chapter: teachers giving grades or making comments. Also the word "validity" has a different sense when we are also talking about interpretation.

down into parts the performance to be evaluated; using more than one observer; and using "movies of the reader's mind."

1. Breaking Down into Parts the Performance to be Evaluated

The classic evaluation research (in my field) was done by Paul Diederich. On the one hand, he confronts us with the extent of our disarray about evaluation—with the extent to which good readers disagree. He shows that if several competent readers grade pieces of writing, any *one* piece will more than likely get the full range of grades, from highest to lowest. This finding has been replicated with readers of various sorts (academics, general adult readers, people from the professions).

But he goes on to show, on the other hand, that our plight isn't quite as bad as that finding might suggest. That is, he shows that if the readers grade *features* of each of the pieces of writing (for example, "ideas," "organization," "mechanics," and so forth— and he derives these features from open-ended statements by the readers themselves) the readers agree remarkably better. That is, where they disagree radically about what grade to give the paper as a whole, they more or less agree that a given paper has, for example, strong ideas and weak organization. Thus, the initial holistic disagreement isn't so much because readers have completely different eyes or because they live in separate, epistemologically closed universes. Rather they often *see* similar features but *weight* them differently: some readers are swayed more in their grading by ideas, others more by organization, others by mechanics.*

---

* I don't mean to give too naive a picture of perception. Of course we don't all walk around the universe seeing exactly the same individual details or features (facts) and merely disagreeing about how to integrate or grade them (values). Our values often determine what facts we see; our "schemata" for integrating or evaluating often determine the nature of the details or features that come to our attention. That doesn't mean, however, that we should give in to the equally naive assumption that sometimes takes over in the first flush of reading Kuhn & Co.—namely, that we can skip disciplined wrestling with perceptions and jump immediately to talk about theory; that there's no use talking about "facts" till we agree about values. In the disciplined work of observation and judgment, we can reap enormous gains in trustworthiness if we concentrate first on the smaller features of a phenomenon which tend, in fact, to yield greater intersubjective agreement.

Grading all around the university would benefit from applying the principle implied here. Grades are universally inconsistent with each other because different teachers weight different features: some teachers grade more in terms of memory, others more in terms of manipulation of concepts, some consider writing skill and participation in class, others don't, and so on. Besides, even if all teachers used similar weightings among features, outside readers would learn very little from reading the conventional grade in a history or psychology or even a physics course about a student's knowledge or ability: an enormously complex and diverse range of knowledge and skills over a whole semester is summed up into a single number. Thus the need for a scheme such as the one in Chapter 8.*

Competence-based (or mastery-based) education is another way to increase the trustworthiness of evaluation by breaking down the knowledge or skills into parts—but with a particular emphasis: a change from "norm-referenced" to "criterion-referenced" evaluation. Competence-based evaluations tell us whether the student has actually learned the particular skills (has met the criteria) that a course is designed to teach. Conventional grades are norm-referenced in that they tell us only where the student's performance stands relative to the norm of others. And competence-based evaluations break the course's content into parts rather than treating the whole semester's work as one "performance" and summing up the evaluation into one number.

Thus competence-based evaluation is usually more trustworthy than conventional grading—and I tried to show in Chapter 6 that it often brings better teaching too. I'd like to see more teachers, departments, or schools willing to try it. But there are some dangers involved in the process and it is much more difficult and disruptive for most colleges and universities to use than the kind of scheme described in Chapter 8.

Another way to increase the trustworthiness of evaluation by breaking a performance down into features is by using *narrative*

---

* This practice of breaking the performance down into features can also be seen as an attempt to gain "reliability" because, at last, one is *naming* what it is one is grading. (It would also represent a willingness finally to allow the possibility of being *unreliable*, since that charge is virtually meaningless when the entity graded is as large and crude as "how good the paper is" or "physics I.")

evaluations (instead of, or in addition to, quantitative grades). If I write out an evaluation of a student's work in my course, I will necessarily articulate and distinguish various *features* of her performance—not just sum everything up into one number. As a result, I am also less likely to base my judgment of her on just one feature of learning—and even if I do, I will tend to reveal my emphasis to my reader. In short, written evaluations are more apt to be accurate, less likely to mislead.* Nevertheless, written evaluations are not feasible in most colleges and universities because the faculty have too many students to evaluate. (At Evergreen we only had twenty students per semester to evaluate because students took one full-time program instead of four or five courses.)

2. Using More Than One Observer

In addition to breaking down a performance into features, we can increase the trustworthiness of grades and comments by getting help. Current thinking in hermeneutics and critical theory stresses that even perception (not just judgment) derives from communities of discourse.

When groups or even pairs of teachers negotiate agreement about the grades on specific student papers or exams—or even when they just agree on criteria or standards for each teacher to use in solitude when she returns to her own office—their grading or commenting becomes much more trustworthy. Of course it's not feasible to bring in multiple graders for all of the grading we must do, but for *certain important judgments* it is more feasible than it might seem.

For example, it is very common to use small committees for judging doctoral dissertations and exams—even for judging undergraduate theses. This practice says, in effect, "Here is a decision that is too important to be left to one evaluator—despite the added cost in time, trouble, or even money."

* The evaluations suggested in Chapter 8 are in a sense wholly "quantitative," yet they represent a crucial move in the "qualitative" direction because *several* features are being quantified, and each feature must be described in words. Thus the student's performance cannot be misleadingly summed up into only one number.

Similarly, when judgments about writing proficiency are important enough to carry weighty consequences, teachers and testers have managed to base these evaluations upon agreements among *multiple readers* by learning to use what is called "holistic scoring": readers are briefly trained (using sample papers that represent each score) to rank large numbers of student papers very quickly indeed—and relatively consistently. The procedure achieves impressive reliability. Every paper gets at least two readings, and where those two differ, or differ by more than one rank, there is always a third reader. (In the scrupulous use of holistic scoring, there are added procedures to try to prevent readers from "drifting" over the course of a long period of reading: periodic "recalibration" of readers by means of more samples and periodic rereadings of already-graded papers by more experienced readers. In smaller programs and sessions, these extra procedures are often omitted, but even with them many essays can be evaluated with remarkable speed.*)

But unfortunately careful research shows what common sense tells us is obvious: no matter how trustworthily we may evaluate any *sample* of a student's writing, we lose all that trustworthiness if we go on to infer from just that one sample the student's actual *skill in writing* (see Cooper, just cited). We cannot get a valid picture of a student's writing skill unless we look at more than one sample produced on more than one day in more than one mode or genre. (And of course it is misleading to talk about "writing" as one skill since there are different kinds of writing and different skills involved. It's like talking about "intelligence"

---

* Of course holistic scoring yields evaluation only—not feedback or commentary. For more about it, see Charles Cooper and Edward White. For an eloquent warning against exaggerated claims about holistic scoring (for of course its results are impressive only when compared to the use of individual readers), see Davida Charmey. There is one *kind* of holistic scoring that tries to increase trustworthiness by *both* procedures I've talked about: not just using multiple readers but also articulating different *features* of a piece of writing. This technique is called "primary trait scoring." It calls for specifying the major trait or skill or feature that the writing task requires (for example, the giving of reasons) and then asking readers to judge more explicitly in terms of that trait. (Sometimes more than one trait is specified.) Primary trait scoring is a way of minimizing the distortion that comes from different readers weighting different features of writing.

as one thing.) Unfortunately, proficiency in writing is typically judged on the basis of a single writing sample—usually produced under timed or exam conditions. (We see the same problem when instructors base their grade on just one or two papers or exams.) At Stony Brook we are experimenting with holistic scoring on small *portfolios* of writing produced by students over the course of a semester—thus involving more than one sample, genre, and writing occasion—in an effort to increase the trustworthiness of evaluation. (See two essays by Elbow and Belanoff in the Bibliography of Works About Writing by the Author.)

In doing so we are bringing in more than one evaluator *only* for the most important decision—trying to avoid a large expenditure of time and effort by leaving the rest of the (less consequential) evaluations to the individual teacher. That is, the individual teacher does all the commenting and grading during the semester and determines single-handedly the final course grade, *but* she must do so in the light of one crucial "gateway" judgment which must be collaborative: the teacher may not give a course grade of C or better unless the student's portfolio has been judged acceptable by at least one other teacher, who of course does not know the student. (When a teacher and first reader disagree, the portfolio goes to a third reader; teachers meet in small portfolio groups.) This judgment is crucial because students must repeat the course if they don't get a C or better. Even though only two readers must agree on any given portfolio, we meet in a large group to agree on sample portfolios. We also save time because portfolio decisions are binary: Yes or No—above or below a C. Thus most passing portfolios can be read quickly.

Some kind of multiple-reader or portfolio procedure could be used for any university grade or evaluation which carries more than usual weight. The procedure could even be used for regular course grades—especially if it is used only for crude "gateway" decisions (as opposed to trying to agree on the whole gamut of grades). This would be a way for faculty members or a department to say, "Yes, the individual teacher does most of the evaluating, but no student should get a C or better (or should get an A) unless she can show on some papers that her performance meets a certain rough standard that someone *else* in the department can agree about." The system can easily be set up by two faculty members working unilaterally on their own.

❁

When we think of trying to increase trustworthiness in evaluation by using multiple observers, we tend to imagine situations such as those I've just described where observers somehow agree on *one* verdict. Part of the power of using more than one observer comes from forcing them to negotiate to agreement. But we needn't go along with this assumption that evaluation always means *one* verdict. One of the most trustworthy evaluations we can produce is a "mixed bag": an evaluation made up of the verdicts or perceptions of two or more observers who *may not agree*. It stands to reason that if the performance is at all complex, I can get a much more trustworthy picture of it and of its worth if I get reports from two sources. The verdict of many evaluating or licensing committees consists of a statement of how a small committee voted. In fact, a hiring committee is often given the task not of choosing *one* candidate but of weeding a large field of candidates down to just three or four and making statements about their strengths and weaknesses—so that some reader of this evaluation can make the final choice. For evaluation often does not require a single verdict: that's only necessary where students need to be compared along a single dimension. And I tried to show in Chapter 8 that it's not really so necessary as we might assume from our habits in education to give in to the hunger to *rank* students along a single dimension. A more accurate account of what students have learned invariably breaks us into more than one dimension.

But when a *single* verdict must finally be arrived at—when a single candidate must be chosen, when a scattering of numbers must be reduced to one number, or a set of comments reduced to one comment—then shouldn't the evaluators themselves be the ones to make that synthesis since they are the "experts" and know more about the student or candidate? Isn't it wrong for them to leave that synthesis to some *reader* of the evaluation who is probably no expert and doesn't know the student at all? But though the readers of evaluations may know less about the student than the evaluators do, they invariably know *more* about the purposes to which the evaluation will be put. That is, the employer or the admissions committee will know more about what *features* of learning and skill they are looking for in students. In the hiring procedure cited above where a committee narrows a field of candidates down to three or four, the whole point is to give the final choice to a person or committee that knows more about the nature of the job and the context.

Interestingly enough, the cognitive power in this "mixed bag" kind of evaluation comes from *not* forcing the several observers to negotiate to agreement—from not forcing people to settle for compromises, for lowest-common-denominator thinking, or for discourse with all the interesting angles rubbed off. Maverick perceptions are not lost. When a pair or a committee is forced to *agree,* it must often discard crucial perceptions—all on the basis of a *guess* or *assumption* about the purpose to which the evaluation will be put. ("We can't really count *effort* here," they may conclude, yet I may come along as an employer or graduate admissions committee and in fact be quite interested in effort or diligence—or some other feature or type of information that fell through the cracks when they were forced to agree on one verdict.)

A common kind of multiple observer or "mixed bag" evaluation occurs when small groups of writers share comments on each others' writing. One of the main reasons why the evaluation of writing is so problematic is that the model of evaluation used is at odds with the thing evaluated. Our model of evaluation assumes value judgments that observers would agree on. As a result, teachers have tended to emphasize those features of writing about which evaluative agreement is possible—grammar and spelling. Or they have set up oversimple models of good writing such as the "five-paragraph essay": graders can agree on deviations from it. But when the thing being evaluated is a complex human performance or product like writing, the most natural model for trustworthy evaluation is not one evaluative verdict but a small array of descriptive perceptions—even if they conflict with each other.

Thus when we are forced to come to terms with the complexities of writing, we tend to end up with a healthier and more sophisticated sense of the nature of the evaluation process itself. We are forced once again to see how deeply enmeshed we are in measurement and an unexamined hunger to rank. We see that our evaluations are usually more trustworthy—*and much more likely to enhance learning*—when we find ways to *describe* the performance in question rather than measure it or rank it. (Note that holistic scoring yields measurement only—no description. And note furthermore that the success of holistic scoring in reliability depends entirely on readers being willing to be "trained" or "calibrated": readers must check their own judgments at the door and conform entirely to the judgments of a "trainer" or training committee that picks and ranks the samples on its own.)

I've long tried to promote writing groups not just for "writers" but even for "students." (Perhaps imprudently, I spoke of these as "teacherless writing classes" in *Writing Without Teachers*.) And it has become common practice now for writing teachers to use class time for students to meet in peer groups to give each other feedback and evaluation. This might seem like "the blind leading the blind," and that charge is sometimes made. But if the goal of the evaluation is not so much to give a grade (measuring "how good" the writing is against some alleged standard of excellence)—but rather to describe how these words work on readers—then peer commentary becomes very useful indeed. A whole new set of accurate and useful perceptions becomes available.

Admittedly there may be differences between how a piece of writing "works" on other students and on a teacher. But to the extent that the goal of the evaluation is to improve future writing rather than to measure accurately this piece (in a sense, this is "formative" rather than "summative" evaluation), then the writer needs perceptions from both peers and teacher. One of the main weaknesses in student writing comes from students' tendency to think of writing only as "performing for a verdict" rather than "trying to communicate with actual readers." For students to find out what their words actually *did* to readers— even if we think some of those readers have the "wrong reactions"—often leads to a remarkable gain in skill.

❊

When we think about trying to increase trustworthiness in evaluation by using multiple observers, we probably don't think of a venerable but currently unfashionable practice: the use of student *self*-evaluations. But here too, an extra observer can increase trustworthiness.

The Evergreen State College presents what is perhaps the extreme case: the student's *official transcript* consists of evaluations written by the faculty member and the student. It is a peculiar document compared to conventional transcripts, but it turns out to gain the trust of readers. When we began the practice we feared that students might be disqualified by many graduate programs or employers since these unusual transcripts lack grades and GPAs and are much more trouble to read. But soon it became clear that the transcripts worked quite well as students were accepted at various graduate and professional schools of proven merit. (The tide turned when a student's application to a program at the University of Washington was disqualified because she had no grades, but then the student was accepted at Harvard. The University of Washington came around.) Turning to the empirical world of actual decisions by employers and graduate schools, one sees how little real trust people put in conventional grades.

There are two sources of increased trustworthiness in student evaluations. First, the student knows more than the teacher does about what and how she learned—even if she knows less about what was taught. Second, even though the student's account *might* be skewed—by her failure to understand the subject matter, or by her self-interest, or (what is in fact more frequent) by her underestimation of self—if you read that account *in combination* with the teacher's account, you can usually draw a remarkably trustworthy conclusion about what the student actually learned and how skilled she is. Because there are two perceivers and because they are using natural language rather than numbers, there is remarkably rich internal evidence that usually permits the reader to see *through* any contradictions and skewings to what was really going on. In short, even though the explicit *evaluative conclusions* presented by student and teacher may be more subjective and therefore (we might say) *less* trustworthy than in quantitative grading—nevertheless anyone reading both accounts can form a much *more* trustworthy evaluative conclusion than she could get from a grade.

Of course Evergreen's practice is extreme. (The college continues to have success with it, however, and is far from alone in sanctioning official self-evaluations.) But even in a conventional grading situation, many experienced teachers have learned to improve the accuracy of their grades by requiring students to write self-evaluations. If self-evaluations are solicited in an honest thoughtful way (perhaps with specific questions to spur detail), students usually write a detailed and honest account of what they have done and learned, and thereby give the teacher much more reliable information for grading—*and* for evaluating her own teaching. (None of this speaks to the other benefit of self-evaluations: students gain much more awareness and control over themselves as learners.)

No doubt there are more strategies than the ones I've mentioned in this section for getting help in grading and commenting by bringing in more than one observer. Some are already in use; others can be devised. Bringing in help will invariably take more time and effort, but this "inefficiency" can be offset in various ways. Sometimes the evaluator is another student (as in writing groups) and so the evaluation is part of the teaching; no time is lost. (See Grant and Kohli, "Contributing to Learning by Assessing Student Performance.") And sometimes we can use collaborative evaluation *very* selectively—to bring a firmer foundation to the ongoing individual evaluation.

3. Movies of the Reader's Mind

In an interesting way, the most useful and even trustworthy evaluation of all comes when we stop trying to measure, when we abandon all claims of objectivity, "validity," and "reliability"—for those claims are of course always suspect—and we attempt instead to give as accurate and honest an account as we can of what is happening in our mind as we read or observe a piece of student work. I may have been too self-deprecatory in my earlier account (in Chapter 9, section 9C) of how I came to use movies of my mind in giving responses to colleagues; and perhaps the practice did grow out of an idiosyncratic mixture in my character of timidity and pushiness.* Nevertheless the procedure has considerable strength. It has the remarkable advantage of offering the lone teacher both epistemological validity and increased effectiveness. That is, on the level of theory, movies of the observer's mind have a greater truth value than other forms of evaluation; on the level of practice, they are often the only message that actually gets through to students to improve their future performance.

In trying to tell what happens to us as we read a piece of student work, we are not trying to produce a *fair grade;* we are not struggling to avoid subjectivity. Quite the contrary. But the procedure involves two kinds of *discipline* nevertheless: trying to tell the truth; and trying to ground one's reactions in specific details and accurate observations. For the whole point of movies of the mind is to increase phenomenological validity by avoiding *translation:* avoiding those evaluations that are at a second or third remove from the reactions, perceptions, and thoughts from which they grew. If someone tells you to move this paragraph from here to there you can't trust what she is saying (even if she is an excellent reader), but if she will tell you the nature of her discomfort that led her to give that advice, *then* you have something really solid and trustworthy—and much more interesting too.

Thus when we give grades or comments that try for objectivity or impersonality or general validity, we are very likely—not to put too fine a point on it—to be telling lies. For example, we might comment on a student paper that its weakness is with its organization (or its argument or its evidence). But if we pause and think about what we've said, we will realize that others would probably have made different judgments. Better yet, try out the piece on other good readers. There is every likelihood that we are *wrong* in our judgment. Indeed, if we compare this

* When I was first working out a rough theory of "movies of the reader's mind" (for *Writing Without Teachers* in 1970–72), I was unaware of the early work in reader-response criticism. Since then that school of criticism has burgeoned and ramified, but I won't try here to work out relationships between various branches of it and my "movies."

paper we are complaining about with another that we graded earlier and liked quite a lot, we will sometimes find that the pleasing paper has exactly the same features of organization (or argument or evidence) as the problem paper. But in the pleasing paper those features didn't bother us.

When, on the other hand, we write about what *happened* to us as we were experiencing that organization or argument or evidence, we are much more likely to be telling the truth. We are writing about the perceptions, feelings, and thoughts that gave rise to the judgments we might make. For example: "I found lots of information in your paper that seemed right and relevant; for the first few paragraphs I was encouraged, impressed, and going along with you; but then I began to get annoyed in the middle when I still couldn't quite tell what you were really trying to *say*. And I kept getting lost. When you finally made it clear what you were saying, I found myself arguing with you and looking for ways to criticize your argument—when I suddenly realized that I actually agree completely with your position."

I got interested in this kind of commentary when I started to wonder about much of what I was writing on student papers. I began to suspect that there was often something wrong with my accounts of what was successful and unsuccessful in student papers when I talked *only* about the text and did not talk about me. I began to sense that my judgment about the strengths and weaknesses of a student performance depended crucially on subtle interactions between the performance *and myself*—interactions which determined whether I would read in a sympathetic or hostile frame of mind. I found I could articulate these determinative interactions much more clearly and accurately (and helpfully) if I simply gave as honest an account as I could of what happened as I was reading.

There is enormous pedagogical power that comes from telling the truth—what happened to us; and avoiding lies—or at least shaky guesses about what is right or wrong in a performance. Students often fight us in our more impersonal verdicts—in part because they sense that these judgments are questionable. Often we win such disputes only by resorting to institutional authority. This further undermines our students' shaky faith in teacher judgments. But when we simply tell what happened to us as we read their writing, students cannot doubt or quarrel with us: what we say has a higher chance of being actually listened to. I have often had the experience (and seen it repeated with other teachers) of trying over and over again to convince a student that there was a certain problem with her essay: I'm giving an accurate and valid diagnosis of what is wrong (and of course this time I'm *sure* I'm not lying, I've got it right; but all to no avail. My message doesn't get through until finally I have the sense to tell her the story of what was happening to me as I read—often how I got confused or annoyed. Finally the penny drops. The student finally wants to make a change. And often it is a better change than the one I would have suggested—better in that it removes my difficulty but takes the paper in the direction *she* was trying to take it, not the direction I wanted to take it.*

Besides, when we give students our frankly acknowledged subjective reactions, we are treating them with more respect: "Here are my reactions; here's the data; you decide what to do about them." By treating them so, we increase the chances that they will do us the honor of treating us as real readers—taking us seriously—instead of just treating us as sources of impersonal *verdicts* to be believed blindly or resisted in a knee-jerk fashion.

Finally—in a striking instance of contraries reinforcing rather than undermining each other—it turns out that giving movies of our mind as we read student work can even increase the *objectivity* of our judgment about that work. In an interesting bit of research (designed to extend Diederich's work mentioned above) Alan Purves discovered that readers make more *accurate* and *reliable* judgments about the features of student writing if, while making them, they are also asked to give a quick account of their subjective response or feelings. It seems that when evaluators have a channel for articulating their feelings or subjective responses, they are less likely to let those responses distort their attempts at objectivity.

---

* Teachers not trained in English often feel they are not qualified to comment on student writing because they cannot make correct diagnoses—cannot correctly *name* the problem. They don't realize that their commentary can often be *more* effective than that by English teachers: first because it concentrates on the story of what was happening to them; second because it *isn't* by an English teacher.

Besides, subjective "movies of the reader's mind" are often more *universal* than attempts at dispassionate accuracy—more true to the perceptions of other readers. Something is lost in phenomenological translation. I am able to say, for example, "In your opening paragraph I feel you inviting me in"—or "keeping me at a distance"—rather than, "the diction or syntax is of a certain sort." Of course it can be useful to characterize the nature of the diction and syntax when I am engaged in careful discourse analysis or research, but for the sake of teaching the student or communicating to other readers, I usually do better by talking about things like whether the passage "invites me in" or "keeps me at a distance." Thus Purves's invitation to his readers to give a subjective response not only provided an escape route for pressures in the wrong direction, it may also have exerted a pressure in the *right* direction.

Conclusion

"Evaluation" refers to two very different activities: *measurement* (or grading or ranking) and *commentary* (or feedback). The effect of the ambiguity in the term is to invite confusion between measurement and commentary. The first two methods I've described in this chapter for increasing trustworthiness in evaluation (breaking the performance to be evaluated down into features and using more than one observer) are most helpful with measurement—though they can help commentary too. Movies of the mind is nothing but commentary (though as we just saw, it may also help accuracy in measurement).

Once we highlight the difference between measurement and commentary, we notice that conventional *grading* also tends to mix them up. Students and teacher fall into thinking of measurement *as* commentary, sometimes as the only important commentary. The mixing up of the concepts of measurement and commentary tends to keep people from noticing that they could get by with far less measurement and thereby do a much better job with commentary. For example, within a course, many teachers find that they benefit from using commentary or feedback *without grades* on individual exercises, papers, or even exams. Often students read commentary better when there is no grade.

The unspoken premise that permeates much of education is that *every* performance must be measured and that the most important response to a performance is a measurement of it. The claim need only be stated to be seen through. Yet many teachers are incapable of commenting in *any way* on a student performance such as a paper except by saying how it measures up or doesn't. (See the chapter on "Feedback" in *Writing With Power* for the myriad ways in which we can give helpful comments on a paper that are not evaluative—for example, by restating what we see as the main idea and the implied ideas of the paper.) When an individual teacher, a department, or a whole faculty sits down and asks, "At what point and for what purposes do we *need* measurement?" they will invariably see that they engage in too much of it—especially if they remind themselves that *accurate* measurement is rare and expensive. (Admittedly, some students will be distressed by cutbacks in measurement—at first.)

It's hard to imagine a procedure more untrustworthy than conventional grading:

- It is almost invariably performed by only one person.
- It encourages confusion between measurement and commentary.
- It disguises the many diverse features of any important performance into a single number.
- As a result it is maximally misleading both to students and outside readers.
- As a further result it encourages students and the rest of the community in the myth that a person's intelligence or learning can be summed up on one dimension. (See Howard Gardner.)

Grading on a curve is the worst. Curved grades give no indication whether all or none of the students have actually learned what was taught.

PART IV

❀❀❀

CONTRARIES AND INQUIRY

I seem to be a person who falls easily into contrary views. It's always happening that I talk to one person and find what she says convincing, and then talk to someone else with a contrary view and find her equally convincing (except where she says that the first person was wrong). The same thing happens to me in my reading. Even "thinking for myself," I characteristically start off believing X and then drift into believing not-X— but want to hold onto both.

Perhaps it's because my brain is accustomed to accepting conflicting data and somehow dealing with it but not reconciling it: I started out cross-eyed and childhood surgery left me with two good eyes which happen to look outward in different directions. Perhaps it's because of being brought up Catholic by Jewish and Catholic parents—and hanging onto the faith through a Unitarian boarding school with compulsory chapel and a fifties-sophisticated college where I tried to look smart to teachers who thought it was dumb to go to church. (I didn't let it lapse till it wasn't under attack.) Or perhaps it's simply because of a congenital impulse to *please* everyone.

What a relief, then, to discover that contraries can interact productively instead of fruitlessly fighting or conflicting with each other. If I push an object away from me and pull it toward me at the same time, it doesn't move and my effort is in vain; or if I assert X and not-X, the two assertions just stalemate each other. But once I add the element of time, the contraries can cease fighting and in fact help each other out. If I first push the object away and then pull it toward me, back and forth, each movement is more smooth and effective for alternating with the other. If I argue wholeheartedly for X and then wholeheartedly for not-X, I can count on getting somewhere in my thinking. At the larger level of temperament, I don't have to try to decide whether to be a logical or an intuitive person, I can invite a productive alternation between those qualities. Inquiry by means of opposites has a longer trajectory but a more interesting one.*

I've come to suspect that whenever any ability is difficult to learn and rarely performed well, it's a probably because contraries are called for—patting the head and rubbing the belly. Thus, good writing is hard because it means trying to be creative and critical; good teaching is hard because it means trying to be ally and adversary of students; good evaluation is hard because it means trying to be subjective and objective (seeking both reader-based and criterion-based perceptions); good intelligence is rare because it means trying to be intuitive and logical. In broken-record disputes that have gone on too long and become fruitless, progress tends to come not so much from some compromise or golden mean, but from some way to do justice to both sides in their opposition. (For example, form vs. content; romantic vs. classic; means vs. ends; empirical vs. normative.)

Which brings up a final contrary: there are two very different ways to get contraries to interact. One can heighten the opposition between them and promote an alternation back and forth; or one can promote some kind of blending or merging of the two. The former, alternating process is more mechanical and artificial—less magic. I sometimes stress it because I'm so interested in what we can accomplish without magic. The latter, magical process—of opposites somehow blending or merging—is not, however, so uncommon. We see

* It's a relief also to find reputable backing for this view of opposites. Yeats: "No mind can engender until divided into two." Niels Bohr: "The opposite of a correct statement is a false statement. But the opposite of a profound truth may well be another profound truth." F. Scott Fitzgerald: "The test of a first-rate intelligence is the ability to hold two opposed ideas in the mind at the same time and still retain the ability to function."

it in metaphor-making, in learning by falling in love, and in thinking by participating or believing.

The two modes of interaction show themselves perhaps most palpably in the writing process. When all goes well in our writing—when the muses visit—we are somehow simultaneously fecund and discriminating, rich and pointed. This condition is perfectly natural, but it is magic. When we are stuck, however, and must write in the absence of the muses, we can use the more mechanical and bumpy process—deliberately moving back and forth between extreme creating and criticizing. Paradoxically, this mechanical process sometimes coaxes the muses back.

CHAPTER 11

❀❀❀

My interest in contraries surfaced during my graduate studies as I attempted to read Chaucer. I started by wrestling with the poet's "retraction" of *Troilus and Criseyde*. The poet concludes this novel-length poem by apologizing for everything that went before as wrong and sinful. He asks the reader to ignore it and forgive him for it. Like most readers of Chaucer I couldn't accept this on face value—as the poet speaking in his own voice: the poem is too "right"; one cannot buy such a disowning. Yet, on the other hand, I couldn't accept the common view that this passage was merely "conventional," "tacked on,"—or ironic or mere "gesture." I sensed too much voice or authenticity in this passage too—however problematic. I felt I had to accept this passage too as integral to the poem, despite the blunt contradiction it sets up. I clung to an intuitive (aesthetic?) sense that both the body of the poem and the concluding disavowal had to be "right"— and not just in some simple chronological sense of being the "true story" of a poet (or even a persona) changing his mind through time.

The story of my working on Chaucer, however, is the story of a path I didn't intend to take. In my second year of my second go at graduate school, one of the required "courses" was simply a requirement to prepare and give a public lecture. "Good," I said to myself. "Here's a chance to write about metaphor and its relationship to thinking"—which over the last few years I'd come to believe was the secret of everything important. "Don't do that," my advisor said, "you'll just get into a muddle and make a fool of yourself." But I insisted and plunged in. He proved right, however, and seven weeks later I had to skulk back to him with my tail between my legs and admit I'd gotten into too much of a mess and I couldn't possibly sort anything out for this lecture. (My advisor later went on to write a book himself about metaphor—the burden of which was that metaphor is not worth writing about.) I had to search for something else to work on. I came back to my unfinished train of thought about Chaucer, and it proved an interesting and fruitful project. But the story then repeated itself eighteen months later when I came to start on my dissertation. This time, I thought to myself, I have the time and scope to get somewhere on metaphor. And this time I didn't give up till I'd invested a full year of work. Again I returned to Chaucer, and again it proved fruitful—indeed, it proved a backhanded way to work on metaphor and thinking. As Chaucer would say, "the tongue returns to the aching tooth."

What follows is the major portion of the last chapter of my book on Chaucer.

The Value of Dialectic

Chaucer was interested in the problem of freedom and necessity, and he often wrote about it even when he seemed to be writing about something else. In writing about Chaucer, I find that I have also been exploring the nature of knowledge and understanding. I cannot resist speculating here about why Chaucer's handling of oppositions seems so important. In doing so I plunge in over my head. In previous chapters I have tried to *demonstrate* my contentions; here I can only try to assert them plausibly.

If I were writing about the dative endings in Chaucer, I should perhaps find in them the source of his greatness. I temper the claim here only slightly. I do not think his dialectic is what makes him a great poet, but I do think that it makes him a wise one.

In trying to understand *Troilus and Criseyde* fully, I found a pattern of thinking at the center of the work. As I explored this pattern in more and more works by Chaucer, I came to see it as a source of the poet's wisdom. And in the process I began to see this pattern more and more often outside Chaucer in cases of great insight or intellectual progress. What I want to illustrate in this essay is that wisdom often seems to have this characteristic, dialectical shape.

The ancient sense of the word dialectic refers to the use of conflict—originally just of dialogue—in the search for truth. Hegel gave the narrower sense that is now current: the thesis-antithesis-synthesis pattern wherein two contradictory elements are transcended, and the process leads to a new idea on a higher level. Chaucer's dialectic falls between the ancient and the modern senses. He seldom produces the new idea on a higher level, though he does not just give a simple conflict either. By setting up a polar opposition and affirming both sides, he lays the groundwork for a broader frame of reference, ensuring that neither side can "win." He arranges the dilemma so that we can only be satisfied by taking a larger view. Sometimes he even creates that larger view.

Why should this pattern of thought make someone wiser, help to free someone from the limitations of language, logic, and the single human point of view? The answer has to do with the nature of knowing, with the way humans perceive and categorize. Perceiving is not so much like a camera's taking into itself an image of what is outside; it is more nearly like constructing or sculpting or drawing something from fragments of a view (or fragments of many views, since the eyes refuse to remain still). Even though the eye's lens projects an image onto the retina, the mind or brain cannot "take in" that image. It can only take in electrical impulses that are nothing like an image, and it must construct from these impulses our sense of what we see. In short, "seeing, hearing, and remembering are all acts of construction which may make more or less use of stimulus information depending on circumstances" (Neisser 1967, 10). That perception is active and constructive is vividly dramatized by hallucinations: there is no way to distinguish between hallucinating and perceiving as processes. Both result from taking limited, fragmentary stimulus information and constructing a picture or idea. The only difference is that we do a better job when we succeed in having an accurate perception (Neisser 1976, 120).

A comparable process occurs at a higher level in categorizing and thinking. We do not just *get* concepts and ideas, we *make* them—even when we seem like passive receivers of information. Hence our already existing categories or frames of reference necessarily shape any new category since they are the only source of rules for how to make up a new one (Neisser 1967; Bruner 1964, 1966). Thus new material is often distorted or ignored when it is "cognitively dissonant" in relation to the existing structures.

Contemporary psychologists thus confirm a kind of cognitive relativity formulated by Boethius: knowledge is always a product of the knower as much as of the thing known. To be more exact, knowledge is a result of the interaction between the knower and the object of knowledge. If there are no contrasting channels for verifying our knowledge—if, for example, we cannot touch or otherwise learn about the things that we try to see—then there is no way to know how much or what sort of distortion has crept in.

This epistemological dilemma has shown up particularly vividly in particle physics. Physicists cannot get information about a particle alone. They can only get a package of information about the interaction of the particle and the "observer" (i.e., the equipment). They can know the velocity of a particle, but not its location, or its location but not its velocity; but they can never know both.

In social science too there is a growing recognition of how the "observer" affects the results of an experiment through the mechanics of the experimental situation and the preconceptions of the designer. In the case of subjective knowledge, the act of focusing our attention on a thought or feeling inevitably alters it.

The dialectical pattern of thinking provides some relief from this structural difficulty inherent in knowing. Since perception and cognition are processes in which the organism "constructs" what it sees or thinks according to models already there, the organism tends to throw away or distort material that does not fit this model. The surest way to get hold of what your present frame blinds you to is to try to adopt the opposite frame, that is, to reverse your model. A person who can live with contradiction and exploit it—who can use conflicting models—can simply see and think *more*.* If I think of my behavior as free, the best way

---

* It is interesting to see a modern historian, William McNeill, apply this model of contradiction as a superior source of fertility in history and culture:

It was the Greco-Roman and Judaeo-Christian inheritances, however attenuated during the Dark Age, that provided the fundamental frame for the elaboration of high medieval and modern European civilization. This inheritance was shot through with contrariety. Europeans confronted unresolved and unresolvable tensions between the primacy of the territorial state as the "natural" unit of human society and the claim of the Church to govern human souls; tensions between faith and reason, each claiming to be the pre-eminent path to the truth; tensions between naturalism and metaphysical symbolism as the ideal of art. The barbarian ingredient of

to notice and understand behavior that was hidden from me is to try to see it as determined.

If in particular we are trying to know something that is especially hard to check or verify, our best hope of doing so is to gain as many *different* and *conflicting* knowings as possible. Holding all these conflicting views in mind, we must then try to get a sense of the unknown behind them. People who are good at doing this seem to call upon some subtle tact, judgment, or intuition. I think that they are using a metaphorical, analogical, Gestalt-finding kind of ability.* They are good at maintaining contradictory points of view simultaneously and at living with ambiguity in order to refrain from premature resolution. They can wait for contrary knowings to interact and affect each other so that the metaphors, analogues, or Gestalten that eventually emerge are likelier to reflect more fully the unknown new phenomena and less likely merely to replicate the patterns already present in the mind.

❀

European tradition introduced still other contradictions—violence vs. the law, vernacular vs. Latin, nation vs. Christendom. Yet these polar antitheses were built into the very fundament of European society and have never been either escaped or permanently resolved.

Quite possibly Western civilization incorporated into its structure a wider variety of incompatible elements than did any other civilization of the world; and the prolonged and restless growth of the West, repeatedly rejecting its own potentially "classical" formulations, may have been related to the contrarieties built so deeply into its structure. . . . In this, far more than in any particular intellectual, institutional, or technological expression that western Europe has from time to time put on, lies the true uniqueness of Western civilization. (*The Rise of the West* 539)

* Though Plato's ontology seems peculiar to us, he was clearly interested in this *kind* of thinking:

Elsewhere in the late dialogues a similar account of dialectic is given. . . . In the *Politicus* the method is again described in similar terms: it is necessary "first to perceive the *community* existing between the many, and then not to desist before seeing in it all the *differences* that there are among the Forms; and then having seen the manifold *dissimilarities* in the groups of many, not to be put out of countenance or stop until, bringing all the common features within a single *likeness,* one encloses them in the essence of a Form (285ab). (Lloyd 432–33)

Searching for contradiction and affirming both sides can allow you to find both the limitations of the system in which you are working and a way to break out of it. If you find contradictions and try too quickly to get rid of them, you are only neatening up, even strengthening, the system you are in. To actually get beyond that system you need to find the deepest contradictions and, instead of trying to reconcile them, heighten them by affirming both sides. And if you can nurture the contradictions cleverly enough, you can be led to a new system with a wider frame of reference, one that includes the two elements which were felt as contradictory in the old frame of reference.

When Einstein found contradictions in classical Newtonian mechanics—contradictions concerning the speed of light in the Michelson-Morley experiment that others tried to eliminate—he developed a theory of relativity that saved the contradictory results. He did not really vanquish Newtonian mechanics, but he radically limited its application. What looked like a general universal law (classical mechanics) was shown to be really just a special, limited case within a more general law of wider application (the general theory of relativity). What looks like polar opposition is really a case of one being a subset of the other—just as Boethius sees the cave/sky opposition as really a matter of the cave being a subset of the sky.

Analogously, Chaucer uses contradiction in *The Knight's Tale* not only to uncover the limitations of the system in which he is working (chivalry), but also to suggest a new, larger system (the values Theseus embodies). Chaucer pushes the opposition between the two cousins till it reaches contradiction—till the rules of the original system lead to a dead end or a wrong conclusion—and thereby forces into the open the weaknesses or limitations of the system of chivalric romance. Courage, loyalty, and honor are shown to comprise a special, limited system of values that is only a subset of Theseus' larger system, which contains feeling for others, humor, irony, forgiveness, the ability to change one's mind, and the ability to grow and change through suffering instead of just stoically enduring it. If courage, loyalty, and honor are applied too widely, they lead to brutal, rigid, humorless, and even unfeeling behavior, and hence contradict the larger system.

But if, as a special case, they are limited to their proper sphere of application, they are fine and there is no conflict.

However, Chaucer usually just breaks out of the limited system he is in by finding and affirming contradictions in it, without going on to present a new, larger system. For example, his preoccupation with the conflict between freedom and necessity often takes the form of asking, in effect, "Which of you is in charge here?"—of husband and wife, poet and sources, man and God—and then watching contradictions emerge. Was it Criseyde, Troilus, Pandarus, the war, or Fate which separated Troilus and Criseyde? Again, no single answer is satisfactory. The truth is contradictory. Chaucer, by exploiting contradiction, is uncovering the limits or blind spots in the system for understanding freedom and responsibility when more than one person is involved.

He does not provide a new system, but he suggests, at least, that two or more people together can seem to function like a complex organism or system. When this system functions as it ought, *each* party seems to have complete freedom and authority: things occur just as planned by *both* man and God, husband and wife, poet and sources. But when the system is not working, somehow things do not come out as either planned. Between them, their freedom and authority do not even seem to add up to 100%. The system rides them. With freedom and responsibility, of course, goes fault. Chaucer implies that fault proliferates along with control: the wife's mistake is the fault of the husband and vice versa (*The Franklin's Tale, The Merchant's Tale*); the poet's mistake is the fault of the sources and vice versa ("Do not blame me, dear reader . . ."); and even man's mistake is a "fault" which Christ takes on through participation (in the basic meaning of the crucifixion; compare, by analogy, "patient" Griselda). Husband and wife, poet and sources, man and God are all implied somehow to inhere each in the other in a relationship of participation.

Much work in our own century confirms Chaucer's implication that we need some larger system or systems for trying to talk about individual agency and functioning when more than one individual is involved. A number of quite diverse people are now engaged in trying to develop such systems by different methods—systems analysis, cybernetics, group-process psychology, the school of psychiatry which treats the family as a single organism, and ecology (which treats the individual or the whole population as only part of a system that includes neighbors and environment). After a new system is comfortably worked out, the conventional way of dividing freedom and control—as if each individual were free and entirely self-contained—will remain as a special case that gives valid answers and does not cause contradiction when applied within its appropriate limits.

❁

Exploiting contradiction helps bring to light the unnoticed limitations of that system we work in most closely, the one whose blind spots are hardest to notice: language. Efforts to uncover the limitations of language and logic seem to be the hallmark of the twentieth century. When physicists conceive of light as both wave and particle, they are putting into our hardest currency the idea that the "real thing" is unrenderable with our standard linguistic-logical equipment, and that we render it best by forcibly bending contradictory models into intersection. General relativity is a rebuke to our linguistically ingrained conceptions space, time, mass, and velocity. Benjamin Whorf asserts the relativity of perception because of the relativity of linguistic structure. Existentialists and phenomenologists emphasize how language falsifies actual experience. In the Middle Ages there was a greater sense of the limitations of language than in any other period but our own, and I think this is a major reason for the increased modern interest in that period.

The Nun's Priest's Tale is a late, sophisticated work in which Chaucer deals almost directly with the limitations of language. By exploiting the contradictions that occur at the intersection of behavior and utterance—the contradictions between, as it were, Chauntecleer's smart mind and stupid body (also his smart body and stupid mind)—Chaucer forces out into the open the limitations of the categories for talking about both behavior and utterance. In the confusion, he enriches each by the other. On the one hand, he shows that utterance is often best understood as behavior. All of Chauntecleer's learned talk is not really so much about what it professes to be about—he seems to ignore or forget what he has argued for—but rather serves as behavior expressing his sense of self-importance in the universe and his lordship over his wife. His learned footnotes are momentary preenings of his tail feathers. On the other hand, Chaucer also shows that behavior is often best understood as utterance: Chauntecleer and Pertelote speak more clearly in behavior than in words.

Chaucer is showing the need for a larger system for speaking clearly about behavior and utterance and their interrelation. That is precisely what many significant twentieth-century thinkers are working on. For example, J. L. Austin, in his general theory of speech acts, rethinks speech as a subset of the larger category of behavior. He chides philosophers for always thinking of utterance in terms of true and false:

> What we have to study is *not* the sentence but the issuing of an utterance in a speech situation. . . . It is essential to realize that "true" and "false," like "free" and "unfree," do not stand for anything simple at all; but only for a general dimension of being a right or proper thing to say as opposed to a wrong thing, in these circumstances, to this audience, for these purposes and with these intentions. . . . The truth and falsity of a statement depend not merely on the meanings of words but on what act you were performing in what circumstance. (Austin 138, 144)

Speech, as just a special case of behavior, is subject to the "ills that all action is heir to . . . subject to the usual troubles and reservations about attempt as distinct from achievement, being intentional as distinct from being unintentional, and the like" (105, 109). Austin makes the question of whether statements are true or false into a special, limited case or subset of the whole larger system for understanding the "force" or "effects" of action.

Freud too brings behavior and utterance together into one system. Where Austin treats utterance as behavior, Freud treats behavior as utterance. Ostensibly he uses a system modeled on classical mechanics with the emphasis on cause. But in fact he keeps coming up with what Chaucer implied: "overdetermined behavior"—events with too many causes. We see why he does this when we see *what* behavior he is drawn to look at: language or utterance—dreams and slips of the tongue. Freud's gift may be that he taught us to ask, when we wish to understand a piece of behavior, not "What caused him to do that?" but rather "What does it mean? What is he saying?" And the weaknesses in psychoanalytical practice may come from the extent to which it still clings to a physical, etiological model:

> What Freud did here was not to explain the patient's choice causally but to understand it and give it meaning, and the procedure he engaged in was not the scientific one of elucidating causes but the semantic one of making sense of it. It can indeed be argued that much of Freud's work was really semantic and that he made a revolutionary discovery in semantics, viz. that neurotic symptoms are meaningful disguised communications, but that, owing to his scientific training and allegiance, he formulated his findings in the conceptual framework of the physical sciences. In some aspects of his work Freud saw this himself clearly. His most famous work he entitled *The Interpretation of Dreams* not *The Cause of Dreams* and his chapter on symptoms in his *Introductory Lectures* is called *The Sense of Symptoms*. He was also well aware that many of his ideas had been anticipated by writers and poets rather than by scientists. (Rycroft 13)

To shift explanation from cause to meaning is to shift some of the focus from the past to the future. There is necessarily a teleological aspect to speech, an attempt to make something happen in the future.

There may be a clue here to the larger system that will eventually emerge. Utterance may be the most useful paradigm for rendering behavior. At this point at least, from our knowledge of how language and poetry work, we understand better how there may be two or more contradictory meanings in a set of words than we understand how there may be two or more contradictory causes for an event.*

Karl Popper argues in a no-nonsense tone that the power of contradiction lies merely in its repugnance:

> It cannot be emphasized too strongly that if we . . . decide to put up with contradictions, then contradictions must at once lose any kind of fertility. They would no longer be productive of intellectual

---

* See Colin Turbayne for a discussion of the difficulties inherent in our tendency always to link explanation with *cause,* and for a proposal to use a *meaning* model instead.

progress. For if we were prepared to put up with contradictions, pointing out contradictions in our theories could no longer induce us to change them. In other words, all criticism (which consists in pointing out contradictions) would lose its force. Criticism would be answered by "And why not?" or perhaps even by an enthusiastic "There you are!"; that is, by welcoming the contradictions which have been pointed out to us. (317)

Though contradiction is an itch we naturally seek to remove, Popper seems in such a *hurry* to remove it. A major part of his essay is devoted to showing rigorously that contradiction is meaningless and useless because in logic, two contradictory statements entail *any* statement. This may be true in strict logic, but when it comes to the actual process of getting ideas, seeing where they lead, and even assessing their worth, a particular contradiction can be meaningful indeed, and can point in a very particular direction. Furthermore, contradictions *cannot* always be removed quickly. For a long time physics has put up with the definition of light as both wave and particle. Some physicists say this contradiction is permanent (Bohr). And Thomas Kuhn's account of the history of science implies that the actual process of deciding between competing models cannot derive from logic alone but rather from authorities in the field who are implicitly empowered to decide the question on grounds—pragmatic, aesthetic, analogical—that are difficult to specify.*

Popper insists that dialectic is a "descriptive" theory not a "fundamental" one: descriptive in that it describes stages that actual ideas or theories sometimes go through in their development, but not fundamental, not a "theory of all sorts of inferences [like logic] used all the time by all sciences" (323). He talks as if this were a logical matter, but it is really an empirical question: how often *are* various patterns or thinking actually used? We need to find out. In making this distinction he is trying, in effect, to keep the time dimension out of thinking. He is willing, that is, to accept a temporal or historical account of the stages through which the opinions of some person or group

---

* Popper's own theory of falsifiability surely sanctions actual situations in which scientists have to choose (for a time, at least) between two hypotheses when neither has been falsified—or what is probably more common, when *both* have been falsified in one respect or another.

passed, but he does not want a temporal account of the actual thinking process itself. He insists that valid inference occurs only in the realm of an abstract, timeless logic.

Perhaps he is right. I am no philosopher or logician. But everything I am discussing in this chapter makes me suspect that there is something particularly important about bringing time into a realm where it has been absent. What was perhaps Hegel's central act was to introduce the time dimension into the hitherto timeless realm of "pure" thinking and inference by insisting that you cannot talk about what is true or what follows from something without talking about *when*. And Hegelians insist that time is the *source* of contradiction, that it is in the realm of time that things or ideas move toward their opposites. Though I cannot evaluate the logic or ontology of these kinds of assertions, many important systematic breakthroughs in thinking seem to involve just this pattern of bringing time into a realm where it has been absent.

For example, the three giant theories of the nineteenth century—those of Darwin, Marx, and Freud—are all cases of insisting on an historical or developmental model. Darwin found the key to understanding the *form* of an organism by seeing where it stands in an historical developmental process. Marx did the same thing to explain a social structure; Freud to explain human behavior. At one point in the developmental or historical process, a phenomenon might mean one thing; at another it might mean something entirely different. Without the time dimension, the explanation is meaningless. Einstein's theory of relativity is, of course, the most striking instance of a theory that insists on the time dimension (the "fourth" dimension) to make sense of phenomena in which it had not seemed to be needed before. Piaget, who considers himself a philosopher and logician as much as an empirical psychologist, has given a powerful model for understanding thinking by also insisting on a developmental structure. And he argues that all growth results from the interaction in time of contradictory processes, assimilation and accommodation. His model has been fruitful in spawning others (e.g., Perry; Kohl).

Time needs to be brought into accounts of how language has meaning. Austin's theory of speech acts does so when he says you must consider all the surrounding circumstances in a speech act. I think Owen Barfield's work has power because he insists on the role of time in the meaning of words. For myself, it did not seem possible to give a satisfactory account of the meaning of the words of *Troilus and Criseyde* without talking about a temporal sequence of events within the reader—agreement, disagreement, and then agreement again.

❀

Since Coleridge there has been a tradition of using the reconciliation of opposites as a model for imaginative art and of calling metaphor a microcosm of imaginative art. (See Coleridge, Book XIII; also Wimsatt and Brooks, Chapter XVIII.) My approach obviously grows out of this tradition. But the emphasis is usually on reconciling, bringing together, "fusing." Here I should like to give a bit more emphasis to the element of contradiction.

Monroe Beardsley is one of the few analysts of metaphor who bring to the fore what is the most important fact about metaphor: there must be a *contradiction,* a piece of *non*-sense, before you can have a metaphor (Chapter III). The word or phrase must be sufficiently *wrong* to produce at least a momentary blockage of sense. This is illustrated by borderline cases: unless you can feel *leg* as the wrong word in the phrase *the leg of the table* (*leg* perhaps as appropriate only to animate organisms), you cannot feel *leg of the table* as a metaphor. For most people the phrase is literal.

From the contradiction or *non*-sense comes the energy or force of a metaphor, the force that makes the mind jump the rails and do something different in the presence of the words from what it usually does. Metaphor has the dialectical pattern I have been exploring in Chaucer. The metaphor does not provide a new system or synthesis, it only provides an abutting of opposed elements. Thus metaphor can be described as a *refusal* to synthesize, a refusal to find new language, an insistence on letting the contradiction stand. When the metaphor is new and unusual, it forces the mind to do exactly what Chaucer forces us to do: simply to live with the contradiction and try to let it reverberate as a way of doing justice to the complexity of its subject.

It is useful to look at imaginative art as a whole in a similar light. Morse Peckham points out that although people talk more about the unity in art, the striking and useful thing is usually its lack of unity. He makes a psycho-biological argument: that the primary activity of the organism is to categorize—to see same-nesses, although really everything is unique in some way. Other-wise prediction and survival are not possible. But categorizing falls into ruts and thereby often blinds one to small but impor-tant differences. Art, Peckham argues usefully, is an activity that serves to break down habitual categories. It trains and rewards living with contradiction and disunity.

❀

Let me conclude by delimiting what I am trying to assert. I am not saying that all these famous people actually used a dia-lectical pattern in their thinking (as I hope I showed Boethius and Chaucer did). I do not know the actual steps they followed in their thinking.* Nor am I espousing the philosophical posi-tion of Hegelianism with its ontology and determinism. My claim is that many important insights or breakthroughs end up as a movement of thought from one frame of reference—originally taken as the whole frame of reference or the most universal way to conceive the matter—to a larger one. There appears to be a contradiction between the original and the new frame of refer-ence—and/or between the original one and some consequence or branch of the new one. But the original one can finally be under-stood as a subset of the larger one, a special case that does not really contradict it if correctly restricted. If breakthroughs often have this shape, then the following strategies are likely to be fruitful: to search for potential contradictions in a given system; to heighten them by affirming both sides rather than trying to resolve or eliminate them immediately; to develop in general an attraction for contradiction, which I think Boethius and Chau-cer had; and even to try negating or turning things upside down just to see what new comes to light. The goal is to encourage the growth of new and larger frames of reference out of the interac-tion of contradictions, but one should remember, nevertheless,

* We need more books that examine the structure of thinking of important thinkers by following closely their language, especially their figurative lan-guage. One such book is Stanley Edgar Hyman's *The Tangled Bank*.

not to be in too much of a hurry to get rid of the contradiction and find a new frame of reference. Taking enough time will increase the chances of doing justice to any possible novelty in the matter under investigation.

Certain people are especially smart. They have a talent for having good hunches, nurturing them, and having a sense of which ones to follow. These people are right too often for it to be a matter of luck. Nor could they have their success by simply cranking through blind algorithms. And they do not get there by strict logic—logic often comes only much later. If these people are not using strict logic, brute algorithm, or sheer luck, and they are still consistently insightful, there must be some patterns in their thinking, some lawfulness in their activity. Affirming contradictions and not being in too much of a hurry to get rid of them—Chaucer's dialectic—must be one of the patterns of thought that makes wise people wise.

CHAPTER 12

✿✿✿

When people are impressed with the power of someone's thinking, they are likely to say something like, "She has a mind like a steel trap!" This essay is my attempt to get them to say (equally awed), "She has a mind like silly putty!"

This essay has not been published before. I put it at the end because the issue is the most important of all to me, it's the one I've been working on longest (I published an early set of reflections on this topic as the appendix essay in *Writing Without Teachers*), and it's the one that looks most to the future.

❀❀❀

Methodological Doubting and Believing: Contraries in Inquiry

"I can't believe that," said Alice.

"Can't you?" the Queen said in a pitying tone. "Try again; draw a long breath, and shut your eyes."

Alice laughed. "There's no use trying," she said; "one *can't* believe impossible things."

"I dare say you haven't had much practice," said the Queen. "When I was your age I always did it for half an hour a day. Why, sometimes I've believed as many as six impossible things before breakfast."

Lewis Carroll, *Through the Looking Glass*

In order to understand what another person is saying, you must assume it is true and try to imagine what it might be true of.

George Miller, "Thirteen Maxims for the Mind"

Certainty evades us. In Plato's *Meno,* in his metaphor of "hypotheses" as planks one "puts down" and then climbs up in order to get high enough to see first principles (in *The Republic*), and in Descartes's *Discourse on Method,* we find the implication that when we *see* the truth we'll know it; and others will agree because we've been able to *demonstrate* it (as in geometry) or because it is so clear and distinct that they *cannot* doubt it. But it doesn't seem to work out that way (not since the good old days, anyway), and recent philosophers, devising more and more sophisticated schemes, cannot find rules or criteria agreeable even to that one discipline for deciding when something counts as demonstrated. The disappearance of certainty is most striking where we most assume its presence—in mathematics:

[M]athematics generally (including geometry and number theory as well as set theory) is from an evidential point of view more like physics and less like logic than was once supposed. On the whole the truths of mathematics can be deduced not from self-evident axioms, but only from hypotheses which, like those of natural science, are to be judged by the plausibility of their consequences. (Quine and Ullian 46)

The intriguing question, then, is not so much why people disagree so much, but why they ever agree. Or to state more precisely the question behind this essay: What really goes on when people start out with positions completely at odds and end up in agreement? (When the people are smart and critical—not just bending to fashion, influence, or power.) What kind of thinking and discourse make this precious event possible? In addition: How shall we describe the mental activity that permits us while operating alone to see that we are wrong and come to a new and better conclusion?

I will argue that we can improve our understanding of careful thinking or reasoned inquiry (and thereby improve our practice) if we see it as involving two central ingredients: what I am calling methodological doubt and methodological belief. The fact that good thinking involves two mental processes that conflict with each other helps explain why the activity is complex and rare.*

Let me start with a meditation on *Othello* as a way to sketch a crude mythology of stages in our relationship to belief and doubt. For the first stage I point to Othello at the beginning of the play. He *knows* Desdemona loves him. It would never occur to him to doubt her love since she risked so much to marry him. He never stops to ponder why or how he knows, or how trustworthy his knowledge is.

But Iago teaches him to doubt his wife's love and fidelity. This

---

* I should specify for learned readers, at the start of this essay, the "field" into which I am venturing. But if I tried I would probably just convict myself of having insufficiently mastered it to justify the attempt. I suppose I am making an assay into what philosophers and rhetoricians have called the "rhetoric of good reasons." But I am more interested in what are good and bad *ways of experiencing and using* reasons than in what makes reasons good and bad in themselves. Perhaps my field is really the rhetoric of bad reasons.

is the second stage. Desdemona's love is *not* beyond a reasonable doubt.

In the third stage, tortured by doubt about whether his wife is faithful, Othello comes to hunger for relief. "Be sure thou prove my love a whore!" he says to Iago because at some level he knows that he can never get relief until he is *certain*—which means being certain his wife is false.

We encounter here that curiously pregnant asymmetry in logic by which only negative claims can be certain. We can never be certain that all swans are white no matter how many swans we examine, but we can be absolutely certain that all swans are not white just by seeing one black swan. Thus, Othello instinctively realizes that he can only find relief from his painful uncertainty if he finds his wife untrue. Doubt and the need for certainty reinforce each other.*

Shakespeare was disturbed about the onset of a new era breeding overly rational men—an era we often symbolically usher in with the work of Descartes, writing just a few years later. It was Descartes who systematized doubting. He didn't just doubt vigorously—he wasn't even very skeptical. But he sought some foundation for knowledge by trying systematically to doubt *everything,* no matter how obvious it seemed. He sought what *cannot* be doubted and therefore remains certain. Through this maneuver, which he proudly called his "method"—what I am calling methodological doubt—he seemed to achieve the certainty he and Othello sought.†

It seemed for a long time as though Descartes really did achieve what we might call his larger methodological goal. That is, he

---

* There are important etymological links which reflect the psychological links between "criticizing" "doubting," and seeking "certainty." "Critical" comes from a word meaning to cut or separate into two parts in order to judge; "doubt" is cognate with "two" ("double"—also in German: *zweifel* and *zwei*); and "critical" is cognate with "certain."

† One of the reasons Descartes believed certainty was attainable was that he had done important new work in geometry. Notice how clever geometers in certain situations can manipulate negative claims to give certainty even to positive claims. They can *prove,* for example, that angles *A* and *B* are equal by showing first that *A* is not bigger than *B* and next that it is not smaller than *B*—both of those negative claims being certain. Thus the two angles must be equal.

may not have convinced everyone of his specific "proof" of his own and God's existence, but his methodological assumptions somehow ended up more deeply enthroned than ever: that certainty is possible if we are willing systematically to doubt everything. The era stretching from the late Renaissance to some time early in the twentieth century can be characterized as an era in which we not only accepted Descartes's goal of certainty as attainable, but we came to assume certainty as a necessary feature of knowledge: if it's not certain, it's not knowledge.

Thus where the first stage is innocent unexamined belief and the second stage is serious doubt, the third stage is a need for certainty—which rests on an assumption we now recognize as innocent too, namely, that certainty is possible. Our present (fourth) stage was also shrewdly suggested by Shakespeare in *Othello:* the realization that certainty is rarely if ever possible and that we increase the likelihood getting things wrong if we succumb to the hunger for it.

For a while it looked as though we might characterize the goal of the modern era merely negatively: how to live in a world where knowledge is unavailable and inquiry thus fruitless. Think of works like *Waiting for Godot* or the writings of certain existential thinkers. But we are seeing the emergence of a more positive and less skeptical way of describing our epistemological job, namely, how to decide which knowledge is most *trustworthy,* even if it is not certain: how to decide which nickels are not wooden. Thomas Kuhn (1970), Stephen Toulmin, Richard Rorty, and Wayne Booth (1979) give noteworthy accounts of how we might characterize trustworthy knowledge. I'm trying here to give an account of the mental processes that are most likely to *lead* to trustworthy knowledge.

My claim, in summary, is that methodological doubt is only half of what we need. Yes, we need the systematic, disciplined, and conscious attempt to criticize everything no matter how compelling it might seem—to find flaws or contradictions we might otherwise miss. But thinking is not trustworthy unless it also includes methodological belief: the equally systematic, disciplined, and conscious attempt to *believe* everything no matter how unlikely or repellent it might seem—to find virtues or strengths we might otherwise miss. Both processes derive their power from the very fact that they are methodological: artificial, systematic, and disciplined uses of the mind. As methods, they help us see what we would miss if we only used our minds naturally or spontaneously.

With our intellectual tradition stemming back to Socratic argument and Cartesian skepticism, we inherit a model for careful thinking that emphasizes methodological doubt or critical thinking. We tend to assume that the ability to criticize a claim we disagree with counts as more serious intellectual work than the ability to enter into it and temporarily assent. Walter Ong is probably right when he sees *fighting* or "adversativeness" as inherent in the development of logic—even of rationalism: "It was through ceremonial contest that rationalism itself had come into ascendancy" (1981, 147; see also 21–22; 34–35).

This emphasis on learning to be critical helps explain the tendency toward critical warfare in the intellectual and academic world—the fact that intellectuals often find it surprisingly difficult simply to hear and understand positions they disagree with. Because of the pervasiveness of this tradition, I will spend more of my energy arguing for methodological belief—for what Polanyi calls the "fiduciary transaction"—than for methodological doubt. Indeed I cannot resist sometimes arguing *against* methodological doubt. (Perhaps I succumb to a Manichean crudeness in my mythology above.) But I trust it is clear throughout that I consider both strategies equally necessary: methodological doubt is only a problem when it tries to hog the whole bed.

Stumbling onto Methodological Belief

It emerged gradually for me while teaching writing. I was exploring ways for students to give helpful responses to each others' writing in small peer groups. I didn't want them so much to *evaluate* each others' texts as to *describe* them: to tell what they see and understand. Sometimes a student would write a piece which didn't seem, say, angry in any way, but one of the responders would see it as angry. This seemed obviously false to the writer and to the other readers (and to me if I was present). But no one objected because I had developed for purely pragmatic reasons the rule that the reader gets to say whatever she sees and no one is allowed to object or quarrel. I had developed this rule when I discovered how often arguments about interpretation got out of hand, wasted time, and prevented new interpretations from surfacing—especially in small groups where I was not present to keep things moving.

And so it happened once—and then as I got better at making people stay quiet and listen, it occasionally recurred—that the writer finally ended up replying something like this: "Wait a minute. Now that you make me look at it this way, I remember that I *was* angry when I was writing. And I can see now that I *did* express some of that anger in this innocent little story [or essay]. I can feel some of the anger subtly expressed in the words now." And the other readers—or rather the more sensitive ones—looked again and saw subtle traces of the anger. They and I became convinced that the anger was actually in the text (insofar as anything can be said to be "in" a text—see the section below entitled "Methodological Belief and the Interpretation of Texts"), and not just projected there by plausible suggestions.

Of course this did not happen often, but it was striking when it did: someone had an "off the wall" reading which the rest of us came to see as valid because we weren't allowed to argue against it. Sometimes it was a faintly implied meaning, sometimes a tonal matter of flippancy or condescension, sometimes a trace of nonconviction in the very argument being advanced. On the basis of this experience I cranked up the perversity of my rule and made it methodological—indeed ideological: "When a reader is telling what she sees in a text or what happened to her in reading, the writer and the other readers must not just shut up, they must actively try as hard as they can to believe her—to see and experience the text as she does. This may be our only hope of seeing something faint that is actually there which she is particularly good at seeing but the rest of us are ill suited to see." In effect I had stumbled onto a game: each participant promises to try to believe what the others see in return for the others trying to believe what she sees. There is a bargain and an exchange of temporary or conditional assent. In a sense this short story says everything there is to say about methodological belief. I should apologize for writing so much more about it, but it becomes both richer and more perplexing when explored.

After a while I began to realize the value of this enforced or artificial believing process to literature classes—arenas where people so often argue and get nowhere. Some students look for the teacher's interpretation or the "correct" interpretation and don't really attend to their own experience. Others cling stubbornly to their own interpretation and cannot or will not let themselves experience the interpretations of others: "That's how *you* see it and this is how *I* see it," they say, "and there's no use arguing." When this stance is taken by a narrow-minded sophomore who reads badly, we often see something we don't see in a brilliant scholar from Yale: disappointment at the inaccessibility of the truth—translated into a pouting swagger.

I finally realized that when the sophomore or the scholar says, "There's no use arguing," he is right: argument seems to get nowhere in either population. (Though people who stake out this position are often remarkably fond of arguing.) "Yes," I say, "there seems to be no use arguing, but No, it is possible nevertheless to make progress by talking." By enforcing methodological belief I began to see communities of five or twenty-five students reach *some* agreement that they hadn't been able to reach before; *some* improvement in their ability to read—that is, to see things they couldn't see before, or to experience interpretations that don't easily fit their predisposition; and *some* improvement in polity or how they offer interpretations and listen to those of others.

In a sense all this is obvious, trivial, no big deal. Everyone agrees in theory that the only way to assess an interpretation is to try it out. But actually the practice is rare: either people don't really try out interpretations they don't like—they don't really try believing or experiencing them; or they think that "trying it out" means arguing against it and seeing how it holds up. But if you take seriously the banal principle that you cannot assess a reading without experiencing it, then an unusual "method" emerges—and one that is difficult because it has rules and takes discipline.

By methodological belief, then, I mean the disciplined procedure of not just listening but actually trying to believe any view or hypothesis that a participant seriously wants to advance. Imagine five or twenty-five of us sitting around a text. One person has an odd view. We must not just refrain from quarreling with it, we must try to believe it. If we have trouble, we ask for help from the few who do better. We ask them to explain—not defend. For example, if someone proposes that "Tyger, tyger, burning bright" with its glowing eye is really a strange new nineteenth-century steam engine with its bright headlight in the night, we must not ask, "What are your arguments for such a silly view as that?" but rather, "What do you see when you see the text so? Give me the vision in your head. You are having an experience I don't have: help me to have it."

What makes this process different from most academic inquiry is that we are not trying to construct or defend an argument but rather to transmit an experience, enlarge a vision. We end up with ingredients that could be built into an argument (we may even end up with an argument itself if that is what the proposer is primarily experiencing and wanting to communicate), but the focus is not on propositions and validity of inference but on experiences or ways of seeing. Bacon talks about two kinds of knowledge: knowledge by argument and by experience.

When we have looked at the text through as many different lenses as possible, we can see better which reading or readings fit the text. In my teaching I move only slowly toward this concluding process of evaluating or justifying interpretations, and thus I am sometimes perceived by my students as a flaming relativist. I'm more interested in trying to train students to entertain various readings than—at first, anyway—to figure out which ones are better.

The believing game seems, and indeed is, extremely permissive. But a paradoxical principle of extreme rigor emerges: you may not reject a reading till you have succeeded in believing it. If you have merely listened politely, even entertained it intelligently, or restated it to the satisfaction of the proposer (à la Carl Rogers), and decided it is wrong, it might be right and you are simply too blind to understand how.

The Development of Methodological Doubt

Believing came first. We seem to have a natural tendency to believe, but our native, naive gullibility gets us into trouble. We buy the Brooklyn Bridge from the nice stranger and thereby we learn to doubt. Young children seem to be more gullible than older ones or adults. Members of early or nonliterate cultures seem more disposed to believe the majority or the elders. The process of language acquisition by children requires the child to believe the speakers around him. To doubt would make the activity intolerably hard. (See Grice on the "cooperative principle"; also, Quine and Ullian; we can see Searle's speech act theory as implying continual acts of trust on the part of both speaker and listener.) *"Credo ut intelligam,"* says Augustine: "I believe in order that I may understand"—and it helps to believe when we are children or struggling to understand something difficult. Experiments in cognitive psychology indicate that people understand sentences they believe more quickly than sentences they doubt. Thus from a cognitive and evolutionary point of view it is no accident that we are credulous.

Over against that backdrop of natural gullibility and group-think, we see the slow human struggle to develop skepticism and individualism. It is an effort to learn to question what the context and our culture lead us to take for granted. The development of logic has been crucial in this battle. It is logic that permits the individual to outvote the group. Socrates and Descartes are heroes in this story of the development of logic and conscious critical inquiry. Socrates had a voice that sometimes spoke to him, but it only said one word, No. He had, that is, a heightened sensitivity to dissonance. He could hear or feel when something was logically fishy even if he could not yet articulate the faulty inference. Socrates loved to show people that their beliefs were misplaced and didn't stand up to critical scrutiny. He cast himself as an individual questioner over against authority, tradition, and the majority culture. He was interested in using dialogue to get ideas or propositions to wrestle with each other so as to expose contradictions in what had been assumed. Descartes, with his Gallic enjoyment of methodological self-consciousness, made doubting into the kind of systematic procedure he loved from geometry.

As intellectuals, then, we have a special role as doubters. A culture needs people who stand back and view critically what the majority assumes, who question society and its values. There is an inevitably combative or adversarial element here. Ong asserts that we need enemies and fighting to sharpen our thinking; he speculates that the Chinese failed to develop logic because they failed to institutionalize combat in oral rhetoric (*Fighting for Life* 122; 170). As intellectuals we need to learn to doubt things by weaning ourselves from naive belief: we need to learn the inner act of extricating ourselves from ideas, particularly our own. We need to learn how to cease experiencing an idea while still holding it, that is, to drain the experience from an idea and see it in its pure propositionality. That's why learning to doubt goes hand in hand with structured uses of language and logic such as syllogisms and symbolic logic.

By championing methodological belief, I might seem to be inviting us to turn back to natural credulity. But of course I am not. Methodological doubt represents the human struggle to free ourselves from parochial closed-mindedness, but it doesn't go far enough. Methodological doubt caters too comfortably to our natural impulse to protect and retain the views we already hold. Methodological belief comes to the rescue at this point by forcing us genuinely to enter into unfamiliar or threatening ideas instead of just arguing against them without experiencing them or feeling their force. It thus carries us *further* in our developmental journey away from mere credulity.

Oppositions Between Doubting and Believing

I can give a richer sense of these two fundamental cognitive processes by sketching a series of oppositions between them. I am speaking here of doubting and believing as root human impulses, not as systematized or methodological.

Psychologically or developmentally, we learn to doubt after believing gets us into trouble. Yet doubt and belief seem to alternate dialectically as we grow up. We define ourselves by saying Yes—for example to parents and teachers—but then by saying No, and then back and forth. Babies begin by putting everything in their mouths, but they move on to spitting out or rejecting. There is the period called "the terrible twos" when the tiny person says nothing but No—she seems literally to be flexing a doubting or rejecting muscle. This usually subsides, yet often recurs around age four. And then comes the striking period of adolescent refusal. In short, we relate to the world by merging and incorporating, but also by rejecting and quarreling. (See Piaget on assimilation and accommodation.)

Thus, phenomenologically, when we doubt we spit out or fend off; when we believe we swallow or incorporate. To doubt well we learn to extricate or detach ourselves; to believe well we learn to invest or insert ourselves. Doubting asks us to heighten our sensitivity to dissonance—to the presence of foreign bodies; believing asks us to learn to accept and integrate foreign bodies and put up with dissonance in the process. The idea of methodological belief—trying to believe many views—may arouse our natural fear of being invaded, polluted, or forced to swallow.

Doubting is the act of separating or differentiating and thus correlates with individualism: it permits the loner to hold out against the crowd or even—with logic—to conquer. Belief involves merging and participating in a community; indeed a community is created by—and creates—shared beliefs.*

Doubting correlates with resisting authority; believing with acquiescence:

> The learner, like the discoverer, must believe before he can know. . . . [T]he intimations followed by the learner are based predominantly on his confidence in others; and this is an acceptance of authority.
>
> Such granting of one's personal allegiance is—like an act of heuristic conjecture—a passionate pouring of oneself into untried forms of existence. (Polanyi 1958, 208)

Methodological doubt is the rhetoric of propositions; methodological belief is the rhetoric of experience. Putting our understandings into propositional form helps us extricate ourselves and see contradictions better; trying to *experience* our understandings helps us see as someone else sees. Thus believing invites images, models, metaphors, and even narratives. A paradigm for systematic doubt is the process of trying to reduce a train of

---

* When doubt becomes *methodological* however, it can flourish as a group process—as in debate or critical discussion. It can even cement the group. And when belief becomes methodological, it can reinforce individualism and odd-ball views by obliging the community to try to believe lone voices.

thought to a syllogism in order to find a contradiction; a paradigm for systematic belief is the process of trying to switch one's experience of an ambiguous gestalt drawing (for example, to see the goblet instead of seeing Peter and Paul).

Doubt implies disengagement from action or holding back, while belief implies action. When we doubt, we tend to pause; and by pausing—by disengaging or standing on the sidelines—we doubt better. When we believe fully, we tend to act; and by acting (for example, when we can no longer wait and collect evidence) we often discover beliefs we didn't know we had. Thus, the intellectual or academic person is traditionally seen as a critic disengaged from action. The engaged "do-er" is usually seen as less thoughtful—as though doing and thinking must be opposite. (Role-playing is difficult for many intellectuals because it is a game of understanding-by-doing and requires an inner act of assenting or giving in to an idea.)

We associate doubt with tentativeness and assume people will be conditional in many of their doubts. We associate belief with total conviction or feeling certain and assume people don't *really* believe something unless they act in perfect conformity with it. (Socrates and many subsequent philosophers have simply *defined* belief behaviorally: they have declared *a priori* that a person's beliefs *are* those assumptions that are implied by her actions. According to this usage, no one could ever perform an act that is in conflict with her beliefs.) Thus it feels perfectly normal to say we have "some doubt" about something; but it can feel odd in certain contexts to say we have *"some* belief" in an assertion.

Yet paradoxically enough, we can turn those connotations on their head. Doubt is also linked with certainty: when we want to be as sure as it is humanly possible to be, we usually resort to logic which relies on contradiction and doubting. Belief, on the other hand, is also linked with *un*certainty: we tend to use the word for views we are not quite sure of—saying, "I don't *know* it, but I *believe* it." And so it also feels odd if someone says, "I *believe* the sun will rise tomorrow" (unless the circumstances are peculiar or the speaker is a philosopher). Even "total beliefs" ("Here I stand, I can do no other!") tend to total *commitment* rather than total *certainty*.

Epistemologically, doubting reflects the trial-by-fire foundation of knowledge whereby we feel no position should be accepted until it has withstood the battering of our best skeptics. Believing reflects the *consensus* foundation of knowledge whereby we feel no position should be accepted until a respected group of authorities positively endorses it through *participation* in it. (It's not enough for a position merely to get fewer negative votes than its competitors.)

With respect to gender, doubting invites behaviors which our culture associates with masculinity: refusing, saying No, pushing away, competing, being aggressive. Believing invites behaviors associated with femininity: accepting, saying Yes, being compliant, listening, absorbing, and swallowing. Doubt implies interrupting and making noise, belief implies being mute or silent—behaviors which are differentially rewarded according to gender.

A man tends to be seen as less masculine if his style is that of the believing game—if, that is, he operates by pliancy, absorbancy, noninitiation, and nonaggression. A woman tends to be seen as less feminine if she shines in the doubting game and loves to win arguments and find errors in the other person's thinking. Trying to believe someone we disagree with tends to make us feel vulnerable, and our culture has seen it as the woman's role to be vulnerable (or at least to acknowledge vulnerability). Some of our metaphors for argument and critical thinking reveal these gender associations: poking holes in the other person's argument, making or advancing points, seeing if a claim will stand up. If I am not mistaken, much feminist theory and criticism points to the cognitive and methodological processes I am exploring here—processes that have been undervalued in a culture deriving its tradition from methodological doubt and male dominance.

The enthusiasm with which I list oppositions will no doubt invite the inevitable objection: that doubting and believing are in fact really the same; the apparent opposition is merely a trick of language. Thus to doubt X is simply to believe Not-X: to doubt that the nickel will come up heads is to believe that it will come up tails. But in truth it is the *equivalence* between doubting and believing that stems from the trick of language. It is a wonderful trick—reflecting the power of language and of the doubting game. But it is only in the realm of propositions that doubting-heads and believing-tails are exactly equivalent. The propositional *equivalence* hides a crucial phenomenological *difference*. Between:

> —distancing or separating oneself from the idea that the coin will come up heads (perhaps at a moment when others are betting on heads): being skeptical and thereby finding subtle reasons why it might not come up that way.

and:

> —positively investing oneself or entering into the idea that it will come up tails—rather than just detaching oneself from the contrary view: feeling or identifying with or experiencing a connection with the idea of tails.

The experience of doubting X typically carries no investment in the idea of Y—and we see this in good doubters: "No, I'm not saying I believe it will come up tails, I'm just trying to show that your belief in heads is ill-founded."

We can see the practical importance of this phenomenological difference if we consider the way "critical theorists" like Habermas and Freire emphasize the need to achieve *separation from one's context*—the need to learn to criticize or "problematize" one's own normally-taken-for granted surroundings. If we reflect on the distinction between doubting and believing, we'll see that there are *two* crucially different methods for distancing oneself from one's context or achieving metacognition.

The obvious method is of course the direct one: to try for separation by working at distance or perspective—to look for problems or contradictions—to heighten one's sensitivity to cognitive dissonance or internal contradiction. This is the route of critical doubting. But we can also achieve critical distance by seeking *other* views and *attaching* or investing ourselves in them. This believing route might be called indirect or artificial—trying for separation from X by means of attachment to Y—but it is usually more effective because it yields greater psychological leverage. In the case of our physical muscles, we can exert ourselves only to contract them—not to loosen them. So in the case of our minds,

our attaching muscle is usually stronger than our detaching one.
It's hard willfully to *let go*. When people try directly to doubt
or distance themselves from a point of view they hold, they often
stay enmeshed. Their "new" view, if seen in perspective, is often
some kind of mirror image or analogue of the old one—controlled
or determined by the very position they are seeking to escape.
We can seldom see clearly a position or point of view we inhabit
till we inhabit one that is genuinely different—not just a denial.

Doubting and Believing by the Rules: Methodology as Game

Doubting and believing are thus among the most powerful root
acts we can perform with our minds. But we cannot *harness* that
power dependably until we learn to deploy doubting and believing consciously and by the rules—not just when they come
naturally. Descartes didn't say, "Let's be a bit more skeptical,"
he proclaimed a "method" that involved treating *every* view as
though false. In becoming systematic in this way, our doubting
and believing become artificial and to some degree conditional
or hypothetical. (Thus Descartes wasn't particularly skeptical—
far from it; and methodological belief doesn't imply credulous-
ness.)

A method, that is, doesn't tell us how to make final decisions,
it only tells us what preparatory activities or processes to go
through before entering the world of full consequences. To use
a method is like being a scientist who runs a series of experiments, or a doctor who runs a series of tests on a patient: answers come out but they are answers to the experiments or to the
tests. It still remains to decide how much *weight* to give those
answers in interpreting or applying them or making a final decision.

To put it that way emphasizes the "weakness" or conditionality of a game or methodology, but therein also lies its strength.
Stanley Fish responded to a draft of this essay by saying that it
doesn't make sense to talk about choosing or rejecting a belief
because to do so implies a self that stands outside its own beliefs. But that's the whole point of a method or a game—whether
methodological doubt or belief: even though we can't "really"

stand outside our own point of view or get away from our beliefs, we can artificially do so, partially or hypothetically, in an
act of imagination or game-playing—and by doing so give a considerable jog to our "real" position. (See Fish 1985; Elbow 1985.)

Because the intellectual world tends to recognize only methodological doubt for the justification of ideas, it easily overlooks
the fact that it is indeed a method and thus conditional—in a
sense a game. Those ideas which come out least flawed when
subjected to the discipline of doubt are, we tell ourselves, most
likely to be true, valid, or trustworthy. It's easy to forget, however, that it takes an additional step of thinking—of judgment—
to decide how much weight to give those results. Someone committed to critical thinking might shout, "No, when critical
thinking gives an answer, that is *the* answer, *my* answer." But
the degree to which we bind ourselves to the results of logic and
systematic doubt in any particular case is not a matter of logic or
systematic doubt: it is a matter of judgment.

Walter Ong (1981) gives an account of the development of
Western intellectual culture as a story of doubting and combat becoming ceremonial and ludic—becoming a game. He shows
how this process served to *heighten* combat, make it central, get
it taught more—and yet at the same time also to defuse it. As intellectual combat became enshrined and more deeply embedded
in the culture's very conception of knowledge, people could fight
about ideas with less personal investment. I look for a similar
development with the game of believing. Just as doubt was crude
and unsophisticated till it developed more of a ludic dimension,
now believing tends to be crude and unsophisticated too: we
sometimes feel we cannot believe something without making a
commitment of action and worship. Of course *final* belief may
be total and committed, but so too may be final doubt.

By emphasizing the hypothetical or conditional character of
doubting and believing as methods—by insisting that methods
are games—I hope I can allay some of the fears about systematic
belief—fears about having to "swallow anything." I can say, in
effect, "Don't worry. If you'll just try to believe all the propositions under discussion, you won't bind yourself to anything. You
get to make your *real* decision afterward—by the use of your
judgment." Judgment involves looking over the results of sys-

tematic believing and systematic doubting and making up one's mind. There are no methodological rules for judgment as there are for the preparatory experiments or tests. (Actually there *is* one important methodological rule for good judgment: don't make up your mind until you avail yourself of the good experiments or tests which are at your disposal. That is, don't forget to play the believing game as well as the doubting game.)

Yet this emphasis on the conditionality of method doesn't make all sense of danger go away. Something real and weighty goes on when we play the believing game. The process often manages to change, genuinely if temporarily, the way we see and understand something. We literally "change our mind." That is, if we come to experience the full force of several competing views on a topic, to feel what it is like to believe each of those views, our final position is apt to change.

Trying to Believe

When we make a method or a game out of these basic mental activities, we oblige ourselves to engage in them willfully—on occasions when they don't come naturally: we oblige ourselves to *try*. The idea of trying to *doubt* no longer gives offense. We learned it, as it were, from Socrates when he taught some of his fellow citizens to doubt the very pieties enshrined in their culture—beliefs they breathed in with the air of the polis. And we learned it from Descartes when he taught the utility of doubting even what seems conceptually self-evident.

But for some people the idea of trying to *believe* still offends. Some philosophers smirk at the idea. Bertrand Russell scornfully defines belief as "an idea or image combined with a yes-feeling." "There are reasons for *wanting* to believe something," say Quine and Ullian, "But how do you *try?* Not by taking a deep breath and closing the eyes" (alluding to the Red Queen's technique). We are likely to laugh at Jowett's response as Master of Balliol to an undergraduate who confessed that he was losing his faith: he trusted the young man would find it again by next Thursday morning at the time of their next appointment. We feel more helpless about believing than about doubting.

But in fact there is nothing unusual about the mental process of *trying* to believe something—though it is too little investigated. Certainly children do it frequently and naturally. That is, even though they absorb in an *unconscious* or *unwilled* fashion many of the beliefs of their parents or peers, they often enough try consciously and willfully to believe: for example, that beer tastes better than Coca-Cola; or that a certain aunt who seems repellent is really a good or lovable person. Obviously they often succeed.

Students sometimes try consciously and willfully to believe what their teachers believe, for example, that Donne is a good poet and Tennyson second rate. I remember trying to believe that Bartók quartets were beautiful because I so much admired people who found them so. And I succeeded: that is, the self-delusion was only temporary—and very useful.

When we present students with a position or a train of thought that we think is important or true but which they find alien (perhaps a counterintuitive interpretation of a poem, myth, or a piece of behavior), we're not so interested at that moment in their practicing critical thinking on it but rather in their learning to say, "Wait a minute, there must be something sensible here: how can I see the validity in it?" When we encounter an assertion that seems absurd but it comes from someone we revere as an intellectual giant, we often block the impulse to say, "How could anyone be so dumb as to think that?"—or even to say, "How could that luminary have gone so wrong?" Instead we reflect, "She must be seeing something I can't see. What am I missing? How can I retrieve her insight? In what sense or under what conditions could her words be true?"

Trying to believe, then, is natural in an "upward" direction— that is, for children or in cases where the belief is held by someone who has great authority. But it is also natural "downward" in authority relationships. For example, when children say something odd or wrong, parents often quite spontaneously ignore the wrongness and search for the rightness: they try to figure out why or in what sense the child's statement is true. Almost invariably the child is saying something sensible or accurate, but the meaning was only retrievable by trying to believe the child's words. (Often enough, the statement doesn't just represent a wrong use of words; rather the child is saying something that genuinely violates the adult frame of reference.)

Teachers, counselors, or therapists often learn to engage in exactly this same process: "trying to believe" what is strictly speaking wrong or nonsensical. By doing so, they not only help their students or clients and thus do a better job, they often help themselves by gaining valuable insights unavailable to them till they break out of their own frame of assumptions.

Vision is a paradigm for belief—"seeing is believing." Just as we mistakenly feel helpless about what we believe, so too with what we see. But once we reflect on the facts of experience, we see there's nothing unnatural about "trying to see" what we don't see—and we sometimes succeed. For example, we may see a receding boat out on the water and someone says, "Try seeing it as approaching." We do, and suddenly we see that it really is approaching and that our original seeing was "mis-seeing." We may hear a statement as straightforward and someone says, "Try hearing it as ironic," and we do, and we suddenly realize we "mis-heard": it *was* ironic.

Many recent accounts of the psychology of perception render us as little Popperian scientists who create hypotheses or schemata that are either sharpened or abandoned through disconfirmatory acts. (See Neisser, 1967 and 1976.) Of course disconfirmations are continually thrust upon us as we bark our shins or reach for thin air or reply to statements that were not made. But compelling research in gestalt and cognitive psychology—especially with ambiguous stimuli—establishes that we also play a substantial role in *constructing* what we see. Neisser himself gives much of the evidence for this constructive or creative role of the agent in perception—what Gombrich calls "the beholder's role." When we see an animal way across the field and cannot quite tell what it is, we often use a kind of "seeing-as," or "believing" process. We try seeing it as dog, then as sheep, then as horse, and suddenly it "sees better" as horse. We don't disconfirm or doubt it as dog or sheep—we don't, for example, test hypotheses about tail behavior. We see it more sharply and we see more of it when we see it as horse.

Under certain circumstances then, it is natural and easy to

try to believe what we don't believe. But the question remains, *how* do we do it? How, especially, do we do it when we aren't children or listening to children or reading a revered sage—that is, when the conditions don't naturally encourage us? I could try to give a theoretical answer or suggest a schematic model,* but I may already have stressed theory too much. If the believing game still seems crazy, nothing is likely to change that verdict but seeing it in action. Let me give what practical advice I can.

Learning to Play the Believing Game

The best place to try out methodological belief is with a small group (or pair) of people who trust each other. Without some trust, it is hard for people to try in good faith to enter into views they disagree with. Of course you can play it alone, and it is safer alone (trying to say Yes for a little while to some view you have read or heard about), but then you lack the leverage of another set of eyes or frame of reference.

The most natural occasions are discussions where the issue is in some sense a matter of *interpretation:* the interpretation of a text or a statement or a piece of behavior; or the attempt to understand a person (such as a fictional character, or a candidate for a job, or a problematic student). In such situations, most people *already* accept the idea that there is no single simple right answer; and that it helps to hear lots of views or hypotheses—even odd ones. When people are discussing a piece of literature, art, film, myth—or discussing a piece of behavior from the point of view of anthropology or depth psychology—they

---

* William Entemann, working from a philosopher's frame of reference suggests (in a response to an earlier draft) the following model of stages in the process of trying to believe something you don't believe:

1. Trying to understand proposition X. (I can either try to understand something someone says or I can refuse.)

2. Succeeding in understanding proposition X.

3. Understanding proposition X and trying to find some evidence and argument—or explore some implications and consequences—that support it.

4. Succeeding in finding some evidence, and so on, to support proposition X.

5. Trying to imagine that the evidence, etc., thus far acquired, even though partial, is sufficient.

6. Succeeding in imagining that the evidence, and so forth, is sufficient.

tend to recognize that our intellectual tradition has already sanctioned interpretations that are inherently "hard to believe" (such as some psychoanalytic, literary, symbolic, or anthropological interpretations). In such discussions, methodological belief is only a small extension (if that) of what most good teachers or leaders naturally make happen: getting the others to *try* to see the truth in a point of view which at first they find alien, absurd, or repellent. (See the section below entitled "Methodological Belief and the Interpretation of Texts" for an argument as to why methodological belief has special power in matters of interpretation.)

Thus the believing game is *harder* to learn in debates or discussions where people are already too invested or polarized into dug-in positions. It is also harder to use (at first anyway) on issues where it looks as though there is a single, "correct" answer to be had: people are too likely to feel they are being asked to entertain views which can be "proved" wrong. (However, mathematics and physics have a venerable tradition of getting people to assent to views which seem ridiculous, such as that a body in motion will continue in motion forever unless something stops it. Aristotle was the last scientist not to impose on our credulity.) For these more difficult situations, it's better to wait till people are more experienced. But even though you cannot make *others* use methodological belief, it is possible to demonstrate its power by using it in response to them: by simply showing them quietly that *you* can conditionally believe what they are saying.*

But there is a kind of "five-minute rule" which is a particular easy way to try out methodological belief. A group can simply agree that whenever any participant feels that some idea or view is not getting a fair hearing, she can invoke the rule: for five minutes no criticism of the idea is permitted and everyone should try to believe it. Believing may seem impossible at first, but people can easily join in answering questions like these:

* In a sense, teachers are in an ideal position to experiment with the believing game. People need direction in learning a discipline which goes against their habits, and teachers can be directive with their classes. It is hard to try out the believing game with peers unless everyone has really agreed to try. But of course it's also problematic for teachers to use anything on students they haven't used among themselves as peers.

- What's interesting or helpful about the view? What are some intriguing features that others might not have noticed?
- What would you notice if you believed this view? If it were true?
- In what senses or under what conditions might this idea be true?

People who cannot answer such questions need to be quiet and listen to those who can. If a group tries this out a number of times on issues that are not too personally loaded, and if some participants are just a bit flexible, people will find they sometimes *succeed* at methodological belief: *believing*—though conditionally and temporarily—something they originally found unbelievable. Of course participants will not *end up* believing most of the views they managed to say Yes to. (How could it be otherwise, statistically?) But they will begin to notice how they experience more of a cognitive shift or enlargement of perspective in this procedure than they experience by simply "understanding" the problematic views.

If people have sufficient success with this trial mode, they will be willing to use methodological belief more extensively and in a more focused way. Let me describe two ways to use it. They correspond to the two ways we use methodological doubt.

First, we commonly use methodological doubt in an exploratory, casual, and heuristic way. We are, as it were, just "having a discussion," but in a highly critical mode: the talk moves casually along but as each point or idea arises, people look for problems or flaws or unnoticed weaknesses. The goal is usually to explore—using the critical impulse as a kind of cyclotron or scattering device that yields new "particles" or ideas. But we also use the doubting game in a second way—more focused and disciplined: the goal is to test or assess two or three positions that people have settled on as the most important ones. The debate and the trial at law are paradigms of this more focused mode of doubting.

So too, we can use methodological belief in a casual, exploratory, heuristic way to uncover views we've not yet worked out. Or else we can use it in a more focused way when we have settled on just a few positions and want to push them to decide what we think. In the first case (as in the doubting or "critical thinking" mode) we are simply "having a discussion," the discussion wanders along. But as each point arises, people try to see what's right about it and even believe it. In the second more focused mode, having decided on only a couple of positions, we set aside a substantial amount of time for each one—to put it to the "test of belief."

Some people will find it intolerably artificial to make this separation between doubting and believing. They will say that thinkers or inquirers who know what they are doing (whether operating in a discussion or alone) will naturally move back and forth between doubting and criticizing on the one hand, and on the other hand entertaining views they are trying to understand—even giving a kind of conditional Yes to them. Of course. When humans function at their best they use their best tools naturally. But we rarely operate at our best, and we benefit immensely from sometimes using our basic tools separately—especially if the two tools tend to interfere with each other, or if one of the tools tends to be neglected (as with believing). The analogy with writing is helpful here: any good writer who is functioning well moves back and forth naturally between generating material and criticizing it; yet most writers—even very skilled ones—benefit from sometimes setting aside portions of time while writing something for uninterrupted generating and uninterrupted criticizing. (For more about writing, see the section below entitled "Practical Applications of Methodological Belief.")

Practical Suggestions for Believing
What Is Hard to Believe

The obvious move is to look for favorable evidence and reasons to support the belief in question. A view may seem clearly false, but if people pool their energies in looking sympathetically for support, they are apt to find a surprising amount. The process turns out to be creatively interesting.

It is crucial, in looking for evidence and reasons, to free more time for the proposer: "Tell us more." She may have to be *asked* to speak more, but it's no good if "Tell us more" sounds to her like, "How could you hold such an odd view?" She must experience the request as a sincere call for *help* in trying to see things as she sees them; she must feel an audience *wanting* to believe what she believes. When we feel an audience genuinely take this stance, we tend to speak and think much better.

But in addition to asking the "owner" for help, it is important to ask help from others who have had some success believing the view. Sometimes the most interesting and telling support for an idea is suggested by someone who started out entirely hostile to it. Her frame of reference or mental set is so different from that of the original proposer that if she can once manage to see the validity in the idea, she sees new and helpful ramifications.

If the spirit is right, it can even help for someone who is having a hard time believing a view to voice her difficulties rather than just quietly trying to enter into the new view. That is, even though it's no good asking, in effect, "How can you believe such a view when it has the following defects?" it *can* bring a breakthrough for someone to say, "I'm having difficulty believing you because I see things thus and so; can you make a suggestion for how I can look at them differently?" (But this is dangerous; the right spirit counts for everything.) Such a question is often best answered by someone other than the original proposer.

Role-playing is a powerful aid in trying to believe what you don't believe. *Pretend* to be someone who believes it—an actual person you know who believes it, or an imaginary person. Sitting inside that person's head, you can usually find helpful answers to questions like these: What is it like seeing things so? What do you see or notice now? What are some of the things that led you to this view? What follows for you? There is something crucial in the imaginative act of *pretending*—a note of literal play—that helps people start to get free of the limitations of their present way of thinking. (The same principle goes for the doubting game: it is easier to find flaws in our own thinking—"de-center" from our own convictions and extricate ourselves from our own assumptions—if we do so with a sense of play. I find the best doubters a bit playful. When the stakes are too high and people are too earnest, their thinking can get muddy.)

Thus it also helps to make a conscious act of fiction: tell the *story* of what it would be like if the idea in question were true— tell all the things which follow from it—tell what the world

would be like. Of course you can tell these stories destructively
as an act of doubting—reducing the idea to the absurdity which
follows from it, applying it unsympathetically. But when someone makes up these stories in a genuine effort to *find validity*,
she often succeeds. The resulting fantasies may be odd or peculiar, but they can lead to helpful insights if entered into in a
spirit of positive play. The use of narrative and descriptive discourse usually taps more insight than efforts to "think" or "find
reasons."

The effort to believe is almost always an effort to find a *valid
sense* in words where before there was no sense or an invalid
sense. "In what *sense* might these words be right?"

> When reading the works of an important thinker, look first for the
> apparent absurdities in the text and ask yourself how a sensible
> person could have written them. When you find an answer, . . .
> when these passages make sense, then you may find that more cen-
> tral passages, ones you previously thought you understood, have
> changed their meaning. (Kuhn 1977, xii)

Allegorizing and symbolizing might seem farfetched, but they
often help us find validities. One thinks of Augustine (in *Con-
fessions*) suddenly discovering that he could find meaning and
truth in Scriptures by reading symbolically—where before he had
found none.

Sometimes I experience a tightness when I am trying to enter
into a position I find alien (sometimes even a physical tightness
in my chest). I've learned to try literally to let go. That is, I can
sometimes find evidence and reasons better not by exercising
greater care but rather by a kind of relaxation of care. Think
of what happens when we are trying to understand people speaking a foreign language we don't know well. When we try to be
careful and monitor each syntactic or semantic move, we destroy
any chance of comprehension. We succeed better by loosening
the mind in some odd way and letting the discourse wash over
us somewhat—consenting to listen or read with only *half comprehension,* but with a spirit of trust that meaning is there and
that gradually our mind will begin to grasp it. What's involved
in both situations is the ability to allow one's thinking and per-

ceiving to be restructured—to allow meaning and language to operate somewhat differently inside one's head.

I find I can help people do better at the believing game if I tell them to relax the rules of contradiction a bit. For example, their difficulty often stems from the understandable feeling that, "If *that* is true, then *this* must be false," or even, "If *she* is right, then *I* must be wrong. In order to believe her, I must renounce my view." It is possible, by an act of will, temporarily to put aside the law of contradiction and the zero-sum model of truth: to assume—temporarily, anyway—that both views are right, however paradoxical it might seem.

Saying Yes: A Phenomenology of Assent

Though it may seem hard to *understand* an alien view and to find reasons and evidence for it, what usually turns out hardest—and most important—is the actual process of saying Yes to it. Assent is the crux, even though it's only conditional and temporary. *Credo UT intelligam* is at the heart of things here: believing *in order* to understand.

It's this act of giving-in which distinguishes methodological belief from merely *understanding sympathetically* what others are saying—or from what philosopher's call "the principle of charity" (Davidson), or from Carl Rogers' empathic listening game in which no one can say her own piece until she has restated the previous comment to the satisfaction of its author. Perhaps I should rest content with those admirable activities; perhaps I'm simply stretching words too far to talk about "belief" when I don't mean permanent belief. Even Coleridge, who wasn't afraid of hyperbole, bent over backwards to avoid the word "belief" itself and coined his rubber-gloved double negative: the "willing suspension of disbelief." But the mental benefits I'm talking about (the opening and restructuring of the mind or the re-seeing and the larger seeing) don't usually occur unless the attempt to see is fueled by some kind of assent—unless there is some kind of saying Yes.

So what is assent? We tend to have two different models for it. On the one hand we often think of it in a religious context—no

doubt partly because of Cardinal Newman's explorations. Thus
we are liable to think of assent as a mysterious, nonrational, and
perhaps religious inner act that we perform in the *absence* of
good reasons or evidence.

But when we shake ourselves loose from the religious connotations of the term and turn to everyday behavior—in and out
of the academy—we find a quite opposite sense: assent is what
we do, naturally and unnoticed, when the grounds *are* sufficient.
When reasons and evidence are compelling, our assent, as it
were, gives itself.

Yet those two pictures of assent are exactly what we seldom do.
That is, on the one hand there are relatively few occasions when
we make genuine leaps of faith. And on the other hand, if we
look closely we must admit that our assent is seldom compelled:
no argument is ever compelling (especially if we consider the
premises); in addition we lack any agreed-upon guidelines for
deciding when reasons and evidence are even *sufficient*. Thus we
invariably perform this inner and nonnecessary act of saying
Yes whenever we reach *any* conclusion of *any* sort. (It is interesting to speculate on *why* we seem to prefer to look the other way
as we assent. Wayne Booth insists on shining a strong light on
the process in his penetrating *Modern Dogma and the Rhetoric
of Assent*—to which I am much indebted.) Assent is thus never
compelled, and seldom given solemnly to organ music.

Newman gives a helpful illustration of the willed dimension
of assent: a mathematician goes through a careful train of inference and deduction which leads him to a conclusion he finds
utterly surprising; he goes back over and checks his reasoning
and can find no flaws; still he withholds his assent till he can get
some of his colleagues to check it over. I am not denying the
cognitive dimension of assent. Of course we must understand
and find evidence. Indeed we usually need the help of someone
else (in person or in a book) to explain or provide language or
give us the new picture. But the more I explore methodological
belief over the years, the more I notice the *willed or conative
dimension* of assent.

And so we come back to the word "try." In trying to believe
something, the act of assent would seem to come at the end—
after understanding it and finding reasons and evidence (see

Enteman's model above). But the question of whether one *succeeds* in those earlier steps often depends on an earlier willingness to assent. What first appeared to be external and inimical to belief—the trying and the saying Yes—turn out in fact to be central. As Quine and Ullian and Russell and Alice imply, closing your eyes and taking a deep breath will not do the trick. But on the other hand, the Red Queen has a point too, and her detractors are wrong to think of belief and assent as *purely* cognitive or evidentiary matters. In any act of reaching any conclusion there is necessarily a *willed* dimension which methodological doubt tends to sweep under the rug and which methodological belief must therefore be forgiven for putting in the spotlight. Closing the eyes and taking a deep breath symbolize this act of will needed for saying Yes to an opponent's view—indeed (dare I say it?) sometimes they are literal aids in the attempt.

Fears of the Believing Game

Wayne Booth's study of assent is an eloquent argument, in effect, for *more* of it—an argument that intellectuals should stop hiding behind the "modern dogma" of objectivity or the fact/value split. He advocates

> cultivating a benign acceptance—perhaps temporary and tentative, but real—of every belief that can pass two tests: you have no particular, concrete grounds to doubt it . . . ; and you have *good reason to think all men who understand the problem share your belief.* (His emphasis, *Modern Dogma* 40)

Notice how *stringent* Booth makes his tests for trial beliefs. It's as though in return for asking intellectuals to give up their knee-jerk skepticism, he has to promise that they won't have to try believing anything hard.

Perhaps I should read his prudence as a warning against my recklessness. But I read it as his acknowledgment of how much *fear of belief* intellectuals have. That is, even though the assent we're talking about is only provisional or hypothetical—it's not, for example, "putting on Jesus" but rather just accepting your colleague's interpretation for a few moments *as though* correct—

most people experience something frightening in this willed attempt to assent or "give in."

This fear is understandable. Here is a strong statement by a colleague, Will Humphreys, responding to a much earlier draft:

> More evil results from maintaining false beliefs than from disbelieving truth. I base this on an appeal to history. . . . This is a *moral* dilemma, not an issue in logic or epistemology as such. . . . Any theory of doubt and belief needs to come to terms with such beliefs as these:
>
>> Jews [blacks, women] are inherently inferior.
>> Man did not evolve but was created by an act of God in a single day.
>> All human actions are really based on sexual motives, regardless of what people say or do.
>> The individual is nothing but the expression of the ideology of his or her class, and that ideology is nothing but the product of the economic organization of society.
>
> What cannot be produced—or at least I cannot seem to find them— are examples of the "other side of the coin," *viz.,* morally repugnant consequences of disbelieving the truth.

Beliefs *can* indeed be dangerous. When people perform horrors, they often do so out of certain reprehensible and seductive beliefs. Thus, as Humphreys implies, the intellectual world has more or less concluded that Pascal's wager ought to be made in reverse: it is safer to doubt than to believe.

But what we must fear is credulity or naive belief; and methodological belief will serve as an antidote to it. Humphreys assumes that if we regularly practice trying to believe things that are false we will end up with more false beliefs, but that is unlikely. If we are regularly presented with a wide array of views and we regularly practice trying to believe them all in turn— knowing of course that many or most of them must be false—we will end up with *fewer* false beliefs.

Surely the danger is not so much that false beliefs will defile us if we try them on like garments—as though the muscles of our minds will somehow be made permanently labile by the process of trying to believe what is not so. The real danger comes from *unexamined* beliefs. The invention of the doubting game was a major step in helping us to examine beliefs. ("The unexamined life . . ." says the grandfather of the doubting game.) But the believing game will lead to fewer unexamined beliefs because it is an additional way to examine or test them. A belief is a lens and one of the best ways to test it is to look through it.

Insofar as a person is particularly susceptible to some dangerously seductive view (such as racism, anti-Semitism, Moonie-ism, IQ-ism, or nationalism), quarantine is not really possible any more. The victory of methodological doubt in the Renaissance was in effect the victory of the free marketplace of ideas. We no longer empower any institution to keep reprehensible ideas out of circulation. To resurrect such an institution would be to give up critical inquiry itself.

But what about certain people with a dangerous "will to believe"—people who are peculiarly susceptible to beliefs, especially to "total" beliefs? They gravitate to cults, they seek envelopment in a creed that decides everything for them. Such people, as the Grand Inquisitor says, would rather be *relieved* of the freedom to think and examine. Might not the believing game nurture that pathology of belief? But that pathology consists of the extreme need to *avoid* being torn in two directions at once, and the believing game would constitute *therapy:* a sustained regimen of exercises to strengthen exactly the muscle that is weak.

There are two other pathologies of belief that we rightly fear: solipsism and groupthink. They constitute the two extreme ways for an individual to relate to a community. But of course the believing game fights solipsism by giving people *more* practice in experiencing the point of view of others. And it fights groupthink by privileging minority opinions and giving them *more* power against the monolithic majority. It's the monopoly of the doubting game that has made it seem legitimate never genuinely to experience any point of view against which one can mount a strong attack.

But precisely because the believing doesn't let us settle comfortably into the *one, easy,* or *seductive* belief, it is liable to arouse a very different fear—the fear of promiscuity. For the believing game asks us, as it were, to sleep with any idea that comes down the pike: we might become the girl who can't say No, the Yes man, the flunky, the slave, the large opening into which anything can be poured—force-fed, raped. These are archetypal fears. Notice, for example, how Descartes was engaged in performing a ritual housecleaning: attempting to remove *everything* in his mind and then take complete control over the portals so he could henceforth refuse admittance to any idea except by conscious decision. How can we not wish for such control? How can we help but feel our minds as cluttered with beliefs we never had a chance to decide on? Skepticism and the doubting game are, among other things, attempts to regain some control over the orifices of our mind.

But mental housecleaning by means of doubt is remarkably futile. As in the parable, the evil spirits tend to come back seven times worse—despite the new broom (Matthew 12:43; Luke 11:24). I think I see compulsive doubters as more dominated by unaware beliefs than other people are. Methodological belief, on the other hand, turns out to give a bit more control over the contents of one's mind. Being "promiscuous" and sleeping with the widest range of ideas (in the safety of provisionality) gives us the best chance of *finding out* what's actually in our mind and *deciding* what to keep and what to throw out. We gain some measure of control only by immersing in the dangerous element.

Am I seeming to say that there is nothing about *commitment* in the believing game? Not quite. For though it is practice in being torn and in making multiple temporary investments, it does in fact consist of practice in the basic act of investing the self. I think the practice of it increases our ability prudently to commit ourselves—where the doubting game reinforces a tendency *only* to be a spectator—to be stuck at William Perry's middle stages of skeptical relativism.

Practical Applications of Methodological Belief

Teaching

In talk about teaching, particularly in higher education, critical thinking tends to have a monopoly. Academics sometimes talk as though our main job is to get students to examine ideas carefully, to guard against weak or wrong ideas—as though there were no problem about the ability to *receive* and especially to *experience* or *feel the force* of new ideas and texts. As teachers we are always saying to students, "Learn to read critically, pencil in hand; look for unbuttressed assumptions or weak points. Get into a critical dialogue with the book." Good advice of course—especially in the case of books that students find congenial or seductive. But not so useful when students are weak in their ability to *enter into* what they read.

Teachers are disturbed when a student seems to accept what a book says without question, but this acceptance is often shallow: there has been no real seduction. The student mouths agreement but really experiences no genuine investment or connection with what the book is saying. Is criticism of Plato really any use if the student has not first fallen in love with Plato? And where weak students have trouble "getting it" at all, many *strong* students learn to "get-it-but-not-really-get-it": they learn, as it were, to understand something and summarize it competently—even in writing—without genuinely experiencing or feeling its force.

Even critical thinking will benefit from redressing the balance, for of course this weakness at entering into new views often works to the detriment of critical thinking itself: "Oh, critical thinking. Yes, we had that in twelfth grade." Students will get more excited about critical thinking and about the ability to distance themselves—especially blasé students—when they are more capable of experiencing surrender.

In teaching literature we know that students must learn to enter unreal or hypothetical worlds. But I'm struck with how little our teaching practices really serve this goal—how few of them directly help students learn to suspend disbelief and invest themselves in a set of words which they find alien. All too often our teaching concentrates on the ability to *justify* interpretations of texts rather than on the more fundamental ability to experience the words. Teaching activities designed to help students experience a text are likely to seem old-fashioned: the teacher reading the text aloud; students reading the text aloud; and students memorizing the text. That such activities now feel quaint in higher education (when once they were common) is a sign of our overcommitment to distancing techniques.

Teachers, too, need practice in the believing game. Though

we rightly value one kind of good teacher—the steel trap mind who keeps students on their toes by sniffing out their every mistake—we also value the opposite type: the teacher who can listen to a discussion or read a paper and sniff out every good idea that comes along, no matter how poorly understood or badly expressed it is. This is the midwife teacher who helps students give birth to nascent good ideas.

Even though it's harder to learn the believing game when people are polarized, the game can help *prevent* polarization too. For example, when teachers meet to discuss sample student papers, there is a tendency for individuals to reach an initial conclusion and then dig in. "I wonder how any teacher with intellectual integrity could give a passing grade to this paper." The believing game helps here. First, I ask everyone in the group to try to see the paper as passing and to give as many arguments as possible to justify that grade. Then, the same thing for failing. *After* that process—teachers having stretched their perception in both directions—they find it much easier to negotiate toward agreement.

Writing

It is helpful to see writing as a movement from disciplined belief to disciplined doubt. That is, while generating draft material, it helps to force oneself to assent to everything that comes to mind and follow the words and thoughts charitably wherever they lead—as they occur and even if they seem dubious. This believing stance leads to richness of words and ideas—intelligence too—and often the surprise of new insights. Even though the process is usually messy, it often leads also to a discovery of structure and coherence—a structure that grows out of the material instead of being imposed upon it. Then the revising process can be fueled by the opposite *doubting* mentality—turning a cold critical eye on this raw material and ruthlessly discarding or changing anything that is not right.

The hyperdevelopment of critical thinking or methodological doubt can produce so strong an internal editor or censor that it is impossible to get things written. The problem is not in the strength of critical thinking or doubt: the more the better when

it comes to "critiquing" one's own material. The problem is in the *absence of a complementary discipline of belief* to clear a safe arena for exploratory generating. Without such an arena our writing is bedeviled because we can see nothing but problems even before we've finished having an idea or before a train of thought is written out—if only for the sake of exploration.

It also helps the writing process if *readers* or *responders* can move in a comparable progression from believing to doubting. Thus as we read early drafts by students or colleagues, we do well to read as believers, trying to see the *validity* in what the writer has written and tell her the ways in which what she has written makes sense. We often fear something dreadful will happen if we refrain from pointing out something weak, but if we hold off doubting for a while and help the writer to take the piece where she and it are wanting to go, she often comes to see the weaknesses herself—and in addition discovers important strengths that our doubts would have undermined. If we want a writer to perform the most difficult and precious act in revising, *letting go,* she cannot do it without support. Revising is seldom effective until we feel secure enough to *want* criticism and to seek changes.

Interestingly enough, much bad writing comes from trying to write to doubters—trying to blow a trumpet to an audience of lemon-suckers. The writer writes nervously and defensively, continually trying to fend off objections, and as a result her writing is often tangled. The main ideas are characteristically muffled and insulated. If the writer can be persuaded to write *as though* to sympathetic allies, to people who are ready to *believe* her, often her writing becomes much stronger: the main ideas are put out clearly on the table and the posture of the writing is no longer tentative and nervous but rather direct and firm.

But of course the transition to doubting is necessary. Now the writer has some ideas she trusts; she cares about them enough to make sacrifices for them. And she has so much, she knows she must throw some away. Now she and her readers can start criticizing and doubting as hard as possible. But with her critical readers, the writer needs to play the believing game. "Eat like an owl." The owl pops down the whole mouse, trusting her innards to absorb what is nutritious and discard what is not.

Heuristic

Teachers usually frown on guessing as a method for finding answers. They assume that the right way to find answers is to use that method which yields the *right* answer. Even investigators of the scientific method have tended, till recently, to be fuzzy about the distinction between finding ideas and testing them—emphasizing the process of justifying hypotheses and neglecting the messy process of generating them. (See Medawar.) Heuristic has tended to be colonized by assessment. Similarly, much of the advice given to student writers is really advice for making sure their ideas are good and their sentences well formed. Such advice is seldom much help in the process of generating ideas and sentences in the first place.

Methodical belief, strictly speaking, may not look like practice in having ideas—just practice in trying to believe the misguided ideas of the other fellow. But it is a powerful aid to heuristic. It's like brainstorming, but here the listeners don't just shut up, they help you find fruitful implications in your suggestion. Such practice in looking at things differently in a supportive setting helps us learn to produce more and better ideas. Also, when trying to explore an idea, there is a peculiar fertility that comes from moving back and forth between doubting it and believing it.

Polity

The doubting and believing games bring out different textures of polity. When the doubting game works well, it is a lively and energetic process. The staple ingredients are disagreement and argument. People are having fun wrestling. In effect, they agree to find faults with each other's positions in order to sharpen the group's thinking. Even when it's painful it can be deeply satisfying. Here is a woman remembering the arguments she used to have as a girl at dinner with her lawyer father. "Often I would cry at the table when I couldn't convince him in an argument, but still the exchange was pleasurable. I remember saying once, 'I'm crying, Mother, but not because I'm not enjoying the argument.' I was crying out of frustration, not hurt." (Quoted by Ken Macrorie in an unpublished interview with Huston Diehl.)

But since the doubting game is an attempt to find what's wrong with statements, people often experience it as an attempt to deny their perception or experience. The process tends to imply a scarcity model of knowledge—namely, that one side can win and be right only at the expense of the other being wrong. The believing game, on the other hand, is essentially cooperative or collaborative. The central event is the act of affirming or entering into someone's thinking or perceiving. It tends to imply a pluralistic model of knowledge—namely, that the truth is often complex and that different people often catch different aspects of it; and that we get closer to seeing correctly by entering into each others' conflicting perceptions or formulations.

Because the central process in the believing game is the attempt to see as someone else sees, the texture of polity is usually quieter. Indeed, when it goes poorly (and the believing game is no easier to play well than the doubting game), it can be sleepy and fruitless. But when people learn, there is a subtle kind of intensity. Participants are struggling to find ways to articulate what they see and experience in an idea; others are trying to understand it that way, and articulate what they understand. The quality of intellectual excitement in the believing game comes from more frequent cognitive shifts than in the doubting game.

The believing game encourages what may be the most valuable intellectual process for inquiry in meetings or groups—namely, the act of seeing the strength in someone's else's position and the weakness in one's own. When the doubting game is dominant, discussion tends to be a matter of "winning" and "losing," and people give in only when coerced—and then of course with a residue of resentment and a desire to get back at the winner. The point of having discussions is for people's thinking to develop through interaction with others, yet characteristically people walk out thinking exactly as they did when they walked in. When people cannot really affect each other's thinking, decisions get made on the basis of power, fashion, or loyalties.

We see something like methodological belief in Quaker meetings or meetings which operate by consensus. Such a polity is not
chosen out of a commitment to sweetness or a fear of disagreement (indeed Quakers are well-known scruplers or doubters),
but rather out of an explicit refusal to settle for the lowest common denominator. Instead of inviting the decision that gets least
objections or which can best fight off objections, the process invites that decision which the whole group can best *enter into* or
affirm.

To use a consensus meeting process is not *exactly* the same as
playing the believing game. But giving one person the power to
prevent closure means going a long way toward giving her the
power to force the others to try believing her views. If they want
to get home in time for supper (or ever before 3 A.M.), their best
hope is to try to see things as she does. Having done so, either
they will see that she was right or they will be in a better position to induce her to see through their eyes and thereby finally
change her position.

The court of law is a classic combative arena for the doubting
game. The structure of the trial seems to represent a clear decision that the truth can best be uncovered through the combat
of opponents. The game-likely quality is heightened by using
lawyers who are not personally involved. Only less important
matters are relegated to the decision of a supposedly neutral
third party—the judge.

But if the doubting game is paramount, why use a jury? Why
take so much power out of the hands of experts in the doubting
game, the lawyers and the judge, and put it in the hands of
jurors who are wholly naive and *least* qualified to play the
doubting game? And why prevent jurors from engaging in the
central process in critical thinking: asking questions or cross examining? The jury is forced to sit and engage in the prime activity of the believing game: mute listening. And when they finally
get a chance to talk and decide, they must (except in certain
special conditions) reach consensus. The Anglo-American trial,
then, is a venerable ritual that seems strikingly arranged to
exploit a dialectic between methodological doubting and believing.

Methodological Belief and the Interpretation of Texts

From the point of view of pure theory it is not very ambitious to claim, as I have done, that people who play the believing game will get better at proposing and understanding diverse readings of a text. I wish to try out a more ambitious claim here—in effect moving from the realm of invention to that of justification: that methodological belief used by good readers over time will gradually yield a body of interpretations that we might call *valid* or *trustworthy*. (I build on Toulmin's notion of a hermeneutical court, Kuhn's notion of authoritative elders in a discipline, and Fish's notion of an interpretive community—not claiming, of course, that they would agree with what I say here.)

I will argue that even though we can never have interpretation that is as logically compelling as in geometry, and thus that there will always be hermeneutical disagreement, nevertheless it makes sense to call interpretations "valid" or "trustworthy" if good readers from diverse critical communities can agree on them over time. Needless to say, such agreement will be rare, but the hermeneutic enterprise will make better sense if we simply accept such achievement as a model and realize that when we *approach* it, we are approaching validity or trustworthiness in interpretation. Furthermore, such agreements will become *less* rare if we can induce respected readers to practice the discipline of methodological belief. In effect, I am threading a common-sense path between hermeneutical relativism or deconstruction on the one side, and monism or positivism or absolutism on the other. (See Paul Armstrong's recent attempt at a comparable path between extremes.)

Suppose we are considering some nonobvious readings of a text, for example, the oedipal reading of *Hamlet,* or T. S. Eliot's reading of the final scene of *Othello* (which sees Othello's suicide not as an enlarging act that enlists our sympathy and identification, but rather an act of self-dramatization that makes him look a bit small or even silly and invites us to distance ourselves from him). My claim is that if we get the best readers to practice methodological belief upon these interpretations over time, and if they can reach any agreement, we can trust their readings.

(Presumably I am just describing what actually happens over the generations when a reading gradually gets accepted as canonical through having been accepted by a sequence of diverse critical communities. I sense this to have occurred with at least a weak version of the oedipal reading of *Hamlet*.)

There are two reasons for trusting the verdicts of these readers. Both reasons rest on an account of how natural language works. The first is a negative argument against the adequacy of methodological doubt or critical thinking. The second is a positive argument that methodological belief is peculiarly apt for yielding trustworthy interpretations.

1. Methodological doubt doesn't help in hermeneutical dispute because it depends on the law of contradiction—the law that something cannot be X and not-X at the same time. The law of contradiction breaks down with natural language and human behavior because they are apt to carry more than one meaning at once—sometimes even logically contradictory meanings. For example, I can say, "I'm happy to see you," yet also be saying something else with these words—perhaps even saying, "I'm distressed to see you." The presence of this latter message, or any other message, does not serve to disconfirm the presence of the former message.

Suppose we are arguing about whether the ending of *Othello* invites readers to merge with the hero or distance themselves. No matter how much evidence I find in the text that suggests we are invited to identify with him, it has no compelling power to disconfirm or deny validity to the opposite interpretation. Texts can support multiple and even contradictory interpretations. (And meanings or effects can be "in" a text, but only faintly so: that is, few critics insist that a meaning permeate every corner of a text to be judged "there.") Because no reading can ever be disconfirmed, many critics adopt—some reluctantly, some joyfully —a strong relativist or subjectivist or deconstructive position.

When faced with two interpretations, the best we can do is to "confirm" one as valid, or perhaps both, through the test of methodological belief or systematic seeing-as: we see the text better and more clearly through the confirmed reading than through others. It "works" better. We may decide to reject other readings as not right, as unsatisfactory lenses, because they fail to show us what the better ones have convinced us is really there. But insofar as we are rejecting, we are not using doubt or critical thinking, we are doing so by means of a believing process. Of course methodological doubt can help us find weaknesses in readings which we end up rejecting as invalid, but it was not decisive in the rejection and could not alone be trusted.

2. The second reason for trusting methodological belief is that it is consonant with the communal character of natural language. Natural language only exists to the extent that a community uses it. (Of course we can carry on thinking, writing, and even talking while alone on a desert island, but in doing so we are living off capital accumulated through a community process. As problems of meaning or interpretation come up, our solitary process of resolving them will differ significantly from how they are normally resolved.)

Let's return to the example. "I am happy to see you." Hirsch is right that it is a matter of genuine knowledge what my utterance means (in context). It may be hard to *find out* that answer, but an answer exists, knowledge is out there to be had. And often enough we have grounds to be confident, if not certain, that we have found that knowledge.

But Hirsch says that the meaning of my utterance consist of what I *intended*. Surely he is wrong here (and he himself stakes less on this point than on his larger one that validity is in fact possible). The meaning of my utterance cannot be judged by me alone, but only by me in collaboration with my audience. I get to decide what I *intended* to say but not what I *succeeded* in saying. (Given an unconscious, we may even be wrong about our intentions.) Therefore, speaking more precisely, the locus of my intended meaning is wholly in me, whereas the locus of my achieved meaning is jointly in me, in the utterance, and in the audience.

This locating of the meaning in speaker-and-audience can be defended by an account of natural language. Natural language exists unstably along a continuum between mathematics (or other legislated languages) at one end and dream language at the other end. Mathematical signs or symbols are nailed down: they mean only what they are publicly agreed to mean. Dream signs

or symbols, at the other extreme, mean whatever the individual
dreamer (utterer) wants them to mean. I can dream about penises
with guns or steeples; but also with flowers or barns. I can build
any meaning into any symbol. Thus, whereas the meaning of a
mathematical utterance is wholly in the public domain, the
meaning of a dream utterance is wholly in the dreamer. (Qualifi-
cation: If we dream in mathematics or even in natural language,
we import some public meanings into our private dream world.)

Meaning in natural language is caught in a tug of war between the two semantic principles illustrated by mathematics
and dreaming. Really, it's a tug of war between individuals and
speech communities (or between subcommunities and larger
communities). As individuals we tend to behave like dreamers,
like Humpty-Dumpty, and to intend by our words whatever we
want them to mean. And of course we also *hear* just as prodi-
gally: we tend to hear what we want to hear. Yet language is a
game played with others. There are rules—of a sort. Speech
communities restrain our Humpty-Dumptyism by not understanding some of what we intend—or by not having intended
some of what we hear. They prune back some of our natural
semantic efflorescence. And the same battle goes on between
small communities and larger ones.

"The question is," said Humpty-Dumpty "who is to be master—that's all." Yes, the question is simple, but the answer is
complex. There are agreements and criteria about how to interpret any word or phrase in a natural language, but these agreements are not written down and they are always in the process of
renegotiation—or at least always up for renegotiation. They are
unstated and constantly shifting agreements or shared assumptions among community members. That is, a particularly powerful speaker (or subcommunity) can blow the meaning of a word
into a new shape. And a particularly powerful listener can suck
a word into a new shape. Change isn't random. Power is being
deployed.

We see now why it's such a matter of tact and sensitivity to
interpret complex utterance in natural language—why we cannot
be bound by the speaker's intention, nor yet simply write it off
either. We need methodological belief because meaning is a

result of collaboration between speaker and readers. No one gets a free hand. The meaning is not objectively "there" apart from the interpretation of readers, but readers don't get to make it up apart from how well it fits the speaker and the text. The resulting community agreement must be right for the speaker, the text, and the readers.

This explanation of how natural language works suggests the following model for validity in interpretation: an utterance finally means what the appropriate speech community reads it to mean (not excluding the author, of course)—at least when they are operating at their best. That is, at any given moment they might be too dumb to see something that is really there in the utterance, especially if the meaning is faint or new or surprising. Mistaken consensus may only be exposed in retrospect: the group learned to read better, or better readers came along and showed them what they had missed.

This approach gives us a lens through which I believe we can see more about natural language, texts, and the process of interpretation—and see more sharply. On the one hand, it helps us do justice to the natural human tendency toward ambiguity and polysemy in utterance: complex utterances often *do* have more than one valid meaning; and speakers and listeners often *are* wrong about meaning. On the other hand, this approach does not force us to grant equal legitimacy to all interpretations, for it helps us see the equally natural human tendency to utter meanings about which speaker and listener can agree: in such cases, speaker and listener can validly trust their commonsense conviction that some meanings were "in" the utterance and others not.

In making my path between the extremes of positivism and relativism, I am borrowing from each group its most valuable possession. From the hermeneutical positivists or absolutists I am borrowing their down-to-earth conviction that trustworthy interpretations are often to be had and that humans can sometimes recognize them when they see them. But I avoid the rigidity and unimaginativeness that sometimes goes along with an absolutist epistemology. For when you have an epistemology that says some answers are right, you are likely to attract people who need to insist that *their* answers are right and all others wrong—people who are bad at changing their minds or letting other views stand.

From relativists I borrow their invaluable *method:* their ability to behave as though all readings are true and therefore worth trying to believe. Relativists or deconstructionists are often the best readers in town: smart, flexible, able to see more readings, and able to articulate more delicate nuances. Once we learn to adopt their fecund method, we will be less tempted to adopt their skeptical and sometimes cynical epistemology.

Epistemological Megalomania

When old-time peddlers went around on wagons selling medicine, they were apt to say, "This lotion is good for rashes, snake bites, women's trouble, and measles. It's even good for polishing the family silver." If I am calling this dialectic between systematic doubting and believing an exemplary use of our minds, there's no use pretending that I am not hawking an all-purpose elixir.

So what is our family silver? Epistemology. That is, by claiming that these games help us figure things out, I am implying a claim about the nature of "figuring out." What does methodological belief have to do with the nature of knowledge?

Since certain knowledge is not available, except perhaps in pure logic, I take it that our task in life and scholarship must be to find truthworthy knowledge—what Hirsch calls "valid" and Holton calls "reliable"—that is, to learn to get over saying, "If it's not certain, it's not knowledge." The urge for certainty is understandable—especially since we enjoyed it as children. But that certainty derived from authority, and once it was destroyed by critical thinking or methodological doubt, I take it to be a petulant refusal to examine the evidence around us not to notice that some claims to knowledge hold up well and some do not. It is epistemology's task to describe what we do when we pick out nickels that are not wooden.

What are the grounds for reliable knowledge? It seems obvious after the fact, but it was Toulmin's achievement to insist that the grounds differ from field to field. Thus there are no quick or universal answers here. But I would suggest that in virtually every field (except pure logic), the grounds must consist of some combination of methodological doubting and believing.

Popper says that science doesn't give us certain positive knowledge but that it does, through acts of disconfirmation, give us certain knowledge of when a hypothesis is false. (I paint a rough picture, glossing over his extensive later qualifications.) Thus, though knowledge is never certain, it can be said to rest, as it were, on *foundations* of certainty—acts of indubitable falsification. This influential view implies a special role for methodological doubt in science since the systematic search for contradiction would occupy a privileged position in determining what counts as true.

But the view has been widely questioned, and Popper himself has given ground. Disconfirmation in science is not so neat as the simple version of his theory implies. Even though doubt is logically more telling than affirmation (a single counterexample makes a proposition indubitably false, whereas no quantity of supporting examples ever makes a proposition indubitably true), nevertheless *in practice* scientists have a habit of not feeling bound by disconfirmations. When an unusually attractive or powerful hypothesis is disconfirmed by an experiment, they sometimes find it in their hearts to call it apparatus error or some other mistake. And of course they are sometimes right, as Einstein was when he rejected some of the early experimental disconfirmations of his work.

If "indubitable" disconfirmation is dubitable, then dubitable *confirmation* ends up carrying more weight. Indeed, "weight" itself then becomes the criterion—something that must be determined by judgment and tact, not by a binary litmus test. This picture of how scientists arrive at knowledge makes us talk about the role of *plausibility* and *judgment*. (One still uses falsification of course, but it takes judgment to decide on the plausibility of negative results.) When we are dealing with plausibility and judgment, we are dealing with how things "fit" or how well things "go" with evidence—and thus we are in a realm where methodological belief or systematic seeing-as must lend a hand.

If we move to the accounts of science by Kuhn and Rorty, there is an even greater role for methodological belief, or something very like it, in determining whether something counts as knowledge. In Kuhn's picture, decisions about paradigms rest on the judgment of a community of respected elder scientists. He doesn't say much about how they actually decide or how their verdicts change (other than by some of them gradually dying off). They must exercise something like methodological belief since disconfirmation of paradigms is not possible. (*Within* paradigms, of course, methodological doubt can be decisive.) In Rorty's account, knowledge is grounded and certified by community consent or belief. Since methodological doubt is seldom decisive in these matters, something like the believing game comes into play.

I have been talking as though science were our paradigm for knowledge—a traditional and tempting but now challenged assumption. Galileo gives us a central text in that tradition when he talks of Nature being a book written in the language of number. But of course he was just giving a fillip to a much more venerable metaphor: Nature is a text written in (what else?) natural language. If we go back to this more ancient figure, our paradigm for getting knowledge becomes the process of interpretation. Instead of saying that knowledge is what they get in physics, and what we get in the humanities and social sciences is deficient to the extent that it differs, we would say that knowledge is best exemplified by those interpretations of a text or an utterance we trust as valid. Physics, though it may look basic and paradigmatic, is really a peculiar special case. (This would resemble the gestalt switch produced by relativity: relativity looks odd and Newtonian physics looks "regular," but really it's the other way around—Newtonian physics is the special case.)

If it seems fanciful to speak this way, notice how satisfying and plausible an answer is provided to the perennially modern debate about whether the world is objectively *given* or *made up* by perceivers. The hermeneutical paradigm shows what most people recognize intuitively must be true: that both positions must somehow be right and somehow be fitted together. In interpreting the world, we must engage in a cooperative "game" with nature, comparable to the language game played by members of speech communities when we speak and understand each other. On the one hand, we "make up" reality just as all meaning is made up by readers or listeners; but on the other hand, if we continue the "conversation" with the world at any length and with any sensitivity, we learn to recognize and acknowledge when we have gone wrong and have "made up" meanings that fail to conform to what the world's "text" was driving at. The resulting "reality" or "right answer" must be right for both parties. (Notice how this account implies abandoning the tempting metaphor of vision as our paradigm for knowing, and using instead the metaphor of *utterance* in a community. Colin Turbayne spelled out the dangers of the visual-spatial metaphor well before Rorty and went on to suggest a linguistic metaphor.)

I will stop here and leave my epistemological "argument" at that: nothing but an interpretation, nothing but a metaphor—nothing but (to return to the dangerous metaphor) a lens to look through. If it works it does more than beguile, it removes blurriness and resolves perplexity. I cannot apologize for an argument that is nothing but an interpretation or a lens since my claim is that epistemological validity rests on the process of trying out interpretations or lenses. Of course the process isn't foolproof, it doesn't yield certainty. Yet to say "it's the best we have" strikes a more melancholy note than I think the situation warrants. My point is that the use of methodological belief can be remarkably accurate. I must put it to the test of readers.

Don't overlook one homely way of putting it to the test: consider individuals or groups who are unusually skilled at finding good insights and reaching sound conclusions—who manage to be at once imaginative and prudent. (I think of people like Wayne Booth, E. H. Gombrich, Robert Heilbroner, Peter Medawar, and Helen Vendler.) Look at exemplars of admirable judgment and see if there isn't in them something like an acute capacity for methodological belief that is central to their gift (whether or not they conceive it that way). Or rather something like a dialectical interaction between the methods of belief and doubt. For I hope that this long attempt to stick up for the believing game has not obscured my commitment to the doubting game as well. Our muscles for critical squinting and self-extrication must also be strong if we are to avoid being fooled.

Besides, we need *both* methods not only for their own individual fruits but also for their dialectical reinforcement of each other. For it is not just inexperienced students who are bad at critical thinking. Scholars and teachers are bad at it too—they fall prey to self-deception with surprising frequency—not because they lack skill in critical thinking, but because they lack the benefit of methodological belief to teach them how to bring critical thinking to bear on their own positions.

I have tried to suggest a larger, more inclusive conception of rationality by adding to the traditional emphasis on critical thinking an emphasis on what has traditionally been felt as primitive and irrational: believing everything or swallowing anything. But this powerful mental activity is not primitive, irrational, or dangerous when it is given the discipline we learned in developing methodological doubt.

❀❀❀❀

Bibliography of Works Cited

Armstrong, Paul. "Conflict of Interpretations and the Limitations of Pluralism." *PMLA* 98.3 (1983).

Austin, J. L. *How to Do Things with Words.* New York, 1965.

Beardsley, Monroe. *Aesthetics.* New York, 1964.

Bell, Daniel. *The Reforming of General Education.* New York, 1966.

Boethius. *The Consolation of Philosophy.* Trans. Richard Green. Indianapolis, 1962.

Bohr, Niels. *Atomic Physics and Human Knowledge.* New York, 1958.

Booth, Wayne. *The Rhetoric of Fiction.* Chicago, 1961. Rev. ed. 1983.

———. *Modern Dogma and the Rhetoric of Assent.* Chicago, 1974.

———. *Critical Understanding: The Powers and Limits of Pluralism.* Chicago, 1979.

Bruner, Jerome. *The Process of Education.* New York, 1960.

———. "Going Beyond the Information Given." *The Cognitive Process.* Ed. Robert J. Harper. Englewood Cliffs, 1964.

———. *Studies in Cognitive Growth.* New York, 1966.

Bruner, Jerome, J. Goodnow, and G. A. Austin. *A Study of Thinking.* New York, 1956.

Chapman, James. *Trade Tests: The Scientific Management of Trade Proficiency.* New York, 1921.

Charmey, Davida. "The Validity of Using Holistic Scoring to Evaluate Writing: A Critical Overview." *Research in the Teaching of English* 18.1 (1984): 65–68.

Coleridge, Samuel Taylor. *Biographia Literaria.* 1817. Ed. J. Shawcross. Oxford, England, 1907.

Cooper, Charles. *The Nature and Measurement of Competency in English.* Urbana, Ill., 1981.

Cronbach, Lee J. *Educational Psychology.* 2nd ed. New York, 1967.

Dewey, John. *Democracy and Education.* New York, 1919.

Diederich, Paul. *Measuring Growth in English*. Urbana, Ill., 1974.

Einstein, Albert. *The World as I See It*. Trans. Alan Harris. New York, 1979.

Elbow, Peter. "Shall We Teach or Give Credit: A Model for Higher Education." *Soundings: An Interdisciplinary Journal* 54.3 (1971): 237–52.

———. "Reply to Stanley Fish." *Proceedings of the Conference: Collaborative Learning and the Reinterpretation of Knowledge*. New York (John Jay College), 1985.

———. See also the "Bibliography of Works about Writing by the Author" which follows this list of works cited.

——— and Pat Belanoff. "Using Portfolios to Judge Writing Proficiency at SUNY Stony Brook." *New Methods in College Writing Programs: Theory into Practice*. Eds. Paul Connolly and Teresa Vilardi. New York, in press.

Fish, Stanley. *Is There a Text in This Class?* Cambridge, Mass., 1980.

———. *Proceedings of the Conference: Collaborative Learning and the Reinterpretation of Knowledge*. New York (John Jay College), 1985.

Freire, Paolo. *The Pedagogy of the Oppressed*. New York, 1970.

Gardner, Howard. *Frames of Mind: The Theory of Multiple Intelligences*. New York, 1983.

Gombrich, Ernst H. *Meditations on a Hobby Horse and Other Essays on the Theory of Art*. New York, 1978.

Grant, Gerald, and Associates. *On Competence: A Critical Analysis of Competence-Based Reforms in Higher Education*. San Francisco, 1979.

Grant, Gerald, and Wendy Kohli. "Contributing to Learning by Assessing Student Performance." In Grant and Associates.

Grice, H. P. "Logic and Conversation." In *Syntax and Semantics*. Eds. P. Cole and J. L. Morgan. Vol. 3: *Speech Acts*. New York, 1975.

Hendrix, Gertrude. "A New Clue to Transfer of Training." *Elementary School Journal* (1947): 198–200. (Cited in *Learning Theory for Teachers*. Morris L. Bigge. New York, 1964, 283.)

Hilgers, Thomas Lee. "Training College Composition Students in the Use of Freewriting and Problem-solving Heuristics for Rhetorical Invention." *Research in the Teaching of English* 14.4 (1980): 293–307.

Hirsch, Jr., E. D. *Validity in Interpretation*. New Haven, 1967.

———. *The Aims of Interpretation*. Chicago, 1976.

Holton, Gerald. *Thematic Origins of Scientific Thought: Kepler to Einstein*. Cambridge, Mass., 1973.

Hyman, Stanley Edgar. *The Tangled Bank*. New York, 1962.

Kohlberg, Lawrence. "Moral Development: A Review of the Theory."
   Theory into Practice 16.2 (1977): 53–60.
Kuhn, Thomas. *The Structure of Scientific Revolutions.* Enlarged ed.
   Chicago, 1970.
———. *The Essential Tension.* Chicago, 1977.
Lloyd, G. E. R. *Polarity and Analogy: Two Types of Argumentation in
   Early Greek Thought.* Cambridge, England, 1966.
McNeill, William. *The Rise of the West.* Chicago, 1963.
Medawar, Peter. *Induction and Intuition in Scientific Thought.* Re-
   printed in his *Pluto's Republic.* New York, 1982.
Miller, George A. "The Psycholinguists: On the New Scientists of Lan-
   guage." *Encounter* (1964).
Miller, George A., E. Galanter, and K. H. Pribram. *Plans and the Struc-
   ture of Behavior.* New York, 1960.
Mowrer, O. Hobart. *Learning Theory and the Symbolic Processes.* New
   York, 1960.
Neisser, Ulrich. *Cognitive Psychology.* New York, 1967.
———. *Cognition and Reality.* San Francisco, 1976.
Newman, John Henry (Cardinal). *An Essay in Aid of a Grammar of
   Assent.* London, 1870.
Ong, Walter. *Fighting for Life: Contest, Sexuality, and Consciousness.*
   Ithaca, N.Y., 1981.
———. *Orality and Literacy: The Technologizing of the Word.* New
   York, 1982.
Osgood, Charles E. *Nebraska Symposium on Motivation.* Ed. M. R.
   Jones. Lincoln, Nebraska, 1953.
———. *The Measurement of Meaning.* Urbana, Ill., 1957.
———. *Approaches to the Study of Aphasia.* Urbana, Ill., 1963.
Peckham, Morse. *Man's Rage for Chaos.* New York, 1965.
Perry, William G. *Forms of Intellectual and Ethical Development in
   the College Years.* New York, 1968.
Piaget, Jean. *Language and Thought of the Child.* 3rd ed. New York,
   1971.
Polanyi, Michael. *Personal Knowledge: Toward a Post Critical Philoso-
   phy.* New York, 1958.
———. *The Tacit Dimension.* New York, 1966.
Popper, Karl. *Conjectures and Refutations: The Growth of Scientific
   Knowledge.* New York, 1958.
Purves, Alan. "In Search of an Internationally-Valid Scheme for Scoring
   Compositions." *College Composition and Communication* 35.4
   (1984): 426–38.
Quine, W. V. O., and J. S. Ullian, *The Web of Belief.* New York, 1970.

Robertson, D. W. *A Preface to Chaucer*. Princeton, 1963.

Rorty, Richard. *Philosophy and the Mirror of Nature*. Princeton, 1970.

Rosenthal, Robert. "Teacher Expectation and Pupil Learning." *Teachers and the Learning Process*. Ed. R. D. Strom. Englewood Cliffs, 1971.

Rosenthal, Robert, and Lenore Jacobson. *Pygmalion in the Classroom: Teacher Expectation and Pupils' Intellectual Development*. New York, 1968.

Rycroft, Charles. "Causes and Meanings." *Psychoanalysis Observed*. Ed. Charles Rycroft. London, 1966.

Searle, John. *Speech Acts: An Essay in the Philosophy of Language*. New York, 1969.

Staats, Arthur W., and Carolyn K. Staats. *Complex Human Behavior*. New York, 1964.

Toulmin, Stephen. *The Uses of Argument*. New York, 1958.

Turbayne, Colin. *The Myth of Metaphor*. Columbia, S.C., 1970.

Vygotsky, Lev S. *Thought and Language*. Cambridge, Mass., 1962.

Wimsat, William K., and Cleanth Brooks. *Literary Criticism*. New York, 1964.

White, Edward. *Teaching and Assessing Writing*. San Francisco, 1985.

Bibliography of Works About Writing by the Author

Books

Writing Without Teachers. New York, 1973.
Writing With Power: Techniques for Mastering the Writing Process. New York, 1981.

Essays and Articles

"Thoughts About Writing Essays." Pamphlet handbook published at Franconia College, 1964.
"A Method for Teaching Writing." *College English* 30.2 (1968). Reprinted in *Writing: Voice and Thought.* Urbana, Ill. (National Council of Teachers of English [NCTE]), 1971. Also in *Ideas for English 101.* Ed. Richard Ohmann, Urbana, Ill. (NCTE), 1975.
"Reply to Donald Hassler." (Follow-up to the previous article.) *College English* 30.8 (1969).
"Why Teach Writing?" and "What Is Good Writing." *The Why's of Teaching Composition.* Ed. Philip Brady. Seattle, Wash. (Washington Council of Teachers of English), 1978.
"Midstream Reflections." In *Moving Between Practice and Research in Writing: Proceedings of the NIE-FIPSE Grantee Workshop.* Ed. Ann Humes. Los Alamitos California (SWRL Educational Research and Development), 1981.
"Taking the Crisis out of the Writing Crisis." *Seattle Post-Intelligencer,* November 1, 1981.
"About Resistance to Freewriting and Feedback Groups." *Washington English Journal,* Winter 1982.
"Teaching Writing by Not Paying Attention to Writing." In *Forum: Essays on Theory and Practice in the Teaching of Writing.* Ed. Patricia Stock. Montclair, N.J., 1983.

"Teaching Thinking by Teaching Writing." *Change Magazine* September 1983.

"The Challenge for Sentence Combining." In *Sentence Combining: A Rhetorical Perspective.* Eds. Donald Daiker, A. Kerek, and M. Morenberg. Carbondale, Ill., 1985.

"In the Beginning Was the Word." (Review essay of educational film "Before the First Word.") *Change Magazine* June 1984.

"Reply to Ronald Scheer and to Abraham Bernstein." *College English* 46.5 (1984).

"The Shifting Relationships Between Speech and Writing." *College Composition and Communication* 36.3 (1985).

With Pat Belanoff. "Using Portfolios to Judge Writing Proficiency at SUNY Stony Brook." *New Methods in College Writing Programs: Theory into Practice.* Eds. Paul Connolly and Teresa Vilardi. New York, in press.

With Pat Belanoff. "The Use of Portfolios to Increase Collaboration and Community in a Writing Program." *WPA: Journal of the Association of Writing Program Administrators,* Winter 1986, in press.

Index

Vygotsky, Lev S., 19. *See also* Scientific concepts and spontaneous concepts

Wesleyan University, xiv
Williams College, 67
Wimsat, William K., 250
White, Edward, 221
Whitehead, Alfred North, 8, 35
Whorf, Benjamin, 245
Writing process, Chaps. 2 and 3, xii–xiii, 38, 141–42, 152, 159, 161, 235, 276, 286–87; as growing, Chap. 2, 59; student writing, 161–63, 167–69, 189, 221, 225. *See also* Feedback; Freewriting; Peer groups; Stuck
Writing Without Teachers, 38, 162, 225, 253
Writing With Power, 56, 142, 232
Wurtzdorf, Allan, 115–16

Yeats, 234n